Saskatchewan
Government

Saskatchewan Government

Politics and Pragmatism

Evelyn Eager

Western Producer Prairie Books
Saskatoon, Saskatchewan

Copyright © 1980 by Evelyn Eager
Western Producer Prairie Books
Saskatoon, Saskatchewan

Printed and bound in Canada by
Modern Press
Saskatoon, Saskatchewan

Cover design by John Luckhurst

Western Producer Prairie Books publications are produced and manufactured
in the middle of western Canada by a unique publishing venture owned by a
group of prairie farmers who are members of Saskatchewan Wheat Pool. Our
first book in 1954 was a reprint of a serial originally carried in *The Western
Producer*, a weekly newspaper serving western Canadian farmers since 1923.
We continue the tradition of providing enjoyable and informative reading for
all Canadians.

Canadian Cataloguing in Publication Data

Eager, Evelyn, 1919-
    Saskatchewan government

    Bibliography: p.
    Includes index.
    ISBN 0-88833-066-9 pa.

    1. Saskatchewan - Politics and government -
History. I. Title.
JL308.E2   320.97124   C80-091069-9

To the Kenaston community,
where my parents farmed

Contents

Preface

This book is intended to appeal to both the general reader and the academic. Therefore footnotes have been kept to a minimum, and they have been used only to show the sources of material and not to provide additional information. General readers who wish to read straight through the book may safely ignore both footnotes and footnote numbers in the text without feeling that they are missing any essential content.

Again for the benefit of the general reader, some particularly detailed material which is likely to be of interest only to the academic has been placed in two appendices at the end of the book. Chapters 3 and 8 deal with the main facts and conclusions concerning the matters discussed in the appendices, so the body of the book is complete in itself.

Any book that deals with current situations has to be cut off at some particular time, so this account does not include events later than 1979.

Acknowledgments

To acknowledge individually the archivists and librarians who over the years helped to supply, as it were, grist for the mill, is not possible. To mention only two, my former colleague Doug Bocking in the Saskatchewan Archives, and Christine MacDonald, the Legislative Librarian, is not to deny the debt owed to other librarians and to many other archivists in both the Regina and Saskatoon divisions of the Saskatchewan Archives and in the Public Archives of Canada.

To Dr. Norman Ward of the University of Saskatchewan, who read the manuscript and provided valuable comments and suggestions, my sincere thanks are due. Dr. Elizabeth Arthur of Lakehead University, and colleagues in political science, gave similar help at earlier stages of the work.

Bob and Tanyss Phillips played a very special role. It was in 1972, I believe, that Bob took me in hand and set a deadline for what was to be a speedy conclusion of an already over-long enterprise. In the following interval, and through various successive deadlines, both Bob and Tanyss read the manuscript, made suggestions, and above all gave encouragement. My particular appreciation goes to them.

Holly O'Neill of Thunder Bay and Nora Johnson of Regina were the typists who converted convoluted manuscript offerings into expertly typed pages.

Grants from the Canada Council for short-term and summer work, and a grant from the Saskatchewan Public Administration Foundation are gratefully acknowledged.

1   Political Roots

Three myths surround the prairie pioneer. According to the first myth he enjoyed an independent life free of restraint, he was self-sufficient, and he asked no help. A second and conflicting myth saw him as being instinctively inclined toward co-operation and socialism. A third myth, partly related to the second, was his presumed radicalism.

Reality differed from myth. A pioneer settler was restricted and bound by conditions largely beyond his control. He showed no hesitation in protesting restrictions which were man-made and in seeking assistance for enterprises which were beyond individual ability. In protests and approach, the outlook and methods of the prairie pioneer were pragmatic and conservative.

The independent spirit which had brought the settler west was confronted by two great restrictions that dominated prairie life from the beginning: the demands of the new environment, and the more distant but ever pervasive domination from "the east". Prairie settlement required accommodation to these two forces and, simultaneously, both individual and joint effort to limit their impact.

The federal homestead policy for the west attracted the individualist. The government offer of "160 acre farms in western Canada free" raised visions of an independent little kingdom for a mere ten-dollar registration fee. The precise terms under which the homesteader took up his land encouraged him to retain his individual area and to enlarge it. Official policy gave him a tentative hold on a quarter section of land. It also gave him three years to "prove up" his hold through compliance with certain residence, building, and farming requirements, and to secure title. Official policy held out a further allurement, during part of the homestead period, of an adjoining "pre-emption" quarter section to be held in reserve for his future purchase. Alongside the homesteader, the more affluent settler who purchased land outright, and the newcomers who had been brought by a settlement scheme faced the same practical demand to fulfill and enlarge the economic potential of their holdings.

Although settlement policy attracted the individualist, the realities of pioneer life made survival impossible in a totally independent way of life. Prairie settlers' activities were inevitably dictated by the urgency of the seasons and by the vicissitudes of climate, weather, and a host of unpredictable calamities. To whatever degree a settler might consider himself master of his farmstead, he was nevertheless enslaved by the pressure of routine duties and by the constant attention which the farmstead demanded. Isolation required a high degree of self-reliance, which gave, in the short term, an aura of independence. That same isolation increased the individual's dependence on community effort for those services which are essential for long-term living.

Whatever the hardihood, ingenuity, and tirelessness of a settler, he had to recognize individual limitations. The informal mutual helpfulness which began with the first neighbors developed into more formal efforts at co-operation as broader needs were faced. The same diligent and practical approach that was necessary in the management of an individual farm extended to community enterprises. Joint effort might be no more than pressure on the government for a particular service. Schools, roads and bridges, railways, courthouses, and land titles offices were urgently sought. Then local or province-wide co-operative organization developed in such areas as telephones, creameries, and grain elevators. Such co-operative action might be a second resort, after ineffective petitioning for government ownership and operation.

These two strains of individualism and of co-operation which resulted from the nature and the necessities of pioneer beginnings contended in prairie life. The homesteader remained an individualist but he was not independent. Co-operative enterprises which arose from his dependence were not usually based on idealistic or theoretical premises. Co-operation was pragmatic. It developed in specific areas of prairie life to meet practical needs, and it was meant to serve an individualistic purpose. Co-operation was the means to an end: the end itself was the ownership and operation of an individual farm.

The great burst of prairie settlement occurred between 1896 and 1914. Earlier settlement had been slow. In the area which is now Saskatchewan, English and French half-breed groups had become established at Prince Albert and in the Duck Lake area by 1870. Small settlements sparsely dotted the Territories, made up of religious or national groups, along with some groups established by colonization companies in the 1880s and early 1890s. Early settlement along the Canadian Pacific Railway line followed the railway's coming in 1882. General economic depression and the collapse of the earlier land boom, the Riel rebellion, and drought, frost, and hail all had a part in slowing settlement in the 1880s. The 1891 census showed a population of 67,554 persons spread throughout the Territories—barely enough for a small city if they were all scraped together.

This slack period in settlement was used to advantage for the provision of basic facilities for the advance guard of settlers who had already arrived and for the influx that was to follow. The Dominion Lands Act of 1872 established the free homestead policy. The land was surveyed, and the Mounted Police force was formed and moved into the Territories the following year, in 1874. Treaties were made with the Indians. A telegraph line was in operation by 1896. In 1882 the C.P.R. overcame the barrier of the Canadian Shield which had barred easy access from the east. Less dramatic, but of vital importance in the prairie climate, was the development of an earlier maturing wheat during the late 1880s.

The impetus to fill this elementarily prepared new land came from Clifford Sifton, the Minister of the Interior in Wilfrid Laurier's Liberal government that came to power in 1896. Modern advertising techniques were fully matched eighty years ago in an intensive publicity campaign in the United States, Britain, and continental Europe. Fulsome descriptions and exaggerated claims for the largely unpeopled prairies were sent far and wide. Capping the praise for the land was the overwhelming inducement of 160 acres of it as a free gift to all comers. The stark price of hardship and privation that would eventually have to be paid in establishing the homestead was not recognized until too late, or it was stoically accepted by the thousands who came to claim their prize.

In the United States, where less farming land was still available, pamphlets, newspapers, farming journals, and immigration agents advertised "the richest land on earth", free, just to the north, with "the best climate". In the British Isles printed inducements were supplemented by brightly-painted "farming wagons" which were driven through the countryside, decorated with wheat sheaves and inviting all to "Share in the Last Best West." Lectures and lantern slides were widely used, and Canadian maps decorated British schoolroom walls. In both Britain and the United States, Canadian booths at agricultural shows and fairs overflowed with the riches of Canada's produce.

In Europe, advertising literature and posters in a variety of languages were widely distributed, even though the direct solicitation of immigrants was forbidden in many European countries. If they were not sent in plain brown wrappers, at least letter-sized advertising cards could be mailed in plain envelopes advertising 160 acres free from among Canada's 200 million acres. Immigration agents who could speak their languages were sent to individual countries, immigration offices were opened, and bonuses for bringing in new settlers were paid to steamship companies, which in turn spread paeans of praise for the bounty of the new land.

Settlers swarmed in both individually and in groups. Most came for their free homestead quarter, but those who could afford it also bought land. Friends and acquaintances, or those with religious or ethnic ties, often migrated together and settled in the same area, even though each settler was essentially on his own. Colonization companies were active in gathering together prospective settlers for the large tracts of land which they had acquired. These companies sprang up in each of the major areas from which settlers came, and they varied in background and motives, and certainly in efficiency. There were those pitifully disorganized companies such as the Barr colonists from England in 1903, whose numbers included, for example, the migrant who had been assured by the company's organizer of his eminent suitability for western Canadian life because, having been in Boston for a time, he would be sure to know about conditions in the far west.

On the other hand there were the smoothly run operations of the Wm. Pearson Co. Ltd., which ran fortnightly excursions from the United States into the Last Mountain Valley from 1910 to 1913. These landseekers were brought in by rail and then driven in democrats by "a fleet of some thirty to forty beautiful teams of horses" over the company's land, parcels of which were auctioned off to individuals as the party drove along. The North Atlantic Trading Company, an umbrella organization of German steamship agents, was secretly subsidized by the Canadian government from 1899 until 1906 to bring settlers not only from northern European countries such as Holland, Denmark, and Germany, but even from as far as northern Italy, Roumania, Bulgaria, Serbia, and Finland. From 1905 to 1914, homestead entries in Saskatchewan varied from close to 28,000 in 1906 to more than 14,000 in 1914, 1913 being a peak year for the prairies as a whole, with some one million immigrants of all kinds.

The homestead policy under which the west was settled lent itself to this intermingling of company enterprise and individual initiative. The survey system divided the country into townships of thirty-six sections of land, each section being one mile square and containing 640 acres. Less than half of the total was open to homesteading. Homestead land was the even-numbered sections in each township, minus almost two sections of Hudson's Bay Company land. This was the land which the Company kept when it sold the northwest to Canada after Confederation, under the terms of the sale that the Company would still own one-twentieth of the land in the agricultural area.

The other half of the land, the odd-numbered sections, was either retained for the time being as crown lands, designated as school lands, or given to railway companies in the generous granting system by which railway construction was encouraged. In this way the C.P.R. received approximately one-half of the land for twenty-four miles on each side of its main line, checker-boarded with the even-numbered homestead sections. Further land grants were made for C.P.R. branch lines and to other railway companies. The school lands amounted to two sections in each township (thus to one-eighteenth of the whole), with the proceeds from their sale earmarked for public schools.

Colonization companies therefore might purchase land from the crown's odd-numbered sections or its school lands, or from the Hudson's Bay Company or the railways. The railways were the most willing to sell early and cheaply because the resultant settlers provided them with new revenue, while there was a tendency for the Hudson's Bay Company and school lands to be held for higher prices.

Settlement showed a lumpy sort of homogeneity. There were pockets of those relatively better-off settlers who had taken a free homestead and who had also bought land, probably from the company which had brought them in; there were a few very large, well-to-do farms; there were even fewer communal groups such as Mennonites, who had been settled under special land regulations; there were varied areas where Germans, British, Scandinavians, Americans, Ukrainians, Poles, or any of a large number of nationalities prevailed, and there were those groups which had common ties to eastern Canada. In few places were any of these economic or national blocks solid. Often a varying number of nationalities were intermingled. Throughout the whole area there was the prototype homesteader in his tiny shack—often a bachelor—struggling to win his gamble with the government for his 160 acres.

Homesteaders were inevitably widely-spaced. Only alternate sections were available for homesteading, and these sometimes included the pre-emptive quarter sections reserved for the adjoining homesteader's future purchase. The disadvantages of having blocks of empty land between settlers—whether pre-emption, railway, Hudson's Bay Company, or school or other crown land—were balanced by the opportunity for future expansion which the blocks of land provided. This acceptance of present inconvenience for the sake of future economic prospects accorded with the pioneer outlook. Some settlers deliberately sought particularly remote locations, less from anti-social instincts than for the economic prospects for expansion which they afforded.

Attitudes toward the new land varied as widely as the people who came. Some were buoyed by a high sense of adventure, while others were homesick. Some saw the open prairie as beautiful and exciting; others saw it as bleak and cruel. Many who came left, and others stayed only because they had no money to leave. Some enjoyed the simple fact of a new country, and others cared only for the possession of their own individual portions of it. One thing was common to all: there was a need to adapt and adapt quickly if they were to stay and survive.

The survey system itself set the tone. It was uniformly applied without modification over flat fertile plains, bush country, grazing lands, coulees, creeks and sloughs, hills, and alkali flats. It was a straightforward and practical system for pin-pointing precisely every quarter-mile surface in a vast open area. At the same time the system imposed an unyielding pattern into which human living must fit. It could be defied only temporarily by the pioneers' prairie trails cutting diagonally along the shortest route. As the barbed wire symbol of farming progress gradually hemmed off quarter sections of land, the trails were abandoned, grown over, and eventually plowed under. The prescribed rectangular road pattern—a mile apart running north and south, two miles apart east and west—was a visible aspect of the conformity which the country demanded.

Adaptation differed in detail according to variations in the broad terrain from the Canadian Shield to the Rockies. Nowhere were the terms of accommodation more demanding than on the open prairie, where the major part of Saskatchewan settlement occurred. Here survival and success depended on a single resource, land—mainly fertile land, but land set nakedly in a harsh environment. Adaptation to its demands was evident in the settler's basic activities—in farming, education and religion, and in social life.

Farming in particular showed the need for continual and deliberate adaptation to particular conditions and the disastrous results of failing to adapt. From the beginning the pressure of a short growing season was evident in the spring rush of seeding to catch early rains and in the even fiercer race against frost and early snow in the fall. Summer-fallowing was a much heralded and universally accepted development of dry land farming. In the main, however, the farming practices brought with the settlers were continued, and these included the plowing and frequent cultivation which had been learned in wetter areas. The appalling climatic conditions of the dirty thirties revealed this traditionalism as insufficient adaptation and led to the eventual realization that farming techniques which were suitable elsewhere had been too uncritically followed. Lack of rainfall was the obvious and most devastating calamity. The part played by unsuitable farming practices in the overall disaster came to be realized only gradually and less dramatically. Extensive experimentation and trial with alternative methods and equipment at experimental farms, individual farms, and at the university led to marked changes. There was a belated recognition that even under normal climatic conditions, the prairies would tolerate long-term farming only with those practices and machinery which were tailored to prairie requirements.

Education showed the imprint of the province's major occupation. Agriculture was emphasized at the University of Saskatchewan from the beginning, not only in instruction but in research and extension work. Farm machinery, grains and grasses, forage crops, flowers and shrubs, rust, wireworms, cutworms, army worms, sawflies, horses, cattle, sheep and hogs—all claimed university attention for development, testing, experimentaton, or control. Active extension programs took information to the farmer and took the farmer to the university, so that the rural population saw the institution as being directed to its needs and regarded the university as its own. Not only did the student share the university with the farmer, but even the academic calendar was affected by farming. A short and intense academic year enabled farm students to help with the harvest and to be available again for spring seeding.

The spiritual field as well as the temporal showed the effect of sparse population and of equally sparse resources. Every religious denomination of those early days has its own story of accommodation and adaption to pioneer conditions. It was customary and natural for isolated representatives of a particular denomination to attend the services of some other church that existed in the community, or for various denominations to use the same building. Some went beyond that into more formal association. It is not surprising that the official union which brought the United Church of Canada into existence in 1925 had actually been consummated years before in many Saskatchewan congregations.

Above all, the prairies shaped their own brand of social life. Early dominance by settlers from eastern Canada and the United States was evident in annual Orange parades and in July the Fourth celebrations. These imported festivities gave way gradually to Grain Growers' picnics and local sports days. Day-to-day social customs and the attitudes brought with the settlers were affected even more quickly by pioneer requirements. Thus mutual helpfulness and open-handed friendliness combated space, isolation, and privation. At the same time there was a rejection of previously established standards of what was socially acceptable and an adoption of new standards based on currently existing circumstances. In the elemental conditions of early settlement, pretension was scorned, and if it was not entirely eliminated from prairie life, affectation was seen as one of the cardinal sins. Social distinctions of class and family which gave importance to members of an established society served little purpose in proving up a homestead.

Despite its much vaunted egalitarianism, pioneer life developed its own distinctions and classes, although they were masked by a general participation in many activities, so that there was an illusion of social homogeneity. There were the big farmers and the small farmers, and the settler who came with sufficient capital to buy land often operated on a quite different level from the homesteader who had smaller holdings. Given a head start by his greater resources, the richer settler either began on a grander scale or at least had a better chance to achieve the prestigious ranking of a big farmer.

There was a social distinction between the country people and the town people, too. Even though there would be a friendly mingling of all on occasion, every child knew the difference between being "a country kid" and being "a town kid". The farmer clung to his occupational badge of bibbed denim overalls just as tenaciously as townsmen, even the non-professionals, tended to avoid them. Town housewives were inclined to arrange their shopping to keep aloof from the combined visiting and shopping which characterized the western institution of Saturday night in town. These and similar distinctions were blurred rather than sharp. They were real nevertheless, and they developed out of the conditions of prairie life.

Another broad division existed between Anglo-Saxons and other ethnic groups. Again, although they were unmistakable, ethnic lines of division were irregular rather than uniformly applied. Eastern Canadian and American immigrants, by and large, set the tone and standards of early Saskatchewan life. Other newcomers were accepted to the extent to which they could and would fit into the existing pattern. Because of the language barrier and the difference of customs, continental Europeans in general were not included in social and community activities. They were, in varying degrees of Anglo-Saxon reference, termed hunkies or foreigners, or they were lumped together by a single national name applied to all, such as "Galician", "Ruthenian", or "Austrian". When their language and customs conformed to the established pattern, notably in the second generation, they became full-fledged members of the community and achieved at the same time a place for their cultural traditions. From the beginning they were accepted and respected in the area where they fitted into the required pattern; by and large they knew farming.

Settlers from the British Isles had to face the same utilitarian standards. With no language barrier and frequently with a broader educational and cultural background than their neighbors had, they were often leaders in community activities. This superiority did not necessarily carry over into the workaday world. British living was in general scant preparation for prairie homesteading. "Green Englishmen" consequently rated low by the unrelenting criteria of their farm neighbors. Ultimate accommodation to the basics of prairie life was the price both for survival and for full acceptance.

Adaptation to prairie living did not mean absolute subjection to its material dictates. Along with the need for meeting elemental necessities was an individual and community refusal to be restricted merely to survival. Early informal social gatherings were supplemented by literary, musical, and dramatic enterprises which arose out of the interests and skills that settlers brought with them. One early group operated under the obviously imported title of the Mechanics and Literary Institute. Library services developed early on the prairies, supplementing the loaning and rereading of the books which had been among the carefully selected effects of many settlers. Annual school Christmas concerts, schoolhouse dances, Homemakers' clubs, orchestras and bands, community clubs, and fairs and sports days with their own prairie flavour gradually developed out of local interests and activities.

Politics showed the same pragmatism that was evident in other aspects of prairie life. The yardstick against which political performance was measured was its conformity to agrarian needs. Just as settlers brought with them tentatively accepted social and agricultural practices which could be continued, adapted, or ultimately discarded, so established political parties also were given a trial. To the extent that the traditional eastern Canadian parties, the Liberals and Conservatives, adapted to prairie requirements, they were accepted. To the extent that they failed to satisfy local needs, protest parties arose—first the Progressives, and then the CCF and Social Credit. During the first quarter century of Saskatchewan's history, the Liberals illustrated the success of a traditional party that could adapt to agrarian demands. The CCF later represented the other alternative —that of a protest party developing out of and tailoring itself to local requirements.

Idealism was not absent, and fervent idealists would either oppose or take part in organized political parties. Particularly in the protest parties, theoretical doctrines were advanced and maintained with enthusiasm and vigor. Nevertheless, electoral experience showed that votes were won less by theories than by practical considerations.

A precarious economic base was the key to the province's political pattern as well as to its relationship with the east. Pragmatism and caution were dictated by the insecurity which has always been a factor in Saskatchewan life. It would be an exaggeration to say that pioneer farmers began on ten dollars of capital, the amount of the homestead registration fee, but for some pioneers it would not be a gross exaggeration. A perilous existence continued in a one-crop economy which was sometimes buoyant but always highly uncertain and frequently disastrous.

Resentment was added to insecurity in western relations with the east, and on the prairies the east meant Ontario and Quebec. It was eastern institutions which exercised monopoly control over the economic necessities of the west: railways and marketing facilities, financial services, and farm machinery production. Similarly, greater population ensured political power for the central provinces. Federal policies in such vital matters as tariffs and freight rates were seen to benefit eastern interests to the disadvantage of the west. Resentment against related economic and political domination was directed impartially against Bay and St. James Streets, and against parliament hill.

Western reaction to this domination gave rise to the myth of prairie radicalism. The west protested those policies which were disadvantageous to its welfare. When the protests were ignored it repeated them with greater vigor, and it organized. Because the protests and the organization were directed against established interests they were labelled radical. The late James M. Minifie, a noted C.B.C. correspondent, in recounting the experiences of his homesteader father, described the reaction to a plan worked out by a group of early settlers. His father and others decided in 1909 to co-operate in a scheme, Mr. Minifie said,

which would dispose of grain at top prices and return the profits to the growers instead of to a horde of middlemen who were then skimming them off. The scheme drew the full fire of the vested interests. They used all media to oppose it; in the press they represented the grain growers' leaders as dangerous radicals . . . , [who] would destroy society . . . , ruin the country, and tear down everything the Fathers of Confederation had built up (by which they meant the vested interests—banks, railroads, and international grain speculators).[1]

Contrary to their label of radicalism, Saskatchewan protesters generally did not seek any fundamental change in the structure of society. They wished merely to bring about a shift in direction of the income resulting from the existing system. Their goal was conservative, and their methods were equally conservative and orderly.

Rejecting doctrinaire proposals which were advanced from time to time, frequently from American groups, Saskatchewan farmers developed their own organization as a sturdy pragmatic tool to serve their particular needs.

The Saskatchewan Grain Growers' Association had its beginnings as a territorial organization, and it served the farmers' interests at various levels. Organized to fight eastern monopoly privilege in grain marketing and handling, it used orthodox and well-accepted methods. It petitioned the government, and it employed the established method of marketing grain through the Winnipeg Grain Exchange. Within the province it had strong influence and associations with the governing Liberal party. At the local level it performed many community functions as a tradesman and as a farmers' educational and social organization. The Grain Growers' and succeeding associations had no doubts about their purpose, which was firmly represented in the slogan, "Our Objective—Economic Security."

Modern agriculture is vastly different from that of pioneer days. A complete transformation of farming methods and of farm living has occurred within the lifetime of many who first turned over their own particular areas of prairie sod. Monstrous machinery has absorbed into one holding what was originally a few or even several farmsteads. Capital requirements have increased immensely. Cars, improved roads, rural electricity, central heating, and even plumbing have reduced in substantial measure the early isolation and privation. Population distribution and social patterns have changed. Many of the people and even more of the community spirit have abandoned rural areas. An earlier gradual shift from the farms has accelerated rapidly in the past few decades. An urban population in the province of thirty per cent in 1951 increased to fifty-three per cent in the following twenty years, and the increase has continued.

Efforts have been made to relieve the precariousness of farming. Crop insurance and government assistance help to cushion disaster years. Controlled marketing facilities reduce the unpredictable effects of fluctuating prices. Control over pests and plant diseases has greatly increased. Professional agricultural advice and the results of continued experimentation and testing are available to farmers.

Diversification has been stressed both in areas other than agriculture and within agriculture itself. Encouragement of industry and efforts to broaden the economic base of the province so as to lessen dependence on a single occupation have been emphasized by successive governments. After a period of restricted markets in the 1960s and a consequent wheat glut, which underlined the hazard of one-crop farming, diversification of farm operations to other grains or to livestock was explored.

Despite enormous changes, basic realities of the Saskatchewan scene remain constant. Three-quarters of a century after the province was formed, its well-being still depends mainly on wheat—how much is grown, how much is sold, and how much it brings. The shrinking rural population has not meant a decline in production but merely that more can now be grown by fewer people. Although Saskatchewan's population has become mainly urban, its economy is still predominantly agricultural. Industrialization, diversification, potash, or oil may receive emphasis or publicity, but wheat is still king.

Problems of farm insecurity remain. Although there has been an increase in the capital outlay of modern farming compared with the meager amount required in homestead days, there has not been a corresponding increase in stability. The best efforts of science cannot remove the farmer's basic dependence on environmental factors. Government measures to alleviate the impact of crop failures or price fluctuations have lessened but by no means eliminated farmers' anxiety. Even in buoyant times, a major topic of consideration in agricultural studies, in public discussion, and in farm newspapers is agricultural stabilization.

Political implications similarly remain unchanged. The farmer today, in the lofty cushioned and air-conditioned cab of a modern tractor, has his political roots just as firmly fixed in the land he cultivates as did his pioneer ancestor, dust-swirled behind four oxen on the iron seat of a breaking plow. Those roots do not stop with the farmer. They quickly extend to the urban dweller, whose economic welfare varies in direct relation to agricultural production. A Saskatchewan politician overlooks these agricultural roots to his sorrow. Premier Ross Thatcher, toppled from power in the 1971 election, belatedly acknowledged this basic truth when he said, "The fact of political life in Saskatchewan is that if you have forty problems and one of them is that wheat isn't selling, the other thirty-nine don't count." Seven years later, after two more elections and in a time of extensive resource development, his NDP successor in office pronounced farming to be "the backbone of our Saskatchewan way of life."

Furthermore, even as oil and potash revenues increase and uranium prospects cause euphoria, the political difference between this revenue and that from wheat sales is significant. Royalties and corporation taxes go to the government, but wheat money goes to the individual. Without dismissing the importance of government royalties, the effect of such revenue on the voter is indirect and diluted compared with the impact of grain cheques coming directly to the farmer or of the volume of a store's retail sales.

The modern westerner feels resentment against eastern domination no less keenly than did his earlier counterpart. Some particulars have changed, but basic postures and long-standing grievances remain, with occasionally a new one added. Resolutions of the early Grain Growers' Association for more satisfactory facilities for grain loading and transportation are matched seventy-five years later by protests against rail line abandonment and by re-echoing demands for better allocation of grain box cars.

Through concentration of population and political power, the interests of central Canada continue to be represented as the national interest. A contrary approach is therefore seen as regionalism, and is stigmatized as selfish opposition to the general welfare. The westerner notes that general freight rates which are controlled in the east and oil which flows from the west operate under entirely different criteria. The rules of the marketplace have long permitted higher freight rates across the prairies because of lack of competition. Oil, flowing in the other direction, is exempt from such rules, and its price is controlled—in the national interest.

The accommodation which the western agriculturist must make in relating to his local environment and to his eastern neighbors may have changed in detail or emphasis but not in essentials. His political motivation is basically the same, too. The pragmatic and conservative outlook of pioneer days is still evident in the modern struggle to retain the system of individually owned farms which has prevailed from the beginning of prairie settlement, and upon which the economy of the province still largely rests.

2   Territorial Government and Autonomy

When Saskatchewan became a province on September 1, 1905, it continued the British system of responsible government that had been established in Territorial days. The pattern of constitutional struggle during the Territorial period paralleled earlier developments in other provinces. After the early period of a personal and autocratic rule, the Northwest Territories gradually had achieved an elected assembly and then a fully responsible executive. The transition from Territorial to provincial status was accomplished with a minimum of constitutional disruption. Geographically the new province formed only part of the former Territories; politically the non-partisan system which had existed in Territorial assemblies gave way to party government; and economically the subsidy system replaced the annual grant from Ottawa. New powers were added, and new men held office. The basic constitutional and administrative practices continued, however, from Territorial into provincial government.

In the Northwest Territories' earliest period as a part of Canada, from 1870 to 1876, Territorial affairs were directed mainly from Ottawa. In 1870 the dominion of Canada took control of that vast area stretching west and north from Manitoba to British Columbia which had formerly been Hudson's Bay Company territory. Federal legislation had been passed in the previous year for temporary provision of government, the main characteristics of which were rule by the lieutenant governor of Manitoba, assisted eventually by a local council, but under tight control from Ottawa.

In the second stage, from 1876 until formation of the province in 1905, the area was governed under the terms of the North-West Territories Act which Parliament had passed in 1875. The two major landmarks of this period were the gaining of an elected assembly for the Territories in 1888 and the achievement of responsible government in 1897.

The North-West Territories Act first provided for government organization within the area, even though under its terms Ottawa still exercised considerable control. A resident lieutenant governor was to be assisted by a council, appointed by the federal government, which would exercise both legislative and executive powers. An even closer union of powers was provided by including the three stipendiary magistrates of the Territories as part of the council, which originally had five members in all. The use of the magistrates reduced the number of salaries to be paid. The Act provided for additional members to be elected to sit with appointed members of council as the population increased, and for the council ultimately to evolve into an elected assembly. The Act outlined the areas in which the council had authority to legislate and the restrictions under which it was to operate.

Local governments and school districts could organize only where an electoral district for a council member had been formed. Formation of an electoral district required a population of a thousand adults in an area not exceeding a thousand square miles. Once this magic number had been achieved, municipal organization with power to tax could be set up as soon as the electoral district had been formed. School districts came next in the chain, since they could be established only where there was a system of taxation, and thus only in municipalities. A further provision concerning schools became the basis of later controversy (described in chapter 3); this provision gave religious minorities the right to establish separate schools and to have their tax support go to the separate instead of the public school.

Provision for an entirely elected assembly representing all the Territories was hailed as a notable amendment to the North-West Territories Act in 1888. There had been mounting agitation for a method of representation to include the whole area since 1884, when the number of elected members had surpassed the number of those appointed to the council.

The dual legislative and executive role of the council had also created problems. The lieutenant governor was theoretically responsible to council for the exercise of a variety of powers such as establishment of health, statute labor, school, and other districts, the granting of licenses, and various appointments. Geographical and practical considerations made consultation difficult, and many powers inevitably had to be delegated to the lieutenant governor, so that the council lost effective control.

An assembly which was a distinctly legislative body representing all the Territories now existed. The major problem remained that this new assembly had no more effective control over the lieutenant governor than the old council had had. The amendment creating the assembly made almost no provision for an executive body through which the assembly might work. The nearest approach was that the lieutenant governor could select four of the assembly members as an advisory council. These members held office at the lieutenant governor's pleasure and were to advise in matters of finance which came from Territorial sources. This council was a strange half-caste creation, midway between an assembly committee and an executive body. It lacked real executive power, and it was restricted to consideration of only the smallest portion of Territorial revenue.

The major source of Territorial income was the annual grant from the federal government, which was administered solely by the lieutenant governor. Finances from Territorial sources, in which the advisory council was to have a voice, were minimal, since they came from such things as licenses and fines. The Territories protested the lack of local control over the annual grant; Ottawa replied that it was federal money and should therefore be administered by its representative, the lieutenant governor.

During the period from 1888 until 1897, there was constitutional struggle in the Territories to replace the ineffectual advisory council (and the executive committee which succeeded it) with a true executive council that had financial control and owed responsibility to the assembly.

The assembly was divided roughly between the reformers who wanted an extension of assembly power and those who favored the status quo. The period was characterized by unsuccessful demands from the assembly for an accounting of all moneys, by memorials to the federal government, resignations of the advisory council, and by other maneuvers and counter-maneuvers. As well as the avowed division on constitutional principles, unpublicized factors which divided the members were "differences of temperament, differences of opinion on tactics, and, to some extent at least, personal jealousies and ambitions."[1]

A factor which initially helped the reform group was the willingness of some of the lieutenant governors to let the advisory council exercise broader executive powers than had actually been granted in the amendment to the North-West Territories Act. Immediately after the assembly was formed, the lieutenant governor gave the advisory council a voice in the expenditure of the federal grant as well as in the spending of the smaller Territorial revenues to which they were legally restricted. Federal opposition to such a liberal stand by the lieutenant governor led to a retreat in this area, however. The assembly meanwhile attempted to extend the duties of the advisory council into areas other than finance.

Gradual progress was made, partly by the federal government's granting some concessions and partly by others being exercised in practice, even when they had not been formally conceded. From 1891 a member of the executive committee, F. W. G. Haultain, remained in Regina between sessions for permanent supervision over Territorial affairs, and in 1895 he was joined by a second full-time member, J. H. Ross. They operated without formal executive status, however, and no departmental organization was attempted. The executive committee acted as a whole on matters that needed attention. The assembly eventually gained practical control of finances, even when the principle of responsible government still was withheld.

Full responsible government was granted in 1897 by an amend-

ment to the North-West Territories Act. The amendment established
an executive council which under British parliamentary tradition
implied its responsibility to the assembly. When the legislation came
into effect on October 1, Haultain was asked to form the executive.
Although he did not himself adopt the title of "Premier", common
usage of the term recognized the constitutional change which had
occurred. Administrative departments now were established to assume
responsibility for specific areas of government activity.

Finance remained the foremost problem. Inadequate revenue had
been a source of irritation from earliest days. The problem grew with
increased settlement after 1896 and with consequent demands for
roads, bridges, schools, and other essentials. Local taxation was not to
be considered in a pioneer population that was struggling to establish
itself. Premier Haultain shrewdly pointed out to the government at
Ottawa that direct taxation on early settlers would militate against
immigration appeals. Territorial land was under federal control and
the Territories had neither any basis for borrowing nor any authority
to borrow. Territorial revenues from licenses and fees remained
minimal.

The major source of revenue continued to be the grant from the
federal government. The Territories regarded this grant as inadequate
and uncertain, since it was given on a yearly basis at Ottawa's
discretion. Territorial authorities pressed for the grant to be replaced
by a subsidy, such as was paid to the provinces, to provide a more
secure financial basis. Even requests for those increases in the annual
grant which were needed to provide for settlers brought in by the
federal government's own immigration policy were turned aside. On
one occasion at least, Ottawa refused on exactly the same grounds on
which the Territories had made its request. Prime Minister Laurier
explained that the rapid development of the country had forced such
heavy federal expenditure that it could not add anything to the
Territorial budget.[2]

Demands for provincial autonomy which emerged at the turn of the
century arose directly out of the Territories' financial problems.
Earlier flurries of autonomy talk had arisen for other reasons. In the
1800s autonomy had been included among a confusion of proposed
solutions for inadequate representation in the council. In the early
1890s agitation developed out of the competitive ambitions of
expanding towns. After the achievement of responsible government,
and with the beginning of the immigration boom, provincial
establishment was looked to as a means of financial stability.

Autonomy became a regular subject of assembly debate. In the
budget speech of 1899, the Territorial treasurer cautioned that
financial arrangements were the cardinal points to keep in mind in
autonomy discussions. The Territories should demand the whole of
the lands, and compensation for those lands which the dominion
government had given in railway and other grants. An assembly
Memorial of May 2, 1900 was the first official approach to the federal
government to ask for provincial status. In this and in following

requests, in initial discussions and in intermittent communications which followed, up to the eventual start of autonomy negotiations in January of 1905, financial considerations remained foremost in Territorial concern.

Constitutional grievances were interwoven from time to time with financial considerations, but generally they were given less emphasis. In a letter of December 7, 1901 to Prime Minister Laurier, Premier Haultain recited financial necessities and legislative and administrative problems. These problems included duplication of effort in the administration of justice and resentment that the dominion retained control of land title registrations even after the Territorial assembly had been granted power to legislate on matters of property and civil rights. Other constitutional problems were raised from time to time, but finance remained the principal grievance, even after the annual grant was increased substantially in the years immediately preceding autonomy.

Circumstances outside and within the Territories complicated efforts towards autonomy. These circumstances included Manitoba's wish to annex a part of the Territories, Ottawa's fear of a separate school issue emerging, and political shifts and suspicions within the Territories.

Manitoba's original boundaries included only the southern part of its present area. Its efforts to expand westward into the Territories and Territorial objections to this expansion overshadowed for a time the question of autonomy itself. Territorial residents protested Manitoba's suggestion of annexation in 1896 and 1897, and a Territorial resolution to the federal government in 1897 asked that the boundaries remain untouched. The resolution war continued, with resolutions from Manitoba in 1901 and 1902 urging extension of its boundaries and matching resolutions from the Territories, opposing any encroachment.

The outstanding event of this annexation struggle was a public debate at Indian Head on December 18, 1901, in which Premier Roblin of Manitoba and Premier Haultain of the Territories attempted to outbid each other in inducements to those living within the area. Premier Roblin dangled the tempting prospect of the extension of railway lines if the area became part of Manitoba. Premier Haultain countered with the debt-free position which would be enjoyed in a new province compared with the heavy load of debt which Manitoba had incurred and which any area added to it would have to share.

In addition to a general disinclination in the Territories for annexation, external politics also affected the issue. Since the Conservatives had been returned to power in Manitoba in 1903, provincial bargaining power was seriously weakened in dealing with a federal Liberal administration.

Concern over the school question lurked below the surface. Memories of the violent dispute in Manitoba in 1890 after the province eliminated separate schools still haunted politicians. With separate schools operating in the Territories, the ingredients for a replay existed. Roman Catholics were anxious to keep separate schools, Manitoba had showed the extent of western sentiment against them, and Prime Minister Laurier, a Roman Catholic, was caught in the middle.

Public comment on the question was largely avoided, but hints or charges occasionally surfaced. In 1902 an opposition member from Manitoba bluntly charged in the House of Commons that fear of a controversy over schools was the reason for federal reluctance in negotiating autonomy. Premier Haultain, exasperated by the vacillation and unexplained delay that met his efforts to forward autonomy discussions, suggested to Laurier in 1903 that there were undisclosed reasons for the dominion's unwillingness to discuss autonomy. The Toronto *News* occasionally printed letters, interviews, or editorials which attributed delay to the fear at Ottawa of being caught between the Roman Catholic Church and the independent temper of the west over the question of separate schools. By May of 1904 the newspaper stated that the Church hierarchy had served notice that separate schools must be guaranteed. In October it declared that Laurier and ecclesiastical authorities in Quebec had come to an agreement in the matter, but that nothing would be done or said with respect to it until after the federal election.

Correspondence between Prime Minister Laurier and ecclesiastical officials confirms that, whether by direction from without or from his own convictions, Laurier had determined at least by 1904 that separate schools must be guaranteed in any new province. In writing to Monseigneur Merry del Val, Cardinal secretaire d'Etat in the Vatican, Laurier spoke of probable agitation arising over the school question. He announced his firm conviction of the constitutional right to continuation of separate schools and his confidence that he could carry this right into effect. On the strength of Laurier's guarantee of separate schools, the Apostolic Delegate in Canada used his influence to prevent agitation during the federal election campaign in November, 1904, and upheld a promise that the question would not be discussed in Roman Catholic newspapers.

Territorial government operated on a non-partisan system. Division in the assembly was based on support of or opposition to the government, and so were election platforms, if they were not run on the personality of the candidate. The reason for the non-partisan system was pragmatic. Being financially dependent on the grant that was voted annually at Ottawa, the Territories could not risk incurring the displeasure of either of the two federal parties. Furthermore, it was considered that federal party names had little significance in questions of schools, roads, and public works, which were the major concerns of assembly business.

This restraint in party activity applied only to Territorial politics. The right to participate in federal partisan politics was staunchly defended. Since 1887 the Territories had been represented in the House of Commons by four members (increased to ten in 1904), and

Territorial Liberal and Conservative associations existed to fight federal elections. Ministers of the Territorial cabinet and other members of the assembly openly supported their respective parties in dominion elections, and they were commonly identified in newspapers and elsewhere as Liberal or Conservative in federal politics. It is too much therefore to expect that Territorial politics could have operated entirely in a political vacuum. Assembly members were conscious nevertheless that it was attention to the concerns of their constituents and not a federal party label which elected or defeated them. There seems little doubt that, except for the latter period described below, the non-partisan approach was real, with the parties of the assembly being simply "government" or "opposition". Premier Haultain, a Conservative in federal politics, had two cabinet colleagues who were Liberals federally. He also had other Liberal party supporters in the assembly, and some Conservatives in opposition to him, although there were of course shifts in support from time to time over particular issues.

Premier Haultain lost Liberal confidence, however, just when bi-partisan support was most needed for any move towards autonomy. The disaffection extended to the premier's colleagues in the Territorial assembly and also to the Liberal members of Parliament. The turning point was the Territorial Conservative convention of 1903, which resolved that the next Territorial election should be fought on party lines.

Some agitation for introduction of party lines in the assembly had occurred with the achievement of responsible government, but in general the existing system had been favored. All the cabinet ministers opposed any change when they returned to their constituencies for re-election in the fall of 1897 (under the existing provision that anyone who was appointed to the cabinet had to go back to his constituency for re-election). In the Territorial general election in 1898, the only two candidates who asked publicly for support on a party basis, one Conservative and one Liberal, were defeated.

Contrary to this general feeling, some Conservatives were dissatisfied because Premier Haultain's two cabinet colleagues were both Liberals, and they were not sufficiently appeased even when Haultain brought in a Conservative in February, 1903. Mr. R. B. Bennett, the assembly member from Calgary (later Prime Minister of Canada) spearheaded a drive to introduce party lines. The national Conservative leader was persuaded to call a convention of Territorial Conservatives in Moose Jaw on March 25, 1903. The convention passed a resolution that Conservative candidates, as such, should contest every constituency in the next Territorial election. Also, a Conservative association for Territorial politics was formed.

This resolution to introduce party politics into Territorial elections placed Haultain in an extremely difficult situation. In the convention he opposed the party lines resolution and declared his adherence to the non-partisan tradition. After the resolution was passed, however, he remained in the convention, and he even accepted the office of honorary president of the newly formed Territorial Conservative association.

Haultain failed to reconcile successfully the conflicting claims of involvement in a Territorial party organization and leadership of a non-partisan government. His subsequent course came to be interpreted by Liberals both at Regina and at Ottawa as being dictated by Conservative party considerations. The move towards autonomy was affected by Haultain's altered relations with his own government and assembly, with Territorial members of Parliament, and finally with the dominion government.

Haultain's relations with his colleagues in Regina first came into question. Immediately after the Moose Jaw convention, J. H. V. Bulyea, a Liberal and Haultain's senior cabinet colleague, asked for a clarification of the situation. Premier Haultain gave a press interview in which he indicated that his position on party lines remained unchanged. He followed this statement with another in the assembly on April 22, in which he reaffirmed the accepted political practice in the Territories:

I claim the right to exercise and will exercise to the fullest extent the liberty of speech and opinion with regard to federal matters, subject to the promise that I will not introduce them into local affairs . . . . With regard to my position with the Conservative party, I am in thorough unison with it on all questions of principle . . . . But the policy of that party and those principles have nothing whatever to do with my position in this House or with the business of this House. The country may be satisfied that I will faithfully and sincerely and impartially do my duty and fulfil my trust on the lines I have given time and time again to my constituency, to my colleagues, to the House and to the people of the Territories generally.[3]

That the reassurance felt by assembly members was more apparent than real is evident in a letter from George Brown, a government supporter in the assembly but a Liberal in federal politics. Writing to Walter Scott, the owner and publisher of the Regina newspaper, the *Leader,* and a Liberal member of Parliament, less than two weeks after Haultain's statement, Brown explained:

Haultain's declaration in the Assembly has to a certain extent satisfied his Liberal supporters, but I do not think it fully did so, although I have heard no real expressions of opinion as to dissatisfaction . . . .
. . . it really seems to me that instead of Provincial Autonomy coming next year, when it ought certainly to have come, it should be delayed until we know exactly where we are and know how much confidence the Liberal party in the Legislature here are disposed to place in Haultain. There is no question in the fact that Provincial Autonomy cannot be approached satisfactorily except with the Government in the Territories strong in the confidence of the Legislature and of the country and with no contention from a party standpoint with the Government at Ottawa, and such at the present time is not the case.
Outwardly there is now no opposition, but there seems to be an element of uncertainty among the members as to what is going to happen next.

Apparently Haultain never had so little opposition in the House as he has at the present time, but at the same time, there certainly never was so great a disposition on the part of his real supporters to hold back to see what he means to do before they commit themselves.[4]

The assembly continued its outward appearance of being non-partisan, but beneath the surface the reality had disappeared. During legislative sessions in 1903, caucuses reportedly were held by both Conservatives and Liberals. Withdrawal of support from Haultain by Liberal members was prevented only because of practical political considerations. Liberal strength was not yet sufficient in the Territories to contest a local election if one occurred. Territorial members of Parliament were anxious also that open division should not occur before a federal election. Despite the nominal non-partisanship, the situation from 1903 confirmed the view expressed privately by Walter Scott upon hearing of the Moose Jaw Conservative resolution: "It is nonsense to talk about giving notice to bring in the party lines four years hence. The moment such notice is given the division will occur."[5]

Relations also deteriorated between Premier Haultain and Territorial members at Ottawa just after support from that source had become established. The change in outlook was most evident with Walter Scott, who was later to become the first premier of Saskatchewan. Before 1900, Territorial members of Parliament had notoriously failed to support Territorial financial or constitutional claims. Equally, however, Premier Haultain had failed to ask them for support or to consult with them on his Ottawa visits. After Walter Scott's election in 1900 as the Liberal member from East Assiniboia, he quickly assumed leadership in championing the Territorial cause in Parliament. His presentation of the Territorial position in the House in 1901 was, Haultain wrote to him, "the first real statement of our position by any of our federal representatives either in the House or anywhere else."[6]

Despite his different party allegiance, Scott staunchly championed Haultain. He supported the Territorial premier in his Regina newspaper, quietly solicited support for him in the 1902 Territorial election, in private correspondence expressed confidence in his administration of Territorial affairs, and urged the strong desirability of leaving negotiations for autonomy in his hands. Even after the Moose Jaw convention Scott continued to support Haultain, although he doubted Haultain's good judgement in continuing in the convention after the party lines resolution. Scott also regarded Haultain's statements in the press and in the assembly as being inadequate, and he privately admitted the undesirable effect which Haultain's actions were having at Ottawa. He nevertheless pleaded a certain latitude for Haultain's awkward position, privately defended him against criticism, and expressed confidence that the premier would continue on a non-partisan course.[7]

Scott's views changed later in 1903. By midsummer he noted apparent partisan Conservative positions in Haultain's activity in the

Territorial assembly and also in his relations with Ottawa. Later in the year Scott and other Liberals interested in Territorial politics hoped that Haultain might be removed from the local political scene through a federally arranged appointment. A year later Scott wrote, "Haultain has killed all the strong confidence I had in him. Even after the Moose Jaw Convention . . . . I still believed his pledge that he would continue to do his business on purely local lines, but I now know that ever since that date he has been controlled by Conservative party interests."[8]

An event which especially strained relations was Haultain's failure to use a capital advance after Ottawa had voted it. Lack of borrowing power to provide long-term facilities in the Territories had been a particular grievance of the Territorial government. In 1903 Walter Scott and a Liberal colleague from the Territories, Frank Oliver, took up the cause with particular energy, and a capital advance on which the Territories could draw was voted for the first time. Haultain then took the position that since the dominion government controlled Territorial lands it should pay all expenses without the Territories having to use the borrowing power it had just been granted. On the eve of the presentation of the Territorial budget he informed Bulyea that he did not intend to vote the capital grant. Bulyea was incensed, and his resignation was prevented only through intervention by Liberal members of Parliament and a compromise that Haultain would not refuse the advance outright but would state that it was simply not then being used.

Bulyea and other Liberal members of the assembly believed that Haultain's repudiation of the capital advance was politically inspired, as did Scott and Oliver, who had worked to get the grant. Consequently there was further polarization beneath the surface of Liberal members' feeling, both in the assembly and in the House of Commons, against what they believed to be Haultain's acceding to Conservative party tactics. On the surface the Liberal assembly members continued to support Haultain, largely because of pressure from the federal members. They did not want a split to bring on a Territorial election which would complicate the forthcoming federal election. Scott explained to Clifford Sifton, Minister of the Interior:

The whole explanation is the conviction that to split now would complicate the federal position; and the only way the split was avoided was by Bulyea and the Liberal members pocketing their dissatisfaction. It required a great effort to prevent Bulyea from resigning . . . on the question of the capital advance; he naturally feels that he is stultified and sacrificed by the decision not to utilize the advance now. On the other hand his resignation meant . . . leaving the machinery of government in Tory hands for both local and federal elections; saddling the Liberals unfairly with the onus of bringing the division on party lines; and going into local elections with the advantage wholly with the enemy so far as concerns personnel. In addition it would have made the Autonomy question a much greater issue in the federal elections than it is likely to prove. From the point of view that nothing that could be said or done in the Assembly was going to endanger the position of Liberal candidates in the federal election, I urged Bulyea and the members to at all costs avoid the split now.[9]

That Haultain's vigorous campaigning for the Conservatives in the 1904 federal election further increased strains is not surprising. Participation in federal politics was acceptable, but the timing and nature of Haultain's activity raised questions. He campaigned on autonomy issues, even though Laurier's promise to proceed with negotiations if elected, and the Conservative stand favouring autonomy might have been expected to remove the question from political dispute. Within the Territorial assembly Liberal members again yearned to bring into the open the political division which now existed in fact. Again they were restrained by practical considerations. From the Territorial point of view, at least the appearance of unanimity was desirable until autonomy negotiations were finished. From the party point of view, the Liberals did not want to share with the Conservatives the blame for bringing party division into the Territorial assembly.

Whether or to what degree Premier Haultain's conduct of Territorial affairs was motivated by Conservative party interests is irrelevant so far as his position in autonomy negotiations was concerned. The Liberals saw evidence that his conduct was motivated by party interests. With a Liberal as his senior colleague in the Territorial government, with a dependence upon Liberal support in the assembly, with seven out of ten Liberal members representing the Territories at Ottawa, and with a Liberal government there to decide the fact and terms of autonomy, it was their interpretation of the premier's actions which determined the acceptability of his views. Indicative of the climate of feeling on the eve of autonomy talks was Scott's comment that "We may as well make up our minds now that Haultain will not be suited with any possible terms which may be offered."[10] An interested observer in Ottawa during the talks was "struck by the absence of any official attention to him,"[11] and Haultain himself complained in later years that western Liberal members of Parliament were consulted more than he was during the negotiations.[12]

It is not surprising that official efforts towards autonomy ran a rocky course. Early requests ran into Manitoba's annexation demands, later they were hampered by the political situation in the Territories, and at Ottawa there was the specter of a separate school dispute.

Settlers in the Territories showed scant interest in the question at all. Their attention was fully occupied with immediate problems of establishing themselves, and the public problems which they saw as pressing were schools, bridges, and roads. Constitutional matters were remote by comparison, and their main concern there was to avoid an unnecessarily elaborate and expensive government. Even on the eve of autonomy, the importance of financial rather than constitutional considerations was pointed to editorially in the *Leader:* "Our autonomy demand was never due to any grievous lack of home rule, it was due to a grievous lack of money . . . . Could we be assured of adequate money grants for ten years to come we should be better off without constitutional change for ten years to come . . . ."[13]

The initiative for autonomy therefore fell to the Territorial government, with support from Walter Scott at Ottawa until 1903. A highly optimistic tone prevailed in the first stage of autonomy talks, from the Assembly Memorial of May, 1900, to early in 1902. Soon after the memorial was sent to Ottawa, discussions were held with Clifford Sifton, Minister of the Interior, and Territorial proposals were favorably received. Early in 1901, conferences were held between the Ottawa minister and Territorial officials. A letter from Premier Haultain on January 30 setting forth the need for provincial establishment was followed by Sifton's suggestion of a conference by way "of bringing the matter to a more definite position."[14] As a sequel to the resulting conference in October of 1901, in December Premier Haultain presented, at the Prime Minister's request, a comprehensive statement of the Territorial case.

The atmosphere had suddenly cooled by the time a response was made to Haultain's statement in March of 1902. Unresponsiveness from Ottawa was to prevail until the promise made before the 1904 election, to begin autonomy negotiations immediately after it. In the intervening period requests for autonomy from the Territorial government and assembly were turned aside at Ottawa, while the Territorial government continued to urge upon federal officials the need for greater financial assistance in the absence of constitutional change.

Walter Scott participated actively, but he reversed his stand in 1903 from urging autonomy to recommending postponement. While other Commons members from the Territories remained lukewarm, Scott raised the matter in the House of Commons in 1901 and in 1902, pointing to the need for autonomy and for increased financial resources because of the many new settlers coming into the Territories. He gave various reasons for reversing his stand in 1903, all having to do with finance. Because of submissions that had been made by provincial premiers in the previous year to obtain a change in the provincial subsidy scheme, Scott suggested it was not wise for the Territories to assume provincial status until that matter had been settled. He pointed to the increase in the Territorial grant for that year, which met immediate needs. Most importantly, he explained, autonomy should be delayed until the question of C.P.R. taxation exemption was finally settled. He was referring to an agreement which the dominion government had made with the C.P.R. in 1881 which included tax exemption for the company on its property and lands. A judgement by the Manitoba Supreme Court in March of 1903 ruled that the C.P.R. exemption did not apply to school taxation in the Territories so long as the area lacked provincial status. Scott suggested that there was little doubt that the same judgement would be made on municipal taxation. He considered it a matter of prime importance which should be settled before autonomy became a fact, so that any possibility of avoiding the exemption in a new province, or provinces, might be seized. Undoubtedly an unacknowledged factor in Scott's reversal of his position in 1903 was the recent Moose Jaw convention and the ensuing political situation in the Territorial capital, of which he was keenly aware.

The irony of the Territorial political situation was evident in Haultain's final argument for autonomy in 1904.[15] He pointed to the unanimous support for autonomy in the assembly in order to refute the recommendation for delay that had come from Territorial Liberal members of Parliament. Yet it was pressure from Liberal members of Parliament on Liberal sympathizers in the assembly which had ensured the continuation of apparent, if not real, support for Haultain. It was a ragged background for the autonomy negotiations which began after the Liberals retained power in the 1904 federal election.

3 Our Constitutional Base: The Saskatchewan Act

The inconsistencies and ironies which characterize politics were fully evident in the formation of Alberta and Saskatchewan in 1905. Transfer of public lands from federal to local control had been one of the foremost arguments for autonomy. Instead, the new legislation left control unchanged under the federal government. This arrangement, furthermore, was staunchly defended even by western Liberal members of Parliament who had earlier argued vehemently for transfer.

The school system which had long been accepted amicably in the Territories exploded in a flaming controversy. Clifford Sifton resigned over the schools issue, and even after he had fully won his point he remained outside the cabinet. Prime Minister Laurier, who lost the schools battle and who had hinted that his own resignation would follow Sifton's, continued in office.

Walter Scott twice submitted his resignation as a member of Parliament over the C.P.R. tax exemption question, partly because he felt committed by a public declaration to do so. He later realized that no one (except himself) had interpreted his statement as meaning that he would resign. His resignation later was accepted, not on any matter of principle, but for the practical purpose of freeing him to become the new premier of Saskatchewan.

The speedy progress of autonomy negotiations gave little hint of such future problems. Despite earlier apprehensions and delays, meetings between dominion and Territorial representatives began in Ottawa on January 5, 1905, without obvious clouds in sight. The federal cabinet committee consisted of Prime Minister Laurier and three other cabinet ministers: Charles Fitzpatrick, the Minister of Justice; Sir William Mulock, Minister of Labour and Postmaster General; and Senator R. W. Scott, Secretary of State. Clifford Sifton, who as Minister of the Interior would normally have taken a prominent part in the negotiations, went south early in 1905 for health reasons. He left behind a memorandum on autonomy questions, and Prime Minister Laurier also corresponded with him on certain points during the negotiations. Territorial representatives were Premier Haultain and G. H. V. Bulyea. Haultain had written in December to senators and members of the Commons for the Territories saying that he was anxious to have their co-operation in Ottawa from the outset of negotiations.

Details of the consultations were not made public, but they apparently proceeded without difficulty. They included daily meetings, formal and informal, between the federal negotiating committee and the Territorial representatives, as well as occasional meetings which included all the Northwest senators and members of the Commons. By January 21, Walter Scott reported to a friend in Regina that "the nature of the deal which we will receive" should assume "something like definite lines" within a couple of weeks. On the federal side, Clifford Sifton, in replying on January 22 to a letter from Laurier, similarly expressed satisfaction over the reported rapid progress being made with the bills.

After the conferences, the actual drafting of the bills was left mainly to the Minister of Justice, Charles Fitzpatrick, who had them ready to present to Parliament by February 21. On that day, in a crowded House of Commons, the Prime Minister introduced the bill to establish the new province of Alberta, and he explained that all its provisions would be duplicated in an immediately succeeding bill for Saskatchewan.

Laurier emphasized four subjects which dominated all others in importance in the autonomy bills. These were the number of provinces to be created; the ownership of public land; the financial terms; and the system of schools. Although the school question had remained largely below the surface, open discussion and controversy had occurred for some time within the Territories on the other three matters.

The number of new provinces to be established had been the earliest point of dispute among members of the Territorial assembly, Territorial members of Parliament, and the public. Premier Haultain argued throughout for one large province. At first he had support cutting across party lines, but by 1905 a straight party division had developed on the issue, with Walter Scott and other Liberals recommending two provinces. The shift was in part at least the result of a renewal of Manitoba's earlier agitation to have its boundary extended further west, which was described in chapter 2. In 1905 that province brought its efforts to culmination by sending two cabinet ministers to Ottawa while autonomy negotiations were under way. But Manitoba could not overcome the political handicap of a provincial Conservative government seeking an extension of its boundaries from a federal Liberal government. The federal government furthermore was well aware of the disturbance which such annexation would be sure to create in the Territories as a whole and especially within the area concerned. But to leave Manitoba at its present size and to establish a single large province stretching from Manitoba to British Columbia would create too obvious an imbalance in size. The solution therefore was to refuse expansion for Manitoba but to maintain basic equality in size by establishing two new provinces.

Once the decision for two provinces had been made, the boundary dispute narrowed down to the dividing line between them. The fourth meridian was included in the bill (and was adopted) as the choice of the majority of the Northwest members of Parliament and senators. Opposing views which did not prevail included Haultain's suggestion for a boundary seventy-five miles further east, and the argument of Conservative members in the house for a line sixty miles east of the meridian to include all the ranching country in Alberta. The legislation fixed Saskatchewan's eastern limit to extend north from the Manitoba boundary to the second meridian, which it followed as far as the sixtieth parallel of latitude, the line of the province's northern boundary.

Local and federal interests conflicted in the matter of public lands. Provincial control of revenue from the lands had been the major impetus for autonomy, but the federal government did not want to risk interruption in its homestead program by transferring management of public lands to the province in the midst of the immigration boom. Therefore the federal government kept control of the lands but made a financial settlement with the new provinces which was on all sides agreed to be generous. Even those western Liberal members of Parliament and senators who had originally been emphatic that lands must be transferred now accepted the new policy, publicly at least, without protest. In fact they went even further and were reported to have been unanimous in urging upon the government that the Northwest preferred to have the extra money instead of lands. It is worth noting, however, that this unanimity among western Liberals emerged only after it was evident that the federal stand could not be shaken. This shift in the position of western Liberals with respect to the ownership of public lands seemed to set the precedent for the next twenty-five years. Until control finally was transferred to the province in 1930, members of both political parties upon occasion reversed their positions on this question.

The lands policy of 1905 was Clifford Sifton's as undisputedly as the vigorous immigration program under which that land was now being settled. Prime Minister Laurier deferred absolutely to Sifton in the matter, intruded the question upon Sifton's temporary retirement from his duties, and accepted his decisions unquestioningly. Both Sifton's firm grasp of this area and Laurier's lack of it were readily evident in correspondence and events. Even Sifton's far-reaching understanding did not prevent the future provincial claims for better terms that he had anticipated in 1905 and had attempted to forestall in the constitutional provisions.

Sifton explained his reasons for continued dominion control of land suitable for settlement in a letter to Prime Minister Laurier on January 22:

... giving them to the Provinces would be ruinous to our settlement policy and would be disastrous to the whole Dominion. The mere report that the lands had been handed over and that there might be a change in the policy of administering them would cost us tens of thousands of settlers in the next two years to say nothing of the more distant future—the continued progress of Canada for the next five years depends almost entirely on the flow of immigration.[1]

As an alternative to straight dominion ownership, Senator J. H. Ross of Moose Jaw, Haultain's first administrative colleague and long a champion of western rights, proposed that the dominion should hold the lands as a trust, retaining control of their administration but handing over the proceeds annually to the province. He suggested that this proposal would solve the problem on every hand. It would sufficiently safeguard dominion interests for purposes of immigration, it would satisfy the people of the province, and it would be of great importance politically.

Laurier favored Ross's suggestion but Sifton did not. He pointed out the difference between the original provinces which had owned their lands before entering Confederation and the new provinces which were now being created from land that the dominion government had purchased from the Hudson's Bay Company. He set out the basis for his rejection of Ross's suggestion:

It involves setting up a fiction in place of a fact, i.e., it involves an admission that the new Provinces were or ought to be constitutionally owners of the land. This is wholly untrue. The original provinces owned the crown lands. The Dominion owns these lands and decides now to erect provinces. It is for the Dominion to say upon what terms .... To crystallize an assumption that the provinces are owners and entitled to the rights of a *cestui qui* trust is to set up an elaborate and untenable fiction.

Once a trust was admitted, he continued, it would not be possible to refuse the provinces the right to demand an account of everything from the beginning: "You may seek to limit the admission now but the future will see the limitations broken down. You will lay the foundation for a perennial agitation in these new provinces for more," he warned. He dealt also with the immediate practical difficulty of seeking to make up an account, in that it would be impossible to know what should be charged against the provinces in the land account, so that every item would become "a subject of dispute and interminable argument." Furthermore, he predicted, as soon as the provinces were strong enough they would demand an adjustment of the account— and they would get it. His advice was that "the facts should be taken as they are—we should say to the provinces—You have no lands and we cannot give them but we shall provide a liberal revenue in lieu of it."[2]

Laurier accordingly justified retention of the lands on the basis of dominion ownership when speaking in the House of Commons. The basis of compensation for the lands had slipped into the bill without Sifton's guiding hand, however, and it had to be changed. The original terms of the bill based compensation on a calculated acreage and price. In subsequent House of Commons debate, Sifton argued against his government's proposal, saying it could be used by the new provinces as an admission that the lands belonged to them beneficially at least, if not in law. He noted that Haultain had already seized upon this point, and that in future the provinces could say that the dominion had not accepted the dominion valuation. Sifton urged that compensation should be fixed arbitrarily on a basis that had no reference to the value of the land, and the bill was amended to base compensation for lands entirely on population.

The lesser matters of grazing lands and of water rights had also to be determined. Having been denied transfer of settlement land, western representatives pressed for grazing lands to be transferred to the province. Since this area would include irrigable land, power over irrigation was included in the suggestion. Sifton vetoed both ideas. He said it would be impossible to distinguish grazing lands. Although admitting that keeping irrigation under dominion authority was in many ways undesirable, the "balance of desirability" he thought lay in that direction. Since interprovincial and international questions would arise with respect to water rights, he considered that

by retaining the plenary power at Ottawa you ensure the fact that a central body which for its own interest is bound to try and do justice to all parties will be able to adjust difficulties as they arise. In the case of the Provinces there would be no way of dissolving a deadlock should one arise.[3]

The lands question was a matter of sharp dispute between the Liberal and the Conservative parties. Within the Liberal party any qualms which western members may have experienced privately were in no way evident in public. They pointed enthusiastically to the money settlement, and Liberals presented a united front on the necessity for continued federal control of the lands on "the highest grounds of policy," and as necessary for the successful continuation of immigration.

Conservatives opposed dominion retention on two grounds. Their emphasis was on violation of provincial rights, and secondly they criticized the amount of compensation. Arguing mainly on the matter of principle, the Conservative leader, Mr. Borden, held that the people of the Northwest were just as entitled to control of their land as were people in the eastern provinces, that they were interested equally with the dominion government in the promotion of immigration, and that federal fears in this respect could be eliminated by a clause relating to free homesteads and the price of land. Haultain supported this stand, maintaining as he had from the beginning that control over the lands rightly belonged to the provinces, and protesting also that federal control over irrigation invaded provincial jurisdiction in property and civil rights.

General financial terms (as distinct from the land settlement) were greeted as satisfactory and even generous. The future premier of Saskatchewan, Walter Scott, reported during negotiations that "we have come out very well with regard to the financial terms. In any case the terms are a good deal better than any of us hoped for right up to the last minute."

Grants from the central government followed the fourfold allowances of the B.N.A. Act. First, the annual grant for support of the legislature was $50,000. The major grant was the per capita subsidy of eighty cents a head, which was stretched by basing it on an inflated minimum population of 250,000, and which could increase to be paid on a maximum population of 800,000. Allowance was made for the rapidly increasing population by providing that quinquennial censuses be taken midway between the regular ten-year periods. Furthermore, estimates of population on which subsidy increases would also be made were to be taken at two and one-half year intervals. Third there was the debt allowance, calculated on the basis of debts which the federal government had taken over from the original provinces. Since Saskatchewan had no debt to be relieved of, she received an allowance of $405,375. The fourth category, special grants, for Saskatchewan consisted of the grant in lieu of lands described above. That amount was to increase with population growth, starting from an original payment of $373,000 (on an assumed population of 250,000) to a maximum of $1,125,000. An additional amount in lieu of lands, $93,750 annually for five years, was also to be paid for the construction of public buildings.

That the grant in lieu of lands should expand with population growth illustrates the trade-off approach which characterized dominion-provincial financial relations, with rationale adjusted to cover financial requirements. Against any assumption that a debt allowance or compensation in lieu of lands might logically represent a fixed amount, each was considered a potential area of flexibility in provincial revenues. Sifton had suggested that the debt allowance be increased on the basis of population at the end both of five and of ten years, but this was not one of his proposals which was adopted. Instead the adjustment in the grant in lieu of lands was to provide flexibility for increasing provincial requirements.

The separate school question soon overshadowed the other three principal issues which Laurier had emphasized in his speech. His appeal in the House that the matter be dealt with calmly and deliberately was quickly lost in controversy and crisis. Even those close to autonomy negotiations were confused at the sudden violence of the storm. Although the separate school question had been pointed to in earlier years as the ghost haunting and delaying autonomy discussions, as described in the previous chapter, it was assumed that this ghost had been laid.

A year before the start of autonomy negotiations, Clifford Sifton had discussed the matter with Walter Scott, and as Scott reported later, the Northwest members of the House had unanimously agreed to the continuation of the existing system of separate schools.[4] Their number included some who disapproved of the principle of separate schools but accepted the political necessity of continuing the status quo. This private and informal agreement apparently was seen as settling the matter, without its being raised for more precise consideration in political or official circles, either before or during the formal negotiations at Ottawa. Although Laurier wrote to Sifton in the midst of autonomy discussions about land questions and related matters, he did not mention the school clause. The only reference to the matter was Sifton's tentative comment in his letter of January 22, 1905 to Laurier: "You do not say anything about the school question and I assume you have not as yet discerned any serious difficulty with it." Laurier's response was only that he was slowly working it out and that he was "satisfied with the progress which we have made on it, though everybody dreads it."[5]

Controversy erupted out of apparent agreement because of a double interpretation of the term "existing system". This existing system clearly included separate schools on a religious basis. The confusion arose over the kind of control to be exercised over these separate schools—whether it must be direct government control, or whether it might instead be clerical. Each type of control had in fact existed at different times in the Territories, and the existence of both federal and Territorial legislation on the subject clouded the precise nature of the "existing system" in 1905.

The North-West Territories Act of 1875 which established the broad outlines of government for the Territories gave the Territorial assembly the right to set up a school system. The federal Act laid down only one specific condition. It was that whenever a school district was established, the minority of ratepayers in that district (whether Protestant or Roman Catholic) had the right to establish a separate school and to have their taxes go to support their own separate school instead of the public school.

The Territorial assembly did not establish a school system until 1884, and it was a dual system divided along religious lines. The Board of Education which was established consisted of two sections, Protestant and Roman Catholic, and each section of the Board supervised its own schools. The school first set up in any new school district was automatically the public school, and it declared itself Protestant or Roman Catholic depending on the majority view. The religious minority in the district then had the right to establish a separate school, if they wished, of the opposite faith. This provided for a four-fold system of schools, all designated on religious lines as Protestant or Roman Catholic public schools, and as Roman Catholic or Protestant separate schools. Legislative amendments from year to year changed the details of school organization, but the essential characteristic of early school administration until 1892 was represented by the dual religious nature of the Board of Education.

Even before 1892, a change was made in that new public schools were to be non-denominational, with separate schools only to be established as denominational in character. In 1892 the religious control of schools which had prevailed through the two religious sections of the Board of Education was abolished. The Board was replaced by a single body, the Council of Public Instruction (later the Department of Education) with responsibility for the entire school system, including both public and separate schools.

The legal position of separate schools after 1892 was therefore quite different. They were now under the direct supervision of a single government body instead of being under an agency of their own religious persuasion. The main privileges left to separate schools were the basic guarantee laid down in federal legislation allowing minority ratepayers to pay taxes to their own schools; the legislative practice of the Territories to give school grants on an equal basis to public and separate schools; and certain exceptions as to text books. A provision allowing religious instruction during the last half-hour of the school day applied to both public and separate schools.

What then was the existing system in 1905?

Certainly it included separate as well as public schools. The confusion lay in assuming that this fact in itself settled the issue, without inquiring into the *kind* of separate schools allowed in the "existing system". Did the term mean only the general guarantee in the federal North-West Territories Act of separate schools with no restriction as to their nature? Under this legislation the Territorial assembly had first allowed direct control of the schools to be delegated to clerical members of the Board of Education. Or did the term mean the system of separate schools after 1892, under direct government control? This system also came under the broad umbrella of the North-West Territories Act, but it was modified by more restrictive Territorial legislation.

The separate school controversy of 1905 therefore developed out of an initial failure to recognize that the "existing system" could mean not one but two quite different systems, depending on whether the broad guarantee of the federal legislation alone was considered, or whether the restrictions of Territorial legislation were also included.

It is not surprising that there was confusion. Besides there being both federal and Territorial legislation, changes in Territorial legislation had resulted in a complicated educational structure in which schools from the dual sectarian system continued even after non-sectarian public schools had been introduced. The total number of separate schools at any time was small, with only seven Roman Catholic separate schools and two Protestant separate schools in 1905. There were in addition, however, still thirty-one Roman Catholic public school districts. Since shifts could occur in settlement patterns, a Roman Catholic concern was to be able to organize separate schools if Protestant majorities overtook some of the Roman Catholic public school districts.

Apprehension kept the Roman Catholic clergy sensitive to educational changes, and there was a direct line of communication from the Territorial clergy through Church officials in Ottawa to Roman Catholic members of the government. This sensitive awareness was in sharp contrast to the ignorance of the intricacies of the educational system subsequently revealed by Protestant members of

Parliament, even when they were from the Territories and included those as knowledgeable of Territorial affairs generally as Walter Scott, soon to become premier of Saskatchewan, and Frank Oliver, who even sooner would succeed Sifton as Minister of the Interior.

When the school clause in the autonomy bills was introduced into the House of Commons in much the same terminology as the broad provisions of the 1875 federal Act, the Territorial members accepted its provisions as the existing system they had agreed to. It was only Clifford Sifton, then in the United States, who was aroused by the wording and who quickly returned to Ottawa to challenge the Prime Minister. He raised the alarm among other western members that the ambiguity of the school clause probably left the door open to wider privileges for separate schools than were at the time actually in effect in the Territories, in that the new school clause continued the general guarantee of separate schools as in the original federal Act, but it did not include the later Territorial legislation which brought all separate schools under the same system of control as the public schools.

Laurier resisted any change in the general wording of the clause. Sifton and the other western members were determined that no possibility should be left open for a return to the denominational separate schools of the earlier period. After crisis and acute uncertainty for some weeks, including Sifton's resignation from the cabinet on February 27, Laurier capitulated. On March 22 he introduced an amendment to the school clause which included specific reference to the Territorial legislation which had brought the entire school system under control of the education department. The school clause which was finally passed was a combination therefore of the general terms of the 1875 federal legislation ensuring the fact of separate schools, together with the restrictions as to their operation embodied in Territorial legislation.

The crisis within government circles was reflected in a public controversy which raged for weeks in Ontario and Quebec. A flood of protest from Protestant and Orange circles in Ontario followed introduction of the original separate school clause. The Toronto *Globe,* until then a champion of the government, defected and denounced the clause, denying that Parliament had any right to compel the new provinces to continue separate schools. Two by-elections in Ontario were fought mainly on the issue. The Conservatives were joined in the election fight by Premier Haultain from the Territories, and they maintained that the original clause and the amended clause both invaded the rights of the new provinces. The Liberals denounced the Conservatives for intensifying religious controversy, and they defended inclusion of a school clause as a moral obligation and a common sense solution.

Quebec remained quiet while Ontario protested the original clause. When it was replaced by the amended clause, Quebec erupted. Petitions poured in protesting the curtailment of any privileges which might have been granted originally. Henri Bourassa, an advocate of "biculturalism" before the modern use of the term, and a Quebec member of Parliament, led French Roman Catholics in denouncing the amended bill as not granting just rights to the Catholic minority. Unlike the earlier Manitoba school dispute in which language as well as religion was a factor, in 1905 the language of instruction was not an issue. The separate school controversy this time was entirely a religious issue.

Largely indifferent to the uproar which its affairs had raised in the central provinces, the Territories remained relatively calm. Here the matter excited "but a languid interest." Senator Watson of Portage la Prairie reported that westerners were thinking more about spring seeding than about separate schools. The correspondent in the west for the Toronto *Globe* wrote to Laurier, "if we hunted up all the fiery Methodist or Presbyterian clergy ... strong expression of opinion might be obtained, but the average western man is not much worked up about it." Lieutenant Governor Forget similarly told Laurier that the agitation raging in the east had not reached the Territories, despite some efforts in that direction, and that resolutions adopted here and there in the Territories had come from small groups and did not represent the general sentiment. The Presbyterian Superintendent of Home Missions for the Territories noted that in going east he had not found interest in the matter until he reached North Bay in Ontario, and from there to Toronto he heard more discussion of it than would be heard in the west in a month.

There was in fact more than a little of an Alice-in-Wonderland atmosphere about the whole episode. Just as the lion and the unicorn fought over a crown which belonged to neither of them, so the central provinces raged over a matter of western affairs which the area itself accepted with relative calm.

An unresolved aspect of the 1905 dispute is the speculative question as to Prime Minister Laurier's actual intention. His defenders argue that the Prime Minister was unaware of the double interpretation possible in the term "existing system", and that he genuinely thought that it was represented by the 1875 federal legislation. On the other side, Clifford Sifton was convinced that Laurier participated in a conscious plan to expand separate school rights and that he knowingly attempted to write into the new legislation a guarantee more far-reaching than had been agreed to.

This matter has been debated by scholars to the present time. For those wishing to pursue it here, the evidence and circumstances of this academic mystery are included in the Supplement to chapter 3 on page 193. For the general reader, the conclusions reached there may be simply stated: that Laurier probably did know precisely the implications of the school clause which he initially presented to Parliament. The extent of his personal participation in the actual wording of the school clause and the closeness of his communication with the Roman Catholic hierarchy throughout allow of only two possibilities. Either Laurier knew precisely what he was doing, or he was elaborately hoodwinked by a combination of members of the Church hierarchy and Roman Catholic members of his own cabinet whose correspondence undoubtedly shows a clear and determined understanding of the situation. In general, history does not record Laurier as a fool.

The Supplement deals also with financial aspects of the separate school issue. These were by no means inconsequential, but they were largely submerged in the emotionalism of the contemporary dispute, and they have tended to be by-passed in historical consideration. The most significant point had to do with the proceeds from the sale of school lands, which had been designated for public schools. Laurier included a provision in the original school clause that they be distributed equally to public and to separate schools. Sifton hotly protested the introduction of this provision, which had never been previously discussed, and it was eventually dropped.

The location of the capital for the new province raised far livelier interest in the area than had been generated by the separate school question. In the midst of the school crisis Regina was reported to be calm and contented because it had been made the capital—but that calm was only temporary. The new legislature would make the final decision, and the geographical distribution of its members was of vital concern to competing regions. When autonomy talks were under way, delegations from various parts of the Territories suddenly appeared in Ottawa, ostensibly concerned with bridges, but with a less publicized interest in the capital question. No agreement as to constituencies was reached in autonomy discussions, and the matter was left to Parliament. With Saskatoon and Regina as the main contenders for the capital, the north-south split of constituencies was awaited with special interest. That score was nine for the north to sixteen for the south in the new twenty-five seat legislature.

Both the Hudson's Bay Company and the Canadian Pacific Railway were alert to protect their respective interests in the new provincial constitution. As noted in chapter 1, each had land holdings in Saskatchewan, and each also had certain rights relating to those lands. Some difference of opinion with the Hudson's Bay Company arose over a proposal that all rights conferred on the Canadian government when it had purchased the land should now be vested in the provincial government, insofar as they related to matters within provincial authority. This proposal was presumably meant to allow the provincial government to take land for roads, but the Hudson's Bay Company objected that the proposal was too general and might cover matters not then foreseen. As a result of the Company's vigorous protest, the proposal was dropped.

The new provinces lost again on the much more serious matter of the C.P.R. exemption from taxation which Walter Scott had first raised in 1903. As described in chapter 2, after the Manitoba Supreme Court decision that the C.P.R. exemption did not apply to school taxes in the Territories, Scott wanted the implications clarified before autonomy was granted. He stated in the 1904 election campaign that he would oppose constitutional change until it became clear what effect this decision might have on provincial status.

During autonomy negotiations early in 1905 and later while the bills were before the House, Scott pursued the question. He attempted to have some proviso included which would leave the way open for eventual cancellation of the tax-exemption privilege. In introducing the autonomy bills, Laurier deplored the tax exemption and intimated future action to obtain its abrogation by legislation, mutual agreement, expropriation, or some other method. Upon finding that the C.P.R., not surprisingly, was sharply hostile to these suggestions, the government refused to incorporate any such provision into the legislation. Scott moved amendments to remove the exemption at both the committee and third reading stage. Upon each defeat he submitted his resignation to the Prime Minister, but both times he was prevailed upon to stay.

On the second occasion, the Prime Minister promised Scott that whenever the exemption became burdensome he would take appropriate action in the matter. He put pressure on Scott to withdraw his resignation because, with the turmoil over the school clause still raging, the reason for Scott's resignation doubtless would be misinterpreted. Scott agreed to let his resignation stand in abeyance, at least until the end of the session or until the school agitation died away. He assured the Prime Minister furthermore that "in conjunction with your statement respecting the tax exemptions, the terms are in my opinion quite satisfactory."[6]

It is scarcely credible that Scott was as sanguine as his statement would suggest as to the possibility of future "appropriate action" on the tax exemption. He had consistently urged the necessity of action before the opportunity was lost in the finality of autonomy provisions, and his acquiescence can be seen only as acceptance of the inevitable.

The C.P.R. exemption from taxation remains to this day. In 1905 the matter was submerged by other issues, but Scott's prolonged if futile efforts to have it eliminated showed the importance he attached to the queston. In one of his urgings to Laurier Scott wrote:

The limitation upon provincial autonomy involved in these exemptions is intrinsically a very serious matter.... I think ... you are depriving the province of an asset almost equal to the amount which at the outset you are proposing to pay the provinces in lieu of the public domain. Were the matter not so serious it would be really laughable to consider the enormous noise which has been made over the education clause which merely asks the provinces to do what they would be pleased to do of their own accord, in contrast with the almost entire lack of any mention of this tax exemption limitation which unquestionably does not leave the provinces free to do as they would do except for this restriction; if the North-West school districts and municipalities and Legislatures were free to tax the C.P.R. I think we may depend upon it that they would exercise the right.[7]

Having lost, Scott felt bound to resign because of the stand which he had taken, and he intended to have his resignation go into effect eventually on that issue. Besides his declarations in the 1904 election campaign, he had stated in effect on the floor of the House that if his amendment was not accepted he would resign. He later realized that he had not made his intent clear in the House, and no one apparently interpreted his statement as an intention to resign. As it developed, when he gave up his House of Commons seat later that year, it was for an entirely different reason, without the original cause for his submitting his resignation becoming public. The resignation came into effect when he was chosen leader of the Saskatchewan Liberals at their convention in August of 1905, and shortly after being chosen as party leader he was selected as premier for the new province.

Representation in Parliament was to be determined by the B.N.A. Act as it applied to all the provinces: that the number of members would bear the same ratio to its population as the number sixty-five bore to the population of Quebec. The readjustment would take place upon the termination of the current Parliament, with the ten members then sitting in the House of Commons for the Territories to remain in the meantime. The province was to be represented in the Senate by four members, with the number to be increased to six after the next decennial census. This increase was in conformity with a suggestion advanced two years earlier by western members that the area west of the Great Lakes should be considered a division for purposes of Senate representation, with each of the four provinces to have six members. The Prime Minister in debate explained that Senate representation was not based upon population but "upon purely arbitrary considerations having in view minorities, and that the great provinces should not override the smaller ones."

Parliamentary government was continued in the province without question. The Saskatchewan Act followed the traditions of omission, obscurity, and elasticity characteristic of British constitutional practice. The existence of a lieutenant governor as the representative of the sovereign was assumed, and the Act assigned to him the customary duty of choosing persons to compose the executive council. It was then left to tradition to continue the principles of responsible government already established in the Territories, with the executive responsible to the elected legislative assembly.

Upon entering the Canadian federal system, the new province received the same exclusive powers as the other provinces, set out in section 92 of the B.N.A. Act. These powers included the amendment of its own constitution except for the office of lieutenant governor, direct taxation for revenue and borrowing on the credit of the province, establishment and maintenance of various provincial institutions, municipal organization, administration of justice in the province, property and civil rights, and "generally all matters of a merely local or private nature in the province."

The name for Saskatchewan was chosen with little dissension, with the choice lying between the names of the two Territorial provisional districts from which the new political entity was formed, Assiniboia and Saskatchewan. Clifford Sifton preferred the name of Assiniboia, although he regarded the choice as being of relatively little significance, since both names were identified with the history of the Territories. Whether it may be regarded as a victory for early pressure group activity, the citizens of the northern district of Saskatchewan asked that their name be used, with no parallel request from the southern district of Assiniboia. Other factors added strength to that choice. The main waterway of the province was the Saskatchewan River, its name being taken from the Cree language and meaning "swift flowing". Historically the name had been known in the east before that of Assiniboia, and through extensive advertising outside Canada of the "Valley of the Saskatchewan", the name suggested vast tracts of fertile land.

The authority for passage of the Saskatchewan Act was set out in the preamble. After Manitoba had been established in 1870, doubts had arisen concerning the power of Parliament thus to create new provinces, and as a result imperial legislation had been passed in the following year specifically ensuring that right. The preamble to the Saskatchewan Act points out that by the legislation of 1871

... it is enacted that the Parliament of Canada may from time to time establish new provinces in any territories forming for the time being part of the Dominion of Canada, but not included in any province thereof, and may, at the time of such establishment, make provisions for the constitution and administration of any such province, and for the passing of laws for the peace, order and good government of such province and for its representation in the said Parliament of Canada.

Although the 1871 legislation firmly established the right of the Canadian Parliament to create new provinces, the constitutionality of the Alberta and Saskatchewan Acts was challenged even before they were passed. Opposition members questioned whether Parliament had the right to alter substantially the terms of entry from those which existed in other provinces. Inclusion of the separate school clause and the withholding of public lands, they contended, were unconstitutional because the provisions encroached upon the rights of the new provinces. Even persons who upheld the right of Parliament to include these provisions in the Act expressed some anxiety for a decision confirming their view.

While the autonomy bills were still before Parliament, the Minister of Justice suggested to the Prime Minister the advisability "of obtaining in some form an authoritative declaration to the effect that this Parliament has the power and possibly the duty to deal with the educational clauses of the new bill in the way that we have done." He added that he was "firmly convinced that in law our position is unassailable and would be so held by the Privy Council."[8] No such action was taken, however, and the legislation creating the new province was proclaimed on September 1, 1905. Walter Scott was named premier on September 5, the day following the inaugural ceremonies and the swearing in of the lieutenant governor. Scott selected a cabinet which took office a week later to carry on the business of government during the interim until an election could be held.

The official launching of the province was by no means the end of the constitutionality question, and the opposition made it their main issue before the election of December 13, 1905. Haultain and his Conservative followers campaigned as members of a newly formed Provincial Rights Party, maintaining that the terms of autonomy invaded the constitutional rights of the province. Haultain declared his intention of submitting the Saskatchewan Act to judicial review if he came to power. Premier Scott upheld the constitutionality of the Act and defended its terms, deploring the disruption in provincial affairs which would result from Haultain's proposed course of action. Scott won the election, and his Liberal administration continued as Saskatchewan's first government.

Despite Scott's victory he was anxious to allay the doubts that had been raised. He suggested to his Liberal counterpart in Alberta, Premier Rutherford, that the two governments join in a request to have their respective Acts submitted to the Privy Council for a decision as to their constitutionality. Premier Rutherford, who had not been subjected to the same pressures in Alberta, was not enthusiastic, and he suggested that if any doubts existed the Acts could be ratified by imperial legislation. Prime Minister Laurier, although expressing a keen desire to remove the controversy, agreed with Rutherford in not taking the question to the courts.

Premier Scott then used his own devices to check the opposition cry of unconstitutionality in Saskatchewan. On May 22, 1906, the legislature passed a resolution on the matter addressed to the Governor General of Canada. It was preceded by an explanation that the Saskatchewan legislature had no doubts of the power of Parliament to pass the Saskatchewan Act, and that the terms and provisions of the Act had been shown to be acceptable by the election results on December 13. The resolution continued:

And whereas nevertheless doubts have arisen and are expressed by a political party respecting the constitutionality of certain of the provisions of the said Act: And whereas it is desirable that these doubts should be removed and that the constitutionality of the said Act and of the several provisions thereof should be finally determined: We do therefore humbly pray that Your Excellency will be pleased to take steps to have submitted to the Judicial Committee of the Imperial Privy Council the Question of the constitutionality of The Saskatchewan Act and of the several provisions thereof.[9]

No action was taken at Ottawa, and knowing the views of the Prime Minister, Scott probably did not expect that anything would be done.

The real purpose of the resolution had already been accomplished. The opposition in the legislature, although approving the request in itself as the course they had advocated, found themselves trapped by the wording, and they were obliged to vote against the resolution. Haultain acknowledged their dilemma in commenting on the matter later: "We could not have supported the resolution as it was brought in and forced through the House, without stultifying ourselves," he wrote, "and there is no doubt it was brought in in that form for that purpose."[10] With the ground now cut from under them, the opposition cry of "unconstitutionality" died away.

The courts did not come into the picture until some years later. In 1927 the Supreme Court of Canada upheld the separate school clause in the Alberta Act after it had been challenged. The judgement included an unambiguous endorsement of the powers exercised by Parliament in 1905:

It seems to be as plain as words can tell that, at the time of the establishment of the province of Alberta, the Parliament of Canada had the power to define and regulate the legislative powers which were to be possessed by the new province . . . . I cannot find, either in the British North America Act of 1867 or of 1871, anything expressed or implied which limited the power of the Parliament of Canada in 1905 to define the constitution and powers of the provinces which were at that time established and constituted within the Territories.

In 1953 an attempt by the Saskatchewan government to break the C.P.R. taxation exemption was frustrated by a similar decision from the Privy Council. The right of Parliament to create provinces with powers which were more restricted or different from other provinces was restated. The judgement said, "There was . . . no set pattern of 'a province' in the Act of 1867 which was bound to be followed in creating the new province of Saskatchewan."

The sequel to provincial autonomy in 1905 was the transfer of natural resources from the federal government in 1930. The intervening quarter century witnessed concerted efforts by the prairie provinces for ownership of these resources. Despite Clifford Sifton's precautions in 1905, the arguments which he had sought to forestall were precisely the ones advanced by the provinces. They included claims of constitutional right to the lands, supported by reference to the compensation terms based on the value of land which Laurier had originally submitted in the autonomy bills; demand for an accounting of the lands from the time the federal government assumed administration; compensation for land granted to the railways and other land alienated by the federal government; compensation for the period they were denied revenue from the lands; and interest on this loss. In the final settlement Saskatchewan received, as well as ownership of its public domain and compensation for lost revenue, the subsidy originally granted in lieu of the lands as compensation for those alienated by the federal government.

With the discovery of oil and natural gas in the province during the 1950s, and with the development of the "energy crisis" during the 1970s, it became clear that natural resources included items of importance other than land. Conflicting claims between the two levels of government which arose in 1973 respecting the imposition of royalties directed attention to the terms of the natural resources agreement of 1930 which stated:

In order that the Province may be in the same position as the original Provinces of Confederation . . . the interest of the Crown in all Crown lands, mines, minerals (precious and base) and royalties derived therefrom within the Province, and all sums due or payable for such lands, mines, minerals or royalties, shall . . . belong to the Province."[11]

Decisions handed down by the Supreme Court of Canada in 1977 and 1978 sharply limited what the province had assumed to be its benefits from such resources as gas, oil, and potash. The Court determined that tax levies on oil and gas which Saskatchewan had imposed were indirect and beyond the power of the province to levy, and that control outside the province came under the federal government's trade and commerce authority. For a province which exports the bulk of such products, the government saw the decision as making a mockery of its presumed control of natural resources, and it stated its intention to seek constitutional adjustment. After what was thought to be the final disposition of the natural resources question by their transfer to the province in 1930 they have thus re-entered the arena of federal-provincial contention.

4　The Political Scene

Saskatchewan politics show the contradiction of a conservative electorate which is willing to elect a radical party to office. The result, that Saskatchewan has had theoretically radical parties in power for more than one-third of its existence, has strengthened the myth of radicalism mentioned in chapter 1. Yet, as shown in the following pages, the electorate is essentially conservative. To suit its own ends the body of Saskatchewan voters has chosen parties in spite of their radical theories, not because of them. This dichotomy makes it necessary to distinguish between electorate and party in searching for an understanding of Saskatchewan political life.

The electorate gave only a cautious reception to early radical groups which came in from outside the province. This cautious response came during unfavorable economic conditions and the failure of traditional federal parties to come to grips with them, circumstances which should have provided fertile ground for radical proposals. Various movements had enthusiastic leaders and attracted attention, discussion, and a core of dedicated supporters, but in the end the electorate rejected them. These movements included such American protest groups as the Farmers Alliance, the Patrons of Industry, and the Nonpartisan League, which gained support in some areas of Saskatchewan but no significant foothold.

During the period of agrarian unrest extending into the early 1920s, when indigenous protest parties turned out governments in Alberta, Manitoba, and even in traditionally conservative Ontario, they were rejected by Saskatchewan voters. One or the other of the two traditional parties formed the government in Saskatchewan from 1905 until 1944. The CCF was brought to power in 1944 only after it had trimmed its radical aspects, and it continued the trimming to stay in power until 1964. In 1971 the party returned to office as the NDP on a basically conservative platform, emphasizing the preservation of the family farm.

In provincial politics the Saskatchewan electorate has impressed its message on the traditional Liberal and Conservative parties with their eastern origins just as unmistakably as on the protest parties which developed out of western conditions. For a party with radical inclinations, the required accommodation was to moderate any extreme proposals that seemed designed to alter the basic pattern of society. For a traditional party the requirement was to abandon its eastern orientation. Prairie agrarian welfare formed the framework within which all provincial parties sought electoral support. In the interplay between party and electorate, the origin, title, or theory of the party mattered little to those beyond the immediate core of loyal party adherents. For success in Saskatchewan every party has had to be essentially a farmers' party, and contests have been based on the most effective means of fulfilling that role.

The paramount position of agriculture in Saskatchewan has enabled the electorate to bend provincial parties more purposefully and completely to its will than would be possible in provinces where interests are more diverse. The provincial scene is in sharp contrast to the situation which Saskatchewan voters face federally. Among competing national claims, with meager voting power, the Saskatchewan electorate finds its interests far down on the list of federal party priorities. As a result, provincial and federal voting patterns show even greater diversity than in some of the other provinces.

Frustration and impotence experienced in federal politics is evident in erratic voting behaviour. A protest party championing regional interests at Ottawa is at best insufficient in numbers, while national parties are guided by the center of power. The Saskatchewan electorate has floundered wildly in this dilemma. At times it has given overwhelming support to one or other of the traditional parties, and again it has veered as sharply to a protest party. Before the First World War, for example, Saskatchewan sent nine Liberals and one Conservative to Ottawa; in 1921 fifteen Progressives and one Liberal were elected; in 1935 it was sixteen Liberals out of twenty-one members; in 1945 there were eighteen CCF out of twenty-one members. A shift to the other side of the political spectrum was the solid Conservative block of seventeen members elected in 1963 and again in 1965.

In contrast, provincial voting shows a stable and purposeful pattern. A disinclination toward change for its own sake is evident in keeping parties in power for considerable lengths of time. The unbroken rule of the Liberals from 1905 to 1929 was almost equalled by the twenty-year regime of the CCF from 1944 to 1964. At the other extreme, only one government was rejected after a single term: the drought-plagued administration of the Conservative coalition from 1929 to 1934. In seventy-five years, governments were turned out of office in Saskatchewan only five times.

The requirements to which all parties in Saskatchewan must direct their attention have followed a consistent pattern. Roads have always been of prime concern among the widely scattered population. In early elections railways also were a prominent campaign subject, with parties promising influence and assistance in this field which was beyond the direct jurisdiction of the local government. Then the question was construction of branch lines; in the 1970s it was their abandonment which was an issue. Education has been important from the earliest election, with a shift only in emphasis. The concern of early voters was for the provision of basic educational facilities, but the degree and manner of government assistance to education at all levels continue to be carefully scrutinized.

In recent years, with the advance of the welfare state, proposals for further social services have been added as an important factor. The early emphasis on the building up of the province is still evident in the interest in resource development. Although many of the vital agricultural issues, such as wheat marketing, are federal rather than provincial, there is nothing to prevent them from being raised in provincial contests. And areas such as land disposal and debt legislation which come under provincial jurisdiction have been significant points of contention. Sound administration and economy in government have been consistent election issues in Saskatchewan, as elsewhere. Others of more temporary concern have formed part of the pattern of individual campaigns. Emotional and irrational issues have not been absent, but results show that abstract appeals have carried substantially less weight than matters of practical benefit.

Before 1905 a pragmatic and conservative approach was to be seen in the non-partisan tradition for Territorial elections, even though party division operated in federal elections. Rejection of party division for local politics was deliberate and was dictated by practical considerations. On the eve of provincial establishment a newspaper editorial explained:

> It was done simply because it was plain on the face of it that neutrality in politics was the best policy for the Territorial Government in its relations with Ottawa. The Territories were in a subordinate relation to the Dominion, and in many matters the Territorial law-givers hung upon the favour of the administration of the day at Ottawa. Anybody could, and everybody in the West did, see that it was not advisable for a dependent Territorial Legislature to get involved in national party politics, with the inevitable result that the rulers at Regina would incur the hostility of either the Opposition or the Government at Ottawa. Plain self-interest caused the Territorial Government to stand outside the ring of party politics until the period of tutelage should expire.[1]

Even in federal elections, many voters showed the same disregard for party loyalty that was evident in later provincial contests. A Territorial political observer commented to Prime Minister Laurier:

> The West differs much from the East. Party lines are not tightly drawn. Out of ten men you may find two out-and-out Liberals, two Conservatives and the other six are nothing politically. They will vote for the man for the Government perhaps because all is going satisfactorily but not because of party and these are the ones that give victory or cause defeat.[2]

Demands from the sheep men of Maple Creek for a duty on wool in 1903 and 1904 well illustrate the looseness of party ties in the face of practical considerations. Walter Scott, who was then member of Parliament for the area, wrote with some concern to Clifford Sifton of a message from one of the sheep raisers, a prominent Liberal who was in Scott's estimation, "the best man we have in Maple Creek." If the sheep men received a promise from the government to impose a duty on wool, Scott had been told, "they will vote solidly; if not they will ask the Conservative leaders for the promise and vote solidly Conservative if those leaders give the promise."[3] Furthermore, Scott revealed in later correspondence, not only would such a promise save the Liberal vote, it would also serve to "get several Conservative sheep men to support me through the common understanding which they had made with each other."[4]

In the first provincial election which was held in 1905, Premier Scott stressed the practical problems of developing the new province. His preoccupation contrasted with opposition emphasis on the constitutional question of invasion of provincial rights in the terms for autonomy. Scott pointed to the financial benefits which the land arrangement had gained for the province, and he argued that the separate school clause provided for a system no different from what would have been practiced in any event. Political counsel from outside the province was in the same practical vein: "Ask the opposition what they did for the country that they should be entrusted with it again," Clifford Sifton advised Scott.[5] The premier followed this approach by stressing the need to bend all efforts toward the building up of the new province, and he campaigned upon a policy of "Peace, Progress, and Prosperity."

The weakness of partisan bonds soon became evident. The non-partisan support which Haultain enjoyed in Territorial elections carried over in his favor. The former premier capitalized on his position by discarding the Conservative title in favor of the Provincial Rights Party as a new name. This proved an effective move. At an early stage one of Scott's cabinet ministers noted, "Party ties are not going to be very strong from appearances." As the campaign progressed, the strength of personal loyalty over party claims was evident, with those in both parties commenting upon the number of Liberals who supported Haultain.

It was a bitterly fought contest with many factors entering into the campaign, and success or failure in the final result was not caused by any single factor. The provincial rights cry was not without effect, especially as it related to the school question. In Scott's estimation, aspects of this issue furnished the main difficulty for the government party. Nevertheless its appeal was not sufficiently strong to win for its proponents either half the votes or half the seats in the legislature. Since the theoretical question of provincial rights formed both the name and the campaign slogan of the opposition party, its defeat showed that other factors weighed more heavily with the electorate than the abstract question of provincial rights.

The 1905 election initiated a series of victories which kept the Liberals in power until 1929. Walter Scott headed an able administration and established provincial institutions on a sound basis. He retired as a result of ill health in 1916, and he was succeeded by W. M. Martin, a prominent Regina lawyer and former member of Parliament. In 1922, in the midst of agrarian unrest, Charles Dunning, long active in farmers' movements in the province, took over as premier, and upon Dunning's move to Ottawa in 1926, James G. Gardiner became head of government.

This period of Liberal rule was characterized by the close attention paid to the expressed wishes of the Saskatchewan Grain Growers' Association, an attention which strongly enhanced the party's position with the agrarian electorate. The Association had had early success in fighting monopolies in the vital matters of transportation and in the handling and marketing of grain, and it had gone on to champion the farmers' cause in many respects. Its activity as a farmers' pressure group was evident in the remark of Sir Wilfrid Laurier: "It always appeared to me that there was more politics than grain growing in the different addresses with which I was favored."[6] Recognized as the official voice of the farming population, it became a strong organization, enjoying high prestige and exercising widespread influence in provincial affairs.

From the beginning, an interlocking of personnel between the provincial Liberal administration and the leadership of the Grain Growers' ensured continuous and sympathetic consideration of agrarian demands. W. R. Motherwell, Saskatchewan Minister of Agriculture from 1905 to 1918, was one of the founders of the Grain Growers' Association, and he became its first president. George Langley, who was taken into the cabinet in 1912, and C. A. Dunning who followed in 1916 and became premier in 1922, were both active and influential in the agricultural association. In 1921, in a direct bid for Grain Growers' support in a period of agrarian upheaval, Premier Martin brought J. A. Maharg, president of the Association, into the cabinet for a short-lived term as Minister of Agriculture. The relationship between the Association and the government was sufficiently close for the Conservative opposition occasionally to challenge the presumably non-partisan nature of the farmers' movement. During the 1917 legislative session so many cabinet ministers deserted the legislative chamber for the Grain Growers' Convention in Moose Jaw that proceedings at the center of government ground to a halt. Efforts were made in later years to avoid such conflict by having the legislative sittings completed before the holding of the Grain Growers' Convention.

This close connection of Liberals and the Grain Growers' Association was more than coincidental, and it was carefully guarded and cultivated by the government. The connection was evident when a group of Langley's constituents in 1908 voiced dissatisfaction with him and requested that the Liberal organizer should not assist in his renomination. Premier Scott, with a shrewd eye to farmer support, warned the dissidents:

There is another consideration of some weight in the present case, which is the possibly damaging effect throughout the Province of the defeat of Mr. Langley in Convention on account of his prominent connection with the Provincial Grain Growers' Association.[7]

Similarly, in 1919 W. H. Harvey, after winning a by-election by acclamation as a "Farmer-Independent," referred to himself as the first representative of the farmers' movement in the legislature, and C. A. Dunning was quick to emphasize the existing association between government and Grain Growers':

When did I cease to be a representative of the Farmers' movement in this legislature? When did forty other men sitting round here cease to be representatives of the Farmers' movement in this legislature? The Farmers' movement since the earliest days of the Saskatchewan legislature has been represented in these seats .... If I had not been a leader in the Farmers' movement, holding every position in that movement from secretary of a country local to the second highest office in the gift of the organization, I do not believe it is likely I would have been invited to become a member of this government.

Touching on activities of the Association, Dunning continued:

I cannot name today one outstanding issue between the government of this province and the Grain Growers' Organization of this province.[8]

The premier and other members of the government were keenly aware of the double service which the connection with the Grain Growers' offered. It provided the government both with a reliable gauge of agrarian wishes, and also with an avenue through which to exert influence. The government gave sympathetic consideration to convention resolutions and to representations made to it by the Association, and government, fiscal, and other policies followed generally the lines advocated by the Grain Growers'. And the government did not hesitate to work through the Association to gain favorable reception of its legislation. When a decrease in school grants was scheduled to come up for discussion at the 1910 Grain Growers' Convention, for example, Scott privately admonished Langley to be prepared to support the government action: "If the Grain Growers' Convention takes a sensible view of the legislation, we shall probably never find any difficulty with regard to it," he wrote. Later the same year the premier made the report of an elevator commission available to the Grain Growers' executive before any public intimation was given of its nature. In 1918 the provincial treasurer took the unusual step of explaining proposed government legislation to the Grain Growers' before it was introduced in the legislature, outlining at their convention the proposed farm-credits measure and answering their questions. It was through such deference to the interests of the organized farmers that the administration came to be referred to and regarded as a farmers' government and that the Liberals continued in power for the first twenty-four years of the province's history.

This Liberal reign was not without dissatisfaction and challenge. Especially in 1919 and the early 1920s, when postwar unrest was exacerbated by economic recession, the rising tide of Progressivism threatened to engulf the Liberals. It was natural that the Progressive movement which developed throughout the agricultural areas of Canada should make its appearance in Saskatchewan through the Grain Growers'. As it happened, formal participation in provincial politics occurred entirely outside the Grain Growers' Association. In the federal field also, an organization separate from the Grain Growers' was established. Nevertheless, the earliest and most significant action arose out of and was closely connected with the existing farmers' association.

The two main issues raised by the movement in Saskatchewan were those requiring federal government action: a revision of the protective tariff, and the establishment of a permanent government wheat-marketing agency. The initial action and the strongest pressure, therefore, were in the federal field, in accordance with the attitude "We've always got what we demanded provincially and where we need to press for power is at Ottawa." Not all subscribed to this theory, and a strongly idealistic section of the leadership advocated both federal and provincial action. Nevertheless, the pressure for entry into provincial politics lagged far behind the insistence for participation in the broader field. It was in federal elections that the greatest activity was evident and that the party received its most enthusiastic and widespread support at the polls.

Interest in federal politics in 1917 moved the Saskatchewan Grain Growers' Association unanimously to endorse the Farmers' Platform drawn up the previous year by the Canadian Council of Agriculture, the national voice of farmers' organizations. In 1919 the Grain Growers' Convention endorsed the Council's revised platform, "The New National Policy," which dealt exclusively with federal matters, and the New National Policy Political Association came into existence in the province the same year, with the name changed in 1922 to the Saskatchewan Progressive Association. Although the political association was separate from the Grain Growers', the latter was its parent body, they functioned in close harmony, and the two were associated in the public mind.[9] In a significant and keenly contested federal by-election in 1919, the farmers' candidate won an overwhelming victory over the former provincial Liberal cabinet minister, W. R. Motherwell. In the federal general election of 1921, Saskatchewan voters elected fifteen Progressives out of sixteen members.

Entry into provincial politics was hesitant, was accomplished only after much delay, and was short-lived. Furthermore, the Grain Growers' official participation in provincial politics occurred, strangely enough, only between elections. Indecision and delay prevented any official action by the Association before the 1921 provincial election. In convention in 1922, the Grain Growers' vote swung in favour of political activity, but at the 1924 convention this decision was reversed, and a policy of neutrality in provincial politics was quietly agreed to.

With the Grain Growers' Association officially neutral during provincial election years, Progressive activity in provincial politics resulted from locally organized groups, or through the provincial political association, which was established in 1923 independently of the Grain Growers'. Mr. Dunning's protests aside, a Farmer-Independent who was elected in the provincial by-election in Kindersley in 1919 was hailed by Progressive supporters as the first representative of the farmers' movement. In the 1921 general election, thirteen candidates who emerged victorious under the designation of Progressive or Independent represented support from those who wished formal Progressive action in the provincial field. Disappointed in their hope of more positive action by the Grain Growers', the dissidents organized the Saskatchewan Provincial Progressive Association in 1923 to contest a forthcoming by-election and to prepare for the next provincial election. Meeting in Saskatoon in the following year, they drew up a platform opposing the party system and urging economy in administration, a reduction in the number of civil servants, a fixed term for the legislative assembly, the reduction of the number of members from sixty-three to forty-two, adoption of the single transferable vote, completion of the Hudson's Bay Railway, assistance to co-operative marketing, and Senate reform.

Caught between antagonism from the Grain Growers' and shrewd action by the Martin government in meeting Progressive appeal, the organization never assumed significant proportions. The strong element of Liberal sympathy within the leadership of the Grain Growers', which had been a major factor in restraining the Association from political action, similarly was responsible for withholding support from the rebel group. In the 1925 provincial election, only six Progressives were successful, and the party gradually waned, although it retained sufficient support to elect five members in 1929.

From the beginning of Progressive activity, Premier Martin was keenly aware of the economic motivation behind the uncertain pressure for provincial participation. He consequently urged upon his colleagues the necessity for action in the crucial area of wheat marketing. Writing to his Minister of Municipal Affairs before the Grain Growers' Convention of 1921, he advised:

The Grain Growers' Convention meets the first of February and from present appearances this is the subject [wheat marketing] which will over-shadow everything else and, if you and Mr. Dunning and Mr. Hamilton were in a position to deal with the question, some government policy having been announced prior thereto, I believe the question of the Grain Growers' going into provincial politics would become comparatively insignificant.[10]

With the Grain Growers' Association continuing its political aloofness, Premier Martin called the 1921 election before the dissident Progressives had time to organize. The result of his swift action was a campaign in which the only real opposition to the government was from candidates of various shades of former political opinion who had no cohesive or overall organization. The government emerged with a strong majority to face an opposition composed of a variety of members designated as Progressive, Independent, Conservative, and Independent-Conservative.

The effect of the Progressives upon the local political scene nevertheless was far from negligible. Since the reform movement came in through the Grain Growers' Association in which the existing administration already enjoyed strong support, the point of its drive was blunted. Despite this handicap, its threat was sufficient to challenge all the ingenuity and tactfulness of Liberal leaders to meet it. When Motherwell contested the federal by-election in Assiniboia in 1919, it was against the counsel of his former colleagues, who saw in his action the danger "that he will dig a gulf between the Grain Growers' and the Liberal Party that may involve us all in the ruin."[11] His participation as a federal candidate was without their open assistance, since they were themselves dependent on Grain Growers' votes and dared not alienate them.

Premier Martin severed his connection with the federal Liberal organization in order to keep his provincial administration as clear as possible of the farmer resentment directed particularly at Ottawa. He repudiated even the Liberal name, and in the 1921 election he and his supporters used the designation "Government" instead of "Liberal." The Grain Growers' Association joined in the effort to dissociate the provincial administration from federal taint. In justifying the entry of the Grain Growers' president, J. A. Maharg, into the provincial cabinet in 1921, the secretary of the association explained, "Time and again it has been made clear that the Government of this Province has no connection with the Liberal Party which is a Federal Party."[12] When C. A. Dunning took over as premier in 1922, his former prominent association with farmers' organizations was of benefit to him. A decline in the intensity of farmer feeling enabled him to restore the former association between the provincial and federal Liberal parties.

It is significant that in the decade preceding the Liberal fall from power in 1929, resignations from the government weakened its former close association with the Grain Growers'. Motherwell broke with his colleagues in 1918 over matters of policy; Langley had been forced to resign in 1921 because of interference in the administration of justice; Maharg terminated his brief tenure in the same year, charging the premier with failure to uphold his part of an agreement to support federal Progressives in return for Maharg's entry into the cabinet; and Dunning went to the federal field in 1926.

In any event, upheaval in farmers' organizations in the 1920s eliminated any one association as the accepted voice of the farmer. The Farmers' Union of Canada was organized in Saskatchewan in

1921 on the premise that it was futile to seek solutions through politicians and governments. The new organization advocated that farmers take direct action in marketing of farm products. Its success in launching the Saskatchewan Wheat Pool in 1924 tremendously enhanced both the membership and the prestige of the Farmers' Union. In 1926 it amalgamated with the Saskatchewan Grain Growers' Association to form the United Farmers of Canada (Saskatchewan Section). Continued activity by a radical left wing which had developed out of the Farmers' Union caused turbulence and division within the United Farmers, and the new organization never achieved the pre-eminent position among Saskatchewan farmers that had previously been enjoyed by the Grain Growers'.

Political confusion paralleled that of farmers' organizations during this period. Despite the decline of the Progressive movement by the late 1920s, the conditions which had brought the movement into existence had not disappeared. The dissatisfaction and uncertainty which shook political alignments in the earlier part of the decade were still evident in the large number of independent candidates contesting the 1929 election.

The Liberals also faced trouble in the 1920s which was related to the support that they received from non-Anglo-Saxon settlers. Liberal party and government organization had been directed to making staunch allies of European immigrants, as described in the following chapter. The problem in the 1920s was not any weakening of the newcomers' loyal support for the Liberal party, but a backlash against these settlers in other areas of the electorate. Federal wartime policies of labelling many of them as enemy aliens, and of setting them apart from other sections of the population through naturalization and franchise laws, gave them an odor of unacceptability which continued after the war. Protestant and Orange groups, suspicious of the European settlers on religious as well as on nationalistic grounds, were increasingly uneasy over the slowness of their assimilation and saw the Liberal government as delaying assimilation by allowing ethnic settlement in community blocks and by enacting provincial legislation to permit some use of languages other than English in the schools. The Saskatchewan Grain Growers' Association, which was largely Anglo-Saxon and Protestant, was one of the outlets for protests against the retention of old-country customs among the immigrants.

With the S.G.G.A. and the ethnic community forming the twin bases of Liberal support in the province, the party was now in the position of having one of its arms attacking the other. Preoccupied with the general threat of the Progressives among the agrarian electorate in the 1920s, the Liberal party tended to overlook the particular dissatisfaction that was directed against the government's policies towards the non-Anglo-Saxon population. And, unlike the concerted farmer protest which was evident, the reaction against the non-English-speaking settlers was scattered, existing not only among the Grain Growers' but spotted among school trustees, in Protestant religious groups, and in fraternal and occupational organizations.[13]

In the 1929 election between the beleaguered Liberals and a renewed Conservative party, the Ku Klux Klan played a significant role. The Klan had organized in the province for two years with considerable success, coalescing the anti-foreign sentiment and appealing to those Anglo-Saxons who feared Roman Catholic influence in public affairs. It concentrated opposition to the Roman Catholic Church and to settlers from central and south-eastern Europe.

The Conservative party, which had abandoned its Provincial Rights name in 1912, had faltered badly in postwar years. Its participation in the 1921 election was so limited that the party allowed the Liberals to win seventeen seats by acclamation. Many former Conservatives ran as Independents, and in some instances there was confusion as to whether an Independent candidate was really a Progressive or a Conservative. Only two Conservatives and an Independent-Conservative were elected in 1921, and three Conservatives were elected in 1925. By 1929 the party had revived, and the flexibility of political alliance was used to advantage by the opposition parties. Through informal co-operation, saw-offs were arranged so that Conservative candidates opposed Progressives or Independents in only nine out of sixty-three constituencies.

The point of attack which became an election issue was the extension of Church influence in public schools in predominantly Roman Catholic areas. For some schools Catholic school trustees hired nuns as teachers, and crucifixes and other religious emblems were placed in classrooms. Since these were public schools, Protestant children also attended them, because the minority might not be large enough to form a Protestant separate school. Although the total number was small, it was the subjection of at least some Protestant children to Roman Catholic influence in public schools which aroused agitation.

This fear of Roman Catholic influence set the stage for an emotional ingredient to be added to the already unstable political background of the 1929 election. The Conservative party fashioned its campaign to capitalize on the existing climate of feeling, and it included the abolition of sectarianism in the public schools as a major issue. Other planks in its platform included the transfer of public lands to the province, a point it had long stressed, the urging of a selective immigration policy, a non-partisan civil service, and, in general, the need for a change in administration. The government underestimated the effect of the opposition appeal and was too complacent in expecting re-election on its record.[14]

The Liberals won twenty-eight seats against twenty-four for the Conservatives. Five Progressives and six Independents who were elected gave their support to the Conservatives, with the consequent formation of what the Conservative leader, Dr. J. T. M. Anderson, preferred to call a co-operative rather than a coalition government.

It was a disastrous victory for the Conservatives. Plagued by drought and depression from the time it assumed office, the new

SASKATCHEWAN ELECTION RESULTS 1905-1978
(Figure in brackets represents percentage of total votes cast)

Election	1905	1908	1912	1917	1921	1925	1929	1934	1938	1944	1948	1952	1956	1960	1964	1967	1971	1975	1978
No. of members	25	41	54	59	63	63	63	55	52	52	52	53	53	55	59	59	60	61	61
Liberal Members	16 (52.25)	27 (50.79)	46[1] (56.96)	51 (56.68)	46 (51.39)	50 (51.51)	28 (45.56)	50 (48.00)	38 (45.50)	5 (35.42)	19 (30.60)	11 (39.27)	14 (30.35)	17 (32.68)	32 (40.40)	35 (45.57)	15 (42.82)	15 (31.67)	— (13.78)
Conservative Members *(Prov. Rts. '05,08)	9 (47.47)	14 (47.88)	7 (41.97)	7 (36.38)	2 (3.94)	3 (18.35)	24 (36.44)	— (26.75)	— (11.87)	— (10.69)	— (7.63)	— (1.97)	— (1.98)	— (13.95)	1 (18.90)	— (9.77)	— (2.13)	7 (27.62)	17 (38.08)
CCF: NDP Members (Farm-Lab. '34)								5 (23.96)	10 (18.73)	47 (53.13)	31 (47.56)	42 (54.06)	36 (45.25)	38 (40.76)	26 (40.30)	24 (44.35)	45 (54.99)	39 (40.07)	44 (48.12)
Social Credit Members									2 (15.90)	— (.06)	— (8.08)	— (3.90)	3 (21.48)	— (12.35)	— (.39)	— (.30)	—	—	—
Independents, Progressives, etc.	— (.28)	— (1.33)	1 (Ind) (1.06)	1 (Ind) (6.94)	15[2] (44.65)	10[3] (30.14)	11[4] (18.01)	— (1.30)	2 (Unity) (8.04)	— (.70)	2[5] (6.12)	— (.80)	— (.95)	— (.27)	— (.01)	— (—)	— (.05)	— (.64)	— (.02)

*Prov. Rts.—Provincial Rights

1. Including Cumberland constituency where the election was declared void and the by-election was held in 1913
2. 7 Independents, 6 Progressives, 1 Independent Conservative, 1 Independent Pro-Government
3. 2 Independents, 6 Progressives, 1 Labor Liberal, 1 Independent Liberal
4. 6 Independents, 5 Progressives
5. 1 Independent, 1 Conservative Liberal
   (In 1917 and 1944 three service members were also elected)

Provincial Elections in Saskatchewan 1905–1979, published by Chief Electoral Office, Province of Saskatchewan, 1979, is the source for the party designations and vote percentages in the chart.

administration had no opportunity to carry out its duties under any approach to normal conditions. Pressing problems of relief and alleviation of distress were thrust upon the government to an extent far exceeding the resources of the province to meet them. The premier and his colleagues were inexperienced. An open split within Conservative ranks added further to the discomfiture of the premier. From 1931 an opposing section of the party outside the legislature criticized the Conservative alliance with the Progressives and Independents, calling for a return to "true-blue" Conservatism. In the 1934 election the Liberals were returned to power with no Conservative winning a seat, and for the next thirty years no candidate in a provincial contest was elected on the basis of Conservative support alone.

After the Liberal victory in 1934, James G. Gardiner returned to the office of premier which he had lost five years earlier, becoming the only Saskatchewan premier to assume the office twice. Upon his move to federal politics the following year a cabinet colleague, W. J. Patterson, moved up to the premiership, which he retained until 1944.

Meanwhile the Co-operative Commonwealth Federation had come into existence. The CCF had its origin in the same conditions of agrarian discontent that had sparked the Progressive movement. Objecting to eastern domination and to control by the traditional parties in Canada, and emerging in a time when conditions were aggravated by the drought and depression of the thirties, the new protest movement grew out of the ruins of the old. Sporadic attempts at the organization of farm and labor groups had occurred with the wane of the Progressives. After discussion of the subject at previous conventions, the United Farmers of Canada (Saskatchewan Section) at its 1931 convention voted to enter politics. On August 1, 1932, at a conference in Calgary, members of the organization met representatives of the United Farmers of Alberta and labor groups from the four western provinces and Ontario to form the new political movement.

Within Saskatchewan, just before the Calgary meeting which established the national party, the U.F.C. and the Independent Labor Party in the province met in joint convention to form the provincial Farmer-Labor Party. The parent bodies continued joint support of the new party until 1935. In that year the U.F.C. voted to withdraw from political action, and the name of the political organization was changed to correspond to its federal counterpart, the Co-operative Commonwealth Federation. The provincial organization thus emerged through local action rather than by branching from the national association. Indeed, provincial preceded national organization, and in subsequent development the provincial CCF enjoyed extensive autonomy and control over its activities.

The first leader of the provincial party, M. J. Coldwell, held the office from 1932 to 1935, when he resigned after his election to the House of Commons. G. H. Williams, president of the party, then assumed the duties of leader, but he aroused considerable resentment through aggressive control of party activities. In 1941, after Williams enlisted in the army, the party chose as its head the member of the House of Commons for Weyburn, T. C. Douglas. He led the party to victory in 1944, and he continued as its leader until 1961, when he became national leader of the newly formed New Democratic Party. Mr. Douglas was succeeded in the Saskatchewan party by a former cabinet colleague, Woodrow S. Lloyd, who continued as leader through the subsequent transition of the provincial CCF to the NDP.

As in protest movements preceding it, the CCF had a strong element of idealism, blending social gospel conviction and imported British socialist principles with intense feeling arising from local conditions. The party's search for power from 1932 to 1944 involved the conflict of doctrinaire principles with practical appeals. This conflict resulted in compromise, in shifts in policy, and in modification of the party program. The platform drawn up at the initial Farmer-Labor convention in 1932 was frankly socialistic, and it advocated a lease system of landholding as a substitute for private ownership. Even before the 1934 election, party spokesmen began to omit references to socialism, and a poor showing in the 1934 provincial and 1935 federal elections led to further doubts about the original approach. In facing the alternatives of adhering to socialism as the ultimate solution to agrarian problems or of modifying its program to include immediate reforms, the CCF chose modification. In its 1936 convention the party dropped all mention of socialism, and during the election campaign of 1938 it stressed government planning rather than ownership. It also adopted a policy of co-operation with other "progressive" parties in election activity.[15] An overture of friendship toward Social Credit was rebuffed by William Aberhart, the premier of Alberta, but CCF and Conservative workers achieved a strange degree of unanimity in an attempt to oust the incumbent Liberals. The CCF doubled its membership in the legislature by winning ten seats, and two Unity candidates supported by the Conservatives, the CCF, and the Social Credit were elected, although the Liberals retained a substantial majority.

In 1944 the CCF campaigned mainly as a social reform group. It emphasized that farms would not be socialized, and it outlined broad plans for post-war rehabilitation, for socialized health and other social services, for collective bargaining for labor, and for the abolition of patronage in the civil service. The Liberals stressed the danger of farmers losing their land under a socialist government and pointed to their own record of the past decade. This last was not a particularly effective appeal. Viewing the return of generally prosperous conditions throughout the country, Saskatchewan residents had not discerned any corresponding reflection in such government benefits as road improvement and social services. Both in terms of popular vote and in the number of members elected, the 1944 contest was a decisive victory for the CCF, which gained forty-seven seats out of fifty-two.

Once in office, the CCF displayed the same flexibility of policy and tactics which had brought it to power. This flexibility is well illustrated in its record on government ownership. In conformity with socialist philosophy, the CCF moved quickly to create provincially-owned companies and to set up a wide variety of crown corporations. In the 1948 election, the government suffered sharp reductions both in its legislative majority and in popular vote. Loss of support was particularly evident in northern areas, where CCF policies of development and control had been most actively pursued. J. L. Phelps, the cabinet minister in charge, was personally defeated. The government's subsequent posture was significant. No real effort was made to find a seat for the fervent and doctrinaire minister, who therefore had no alternative but to resign from the cabinet. Abandonment of the socialist name was seriously discussed in CCF convention, and the government substantially modified its policy of social ownership. Some of the enterprises which proved unsuccessful were discontinued, and few new ones were established. As a result, the business carried out by government-owned enterprises at any time constituted but a small percentage of the total within the province. The development of oil and mineral resources was left largely to private enterprise, although in this matter the practical problem of lack of capital rather than ideological considerations was apparently a determining factor.

Distinctive features of the CCF government's performance did not represent that sharp departure from the practices of its predecessors in government or from those in neighboring provinces which was sometimes pictured. Enthusiasm and a reforming spirit were evident, administrative innovations occurred, changes were made, and new policies and services were introduced in addition to the experimentation in government ownership. These new elements all occurred within the framework of the existing economic and social order. Neither the claim of its supporters nor the charges of its opponents that the old social order would be replaced by a new one were fulfilled.

In an era of increasing government activity and participation, CCF performance showed a difference more in degree and in timing than in kind. The CCF did not create, but inherited, two of the province's most conspicuous public enterprises, the telephone monopoly and the power corporation. Social welfare measures, while being in advance of those elsewhere, did not differ in nature. A scheme of provincial hospitalization which was a pioneer measure had within a decade been introduced for the entire country, and provincial medicare was soon followed by a similar plan at the national level.

In other instances CCF innovations reflected the same idea and intent as those approved by a predecessor but not carried into effect. The system of larger school units found an earlier echo in Premier Scott's idea of "placing a group of rural schools under the supervision of a single Board of Trustees." The idea at least of the Economic Advisory and Planning Board which the CCF set up was not without precedent. In the last session of the Anderson administration, the premier announced the establishment of an economic advisory board which "would consist of the best brains that could be obtained within or without the province to study the intricate problems faced by agriculturalists and ranchers." Even the charges flung at a socialist government were not entirely new. In 1908, in debate on the Liberal government policy of supplying free textbooks to schools, the leader of the opposition "described the idea as socialistic or communistic in origin and practice."

The course of the CCF in Saskatchewan thus followed the political pattern previously established. The party was not successful in leading the electorate into new fields of economic and political thought. On the contrary, to achieve and to maintain power the CCF adapted its early radical policies to conform to the long-standing demands of the electorate, and it adjusted its program to their requirements. S. M. Lipset concluded from his study of the party in Saskatchewan:

The socialists had attempted to convert the people of the province to the necessity of a fundamental societal change that would affect the entire economic structure of the country. They soon learned, however, that the majority of farmers and many of their original followers were more interested in immediate reforms that would improve their economic position than in a new social order. The strong appeal in the middle thirties of the Social Credit and progressive coalition movements was clear evidence that the particular ideology of socialism was not important to farmers.[16]

Taking this lesson to heart, the CCF suppressed the doctrinaire element within its ranks and substituted for government ownership, benefits and services within the existing economic order.

When the CCF was reorganized at the national level in 1961 as the New Democratic Party, the Saskatchewan CCF showed considerable concern to preserve its existing provincial structure. There was an evident desire to retain the agrarian flavour of the Saskatchewan organization and a resistance to emphasizing the relationship with labor. The provincial CCF kept the existing name until after the 1967 Saskatchewan election. It made concession to its federal counterpart only in the cumbersome official title of "The Co-operative Commonwealth Federation, Saskatchewan Section of the New Democratic Party," but the CCF title continued for ordinary use. The Saskatchewan party contributed its leader to the national cause, but it was careful to keep its own name and character.

A deeply divisive factor in the province during the latter years of the CCF was the much publicized medicare dispute. Medical care insurance had long been included in the party's platform, and late in 1959 Premier Douglas announced the government's intention to put it into effect. An intensive campaign which the medical doctors launched in opposition to the proposed plan made it a highly controversial issue in the 1960 election. Subsequent events were even more turbulent, reaching a peak in the summer of 1962, when doctors withdrew services to protest implementation of the scheme. Petitions and counter-petitions went to the government, doctors threatened to leave the province, a "Keep our Doctors" committee appeared, protesting groups marched on the legislative building, and backfence neighbors of long acquaintance refused to speak. Each side finally gave some ground, and Lord Taylor, a British Labor peer and a physician, acted as a mediator. Eventually the plan, with certain modifications, was implemented. The controversy which had been aroused was so intense that the bitterness lingered on long after the launching of the plan and its widespread acceptance in the province.

The effect of the dispute on election results is difficult to estimate. On balance, it appears to have helped the CCF government in 1960 but to have contributed to its defeat in 1964. In 1960 the ferocity and excess of the doctors' campaign defeated its own purpose, and it may even have been the determining factor in keeping the government in power. The controversy and bitterness which occurred in the interval between elections was unsettling, an effect which is never beneficial to the party in power. The controversy had the further effect of exhausting the government's time and energy, and of diverting its attention from the development of new programs to offer to the electorate.[17]

Other factors affecting both the hard core of party workers and the general voting public contributed to the 1964 defeat. In 1961 the loss of the party's highly effective leader, Premier T. C. Douglas, to the federal field weakened the provincial party. The courting of labor which was involved in the party reorganization as the NDP also created resentment among rural followers. "The old faithful CCFers lost a lot of faith with the labor amalgamation," and the need to "tone down" relations with labor was the tenor of certain reports from party workers. To what extent this or other factors were responsible is uncertain, but the early 1960s witnessed a general slackening of party activity. Some of the spark and the apparently tireless energy which previously had characterized the party faithful were missing. Among the electorate generally there were the inevitable grievances built up over twenty years. And in contrast to a government which had grown older in office and had become wearied by recent struggles, there was a Liberal opposition revitalized and presenting new inducements.

For some years after its defeat in 1944, the Liberal party had devoted considerable energy to changing leaders. W. J. Patterson, who was premier from 1935 to 1944, stepped down as Liberal leader to be succeeded in turn by Walter Tucker in 1946, A. H. McDonald in 1954, and Ross Thatcher in 1959.

Mr. Thatcher, a former CCF member of parliament turned Liberal, now employed against the CCF the techniques of grass-roots organization which he had learned as one of them. He addressed immediate energy and purpose to reorganizing and rejuvenating the Liberal party. He also changed their campaign approach. In the 1964 contest the Liberals abandoned their previous emphasis on the theoretical concept of socialism versus free enterprise. They held out tangible allurements of decreased taxation, better agricultural credit, increased industrialization and more jobs, free school books, and extensions of medicare. The Liberals gained power with thirty-two seats out of fifty-nine, and they increased their number to thirty-five in 1967.

The seven years of Liberal government, sandwiched between the CCF and the NDP government which followed in 1971, demonstrated basic differences in approach which are infrequently evident between modern parties and administrations. The differences, however, were more in outlook and in intent than in actual policies. Philosophically, the CCF and the NDP favored government ownership or direct control; for political and practical reasons they accepted a wide area of private enterprise. Premier Thatcher placed strong and vocal emphasis on private effort; political and practical necessity required a continuation and even an expansion of so-called socialist enterprises. Administratively the CCF emphasized research and planning, and they built up a highly competent administrative service; under the Liberals this structure was not so much swept away as deliberately allowed and encouraged to atrophy.

In operating within the relatively inelastic bounds of economic and political necessity, neither the Liberals nor the NDP made a sharp break with its immediate predecessor so as to alter substantially services to the public. The contrast was in the entirely different spirit, emphasis, and goals of the CCF-NDP and the Liberals. What was the aspiration of one was the unavoidable necessity of the other.

A foremost factor in the Liberal loss in 1971 was the abrasive and heavy-handed way in which the government had applied its policies, and a general feeling of distrust which resulted from its approach. The government under Premier Thatcher had antagonized broad sections of the electorate including labor, school teachers, hotel owners, hospital boards, and rural municipal officers. "If there was anyone we didn't alienate, it was because we didn't contact him," was Deputy Leader Dave Steuart's rueful summation following the Liberal's 1971 campaign. Widespread annoyance resulted also from the earlier imposition of utilization fees for medical services.

Among the list of the disaffected was the broad span of disgruntled farmers. A glaring oversight by Premier Thatcher was his failure to take any positive stand on the unhappy farm situation and on the urgent dissatisfaction arising from restricted wheat sales. The government admittedly was at a serious disadvantage. There was little it could do to remedy either the immediate or the general farm situation, and it suffered from the unpopular agricultural policies of the Ottawa Liberal government. But the premier's silence on these policies, in contrast to a previous readiness to quarrel with his federal counterparts on a variety of matters, tacitly allied him with the federal program.

The NDP opposition under its new leader, Allan Blakeney, adroitly made the federal policy a credible provincial issue. He reiterated throughout the campaign that only by defeating the provincial Liberals could the message of farmer dissatisfaction be impressed upon Ottawa. The overall federal program was pointed to as threatening the individual family farm, which it was the NDP's objective to protect. The NDP won fifty-five per cent of the popular vote and forty-five seats out of sixty.

The 1971 election marked the end of Social Credit participation in Saskatchewan elections, while the most notable feature of the 1975 election was the upsurge of the Progressive Conservatives. From the 1930s neither of these two parties had won more than an occasional seat. Despite their lack of success, their sporadic activity resulted in frequent three- and four-cornered contests, which added a further variable in election speculation. This was the extent to which either of the two main parties would be most likely to gain by the election presence or absence of either of the minor parties.

After the Social Credit victory in Alberta in 1935, the party twice made determined efforts in Saskatchewan to challenge the political domination of the Liberals and the CCF. The first try was in 1938, when they won only two seats. Enthusiasm waned and activity was sporadic for the next two decades until an onslaught from British Columbia and Alberta in 1956. The Social Credit's platform in that campaign emphasized the superior progress of the two most westerly provinces and the logic of extending the same jurisdiction into the next neighboring province. Social Credit secured more than one-fifth of the popular vote, but the party won only three seats. These were lost in 1960, and Social Credit ran only two candidates in 1964, each of whom forfeited his deposit. An abortive attempt in 1971 to merge Social Credit and Progressive Conservative forces was indicative of the low ebb of both parties. Social Credit was even further weakened by a split which occurred in its ranks over the attempted merger, and the party faded from the scene.

After its rout in 1934 the Conservative party retained a core of staunch supporters and at times it had dedicated leadership, but until 1975 it achieved only minimal success. In the 1948 election and in a by-election in 1953, candidates with joint Liberal and Conservative support were elected. One of these subsequently ran as a Liberal and was re-elected; the other lost in a second bid when running as a Progressive Conservative. A reflection of rising federal fortunes was evident in an upswing of provincial Conservative support in the late 1950s and early 1960s when the leader, Martin Pederson, was elected to the legislature in 1964 for a single term. After the attempt to merge with Social Credit failed, the Progressive Conservatives were able to muster only token effort in the 1971 election. They were barely able to secure candidates, the sixteen who did run all lost their election deposits, and the party gained only slightly more than two per cent of the total vote.

When Dick Collver assumed the Progressive Conservative leadership in 1973, his announced high optimism seemed ill-founded. With few members, no money, and recent dissension in the party, there was little to indicate that within two years the party would run a full slate of candidates, win seven legislative seats, hold second place in twenty other constituencies, and secure close to twenty-eight per cent of the popular vote.

Balancing this remarkable Progressive Conservative upsurge in the 1975 election was a substantial drop in government support. The NDP still retained a comfortable majority, however with thirty-nine seats out of sixty-one, against fifteen Liberal members and the seven Progressive Conservatives. The popular vote for the NDP dropped from fifty-five per cent in 1971 to forty per cent, against a Liberal drop from forty-three per cent to thirty-two per cent.

The NDP had gone into the 1975 election with the advantage of an overflowing economy and with a specific election issue. At the outset Premier Blakeney asked for a mandate to resist Ottawa on two fronts, first on energy policies, and secondly on federal agricultural policies. The Liberals, who were under the leadership of Dave Steuart as a result of the sudden death of Ross Thatcher only a month after his defeat in 1971, found themselves without any specific issues. They fell back on the election-worn slogan of "Free Enterprise versus Socialism", but they applied it with some effect in the specific issue of the NDP's land bank policy. They charged that the NDP government had no intention of re-selling land which had been purchased from retiring farmers for a land bank, but that they were using it as a means of nationalizing farm land which they would continue only to rent.

The Progressive Conservative's main advantage was simply in being there, to capitalize on a substantial disenchantment with both the NDP and the Liberals. Their really significant achievement was to secure a full slate of candidates, which was noteworthy in itself. They exploited this achievement with a full-page newspaper advertisement, complete with photographs of the sixty-one candidates, more than a month before the election was announced.

The NDP and Liberals campaigned mainly against one another, and it suited Conservative tactics to be left largely on the side lines. Emphasizing the individual and the need for both diminution and decentralization of government power, they also pointed to the ill-feeling between the Liberals and the NDP and to the undesirable political in-fighting which it produced. The loftier ground taken by the Progressive Conservatives was evident in Mr. Collver's slogan that "Mud thrown is ground lost", and in an underlying and general appeal to religion in such references as "a power greater than ourselves." No single issue was overriding, and local concerns and personalities often overshadowed the avowed major issues.

In contrast to a quiet campaign in 1975, the 1978 election was lively from the beginning and uncertain to the end. This time it was against the Progressive Conservatives that the NDP directed their fire, as the 1975 election and succeeding events had marked them as the real threat to the government. The nucleus of seven seats which the Conservatives had won in 1975 had been augmented by their winning two seats from the Liberals in by-elections and by the defection of two Liberal members to the Conservatives, one of whom was Ross Thatcher's son, Colin Thatcher. The Liberals and Conservatives therefore each went into the 1978 election with eleven members, but the Conservatives were clearly on the way up and the Liberals on the way down.

The question of leadership overshadowed a variety of lesser issues and a host of campaign promises from all three parties. In 1975 Progressive Conservative leader Dick Collver's achievement in pulling the party up from next to nothing was little short of miraculous. In 1978 that same leader appeared to be a major obstacle in further advances for the party. Greater exposure had diminished rather than helped his acceptability. Involvement in personal lawsuits over business matters and a less than impressive legislative performance contributed to uneasiness over the prospect of entrusting the affairs of the province to him. By contrast, NDP leader and premier, Allan Blakeney, had increased his stature after taking office in 1971, and he was seen as a bulwark against threatened federal encroachment into areas of provincial natural resources. The resource issue was part of the larger picture of antagonism towards Ottawa, and of what was seen as the need for the best man to do battle in the federal-provincial arena.

The NDP put the Progressive Conservatives on the defensive at the outset of the campaign. An attack on what the NDP declared were Conservative intentions to introduce utilization fees for medical care was so harsh as to threaten a backlash against the NDP, especially since they did not have very substantial evidence for their charge. Their strategy to shift, after attacking, to the positive aspects of NDP government was strengthened by Supreme Court decisions which came down during the campaign. The striking down of Saskatchewan revenue taxation, as described further in chapter 12, was used by the NDP as evidence of the need to stay with a leader who had been proven able to stand against Ottawa.

In 1978 it was not possible for the Conservatives to adopt the same aloofness from controversy as they had done in 1975, especially when they had to refute the NDP charges about utilization fees. Their new prominence also made it more difficult for them to keep only to generalities in emphasizing the individual and the diminution of government. Using many of the same techniques and slogans a second time around, the Conservative campaign in 1978 lacked some of the freshness it had had in 1975.

The Liberals started as perceived losers, and even a valiant campaign by leader Ted Malone could not reverse the process. The handicap of an unpopular Liberal government at Ottawa was fully as great in a Saskatchewan election as in other provinces, if not more so. The Liberals compounded their problems by a cumbersome election platform which proposed a series of referenda to be taken to the people.

The decisiveness of the election results obscured, after the event, the uncertainty which the media, the pollsters, the political scientists, and many of the participants experienced to the end. As seen in the table on page 54, the NDP substantially increased its membership in the house to forty-four out of sixty-one seats, with the remaining seventeen going to the Conservatives. The Conservatives could assuage their disappointment only slightly by pointing to their increase of more than ten per cent in popular vote to bring it to thirty-eight per cent. The Liberals could take comfort on no score, with no seats and their popular vote cut by more than half to less than fourteen per cent. Dick Collver, who in 1975 had staked his continued leadership on winning the next election, announced his intention to step down some months after the 1978 results were in. The change was made on November 10, 1979 when a Progressive Conservative leadership convention chose Grant Devine, an agricultural economist, as their new leader.

The 1975 and 1978 elections have put a new face on Saskatchewan politics. In 1975 the Conservatives emerged from their former role of spoiler to become rivals for power. That election brought immediate anticipation that the next would decide whether the Conservative upsurge was genuine. But the 1978 election, positive as its statistics seem, still left that question in doubt, with much depending on the new Conservative leader and also on what revival may occur within the Liberal party.

A new face has not changed the body politic. As always, the Saskatchewan electorate has refrained from a sharp enough swing to one party to leave itself without an alternative. Even more than that, since the 1920s a protest party has emerged whenever the electorate has become disenchanted with both of the established parties. The 1970s have seen no change in this pattern, but merely a change in the relative positions of the parties within the political field. Thus the CCF protest party of the 1930s, now the NDP, has become in every sense of the word an established party. On the other hand, the Conservatives, the earliest organized and the most traditional of the traditional parties, after forty years of purification in the political wilderness, emerged in 1975 as a new protest party. The CCF protest had been for extended government jurisdiction to enhance individual welfare. The Progressive Conservative protest was for decreased government participation to increase individual freedom. The party has now found its place in the established order as the official opposition and as the visible alternative.

The near extinction of the Liberals in 1978 does not necessarily mean their demise. That the areas newly won by the Conservatives tend to be traditional Liberal territory and include, incidentally, all three seats won by Social Credit in 1956, indicates an anti-NDP base for either of the two opposing parties. The NDP naturally will concentrate its criticism on the Conservatives and leave the Liberals on the side lines to recover from their wounds. To the extent that it is possible without being too obvious, it is to the advantage of the NDP even to lend a helping hand to the Liberals. Nothing can help the NDP cause more than to have the opposition to them divided between parties rather than concentrated in one party. Even before the 1978 election they had on occasion made strangely encouraging comments about their former major rival, opining that the Liberals were not yet finished. In the longer term the political history of the province does not even rule out the possibility that the Liberals will take their turn at emerging afresh as a protest party. The electorate has already shown its acceptance of a new incarnation of a traditional party in that role.

Saskatchewan has been noted for the liveliness of its politics and for the active partisan division which has always existed. This activity is in contrast to the political climate in neighboring provinces, where much more one-sided results and frequently less aggressive political activity have been evident. The political pattern in Saskatchewan cannot be laid to any single cause, but it has resulted from a variety of factors and personalities which have combined and succeeded one another.

The first of these shaping factors was a chance circumstance that gave Saskatchewan politics a turbulent beginning. Because Saskatchewan fell heir to the former Territorial capital of Regina, Haultain carried on his political career there instead of in Alberta, and he carried controversies over autonomy into early Saskatchewan politics. Haultain was originally from the area which became part of Alberta, having set up a law practice in Macleod in 1884 and having represented that constituency throughout his Territorial political career. In 1905 he shifted his political base to Saskatchewan, representing the constituency of South Qu'Appelle, which lies south and east from Regina. Saskatchewan therefore became the scene of Haultain's determined efforts to challenge the terms of autonomy. The hard-fought and bitter election contest in Saskatchewan in 1905 contrasted sharply with a much calmer campaign in Alberta. There the Liberals readily won twenty-three out of twenty-five seats.

In contrast to both Alberta and Manitoba, where scandals have devastated political parties, in Saskatchewan no party has ever been obliterated by scandal to give an opponent a monopoly position even temporarily. Serious charges which were made against the Liberal government in 1916 concerning liquor administration and road building were the closest approach to a damaging scandal in Saskatchewan, and these charges were unsubstantiated as far as the government itself was concerned, as described in chapter 8. By moving quickly against those who were found guilty in both the legislature and civil service, the government maintained its credibility and continued firmly in power.

Saskatchewan emerged from the Progressive upheaval and the political confusion of the 1920s with active political opponents. In contrast to activities in neighboring provinces, the refusal of the Saskatchewan farmers' organization to enter provincial politics placed no obligation on its members to concentrate their votes in one direction. The formation of governments in Alberta and Manitoba by farmers' parties left each province subsequently without strong political competitors. In Alberta, the political action of the United Farmers of Alberta helped to destroy the Liberal party. In Manitoba the result was an ultimate merging of political forces in an essentially one-party system.

In Saskatchewan the farmer appeal presented by the Progressives had to compete with the informal connection between the Liberals and the Grain Growers' Association. Neither party could make any official claim on the farmer. As a result the vote was split, and the Liberal party survived as a political alternative.

Political shifts in the 1930s similarly saw continued opposition even after the decimation of the Conservatives in 1934. While the Conservatives and their allies were in power from 1929 to 1934, the Liberal opposition was headed by the doughty James G. Gardiner, who with his own aggressive personality, his experience in office, and more members than the Conservatives themselves had, continued the tradition of strong opposition. The drought and depression which destroyed the Conservatives had as the other side of the political coin the emergence of the CCF. New opposition thus existed after the Liberal return to power. Though few in number, the five new Farmer-Labor members, soon to be renamed CCF, had all the zeal of a new movement, and they also had their numbers doubled in the 1938 election.

The nature of the CCF and of its NDP successor has contributed significantly to the vigor and continuing division in Saskatchewan's political life. The socialist ideology of the party has for years caused a more distinct separation from its opposition than has normally been evident in the party systems of other provinces.

In Alberta, Social Credit was from the beginning further to the right, and it moved increasingly in that direction. As a right-wing party, it managed more readily to straddle the political spectrum of its electorate, especially with the earlier demise of the Liberals. In Manitoba the merging of the protest party of the 1920s with the traditional parties blanketed the political scene until the mid 1950s.

The practical application of the policies of the NDP and Liberal parties in Saskatchewan did not differ sufficiently to give great concern to the politically casual. The politician at close range and the politically conscious were aware of the difference in motivation and ideology. It was the mutual suspicion arising out of this consciousness that maintained a genuine gulf between the two parties.

The NDP saw a broad reach of government and party control as an essential concomitant of its social goals. The Liberals saw such control as a sinister extension of party tentacles into areas beyond those that they regarded as the proper sphere of government activity. The ideology of the NDP and the distrust which it generated among the Liberals marked a sharp difference in party approach and a strong motivating power in election contests.

These ideological differences exist at the party level. The appeal each must make is to a pragmatic electorate. A candidate therefore needs to distinguish between party and electorate. To whatever degree the candidate may be motivated by ideological considerations, the political reality is that his electorate, in broad measure, will judge on pragmatic grounds.

The distinction between party and electorate explains the lack of any contradiction between the existence of a CCF government for twenty years on one side of the boundary dividing Saskatchewan and Alberta, and the existence of a Social Credit administration on the other. In each province a new party was brought to power as a reaction against the previous administration; each represented in its respective province the available alternative when the particular situation was ripe for a change in government. Once in office, their respective performances were judged on the basis of general satisfaction, without any great concern on the part of most of the electorate as to what particular political doctrines or labels were incidentally endorsed by its vote.

Similarly in the late 1970s the retention of an NDP government in Saskatchewan sandwiched between Conservative administrations in Alberta and Manitoba represents no strong ideological commitment by the electorate in general. The Saskatchewan premier himself explicitly acknowledges the conservative nature of the Saskatchewan electorate. Ideology may motivate the party worker, but the main body of the electorate continues to look to practical considerations.

5   Party Organization

If the party throughout the Province could have a central organization in each district which would keep in touch with one or two active agents in each township during the years between elections we would find it very much easier work when the campaigns come on. It is always the case that many divisions give majorities against us, simply because of lack of organizaton. In most townships there is a sufficient number of men, who do not feel strongly one way or the other, to make the majorities. It is the party which gets the work done that secures the votes of these men.[1]

These comments by Premier Walter Scott in the wake of the first Saskatchewan election were an early recognition of the importance of political organization. His assessment was especially true in a new country where established patterns of living and frequently of political thought had been broken. Experience reinforced this early opinion, and highly developed organization has played a vital role in Saskatchewan politics.

As with other aspects of life in the province, political organization was not easy. Especially in early days, population was scattered and communication difficult. Their preoccupation with endless farming duties meant few settlers had the leisure or means for party service, even if they were interested in it. A variety of community services competed for attention: local government bodies, school boards, farmer and business organizations, and social groups. Population changes with corresponding constituency adjustments disrupted party organization. A disparity in the number of federal constituencies compared with provincial seats compounded the problem of co-ordinating federal and provincial organization.

The processes of settlement gave the government party a tremendous advantage over the opposition. Highway supervisors and inspectors, sanitary inspectors, and other field personnel of the civil service formed the core of Liberal party organization from 1905 to 1929.[2] And during this period homestead inspectors were appointed by a federal Liberal government until 1911 and again after 1921, giving the Liberals full sway in the province both provincially and federally in those years. This political influence was used to full advantage among non-English-speaking immigrants, who were the most reliant on government personnel for advice. As noted in chapter 4, they became overwhelmingly Liberal supporters.

This patronage system of appointing party supporters to the civil service rewarded the faithful while providing the party with a pool of workers who were on the public payroll. Following the prevalent political practice of the day, the sitting member (or defeated candidate) of the party in power held a firmly established right. He recommended the appointee for any government job within his constituency, or the appointment of persons from his constituency to civil service jobs in Regina.

The member also prepared a patronage list of services to be used in his riding. The outside staff of the Department of Public Works was required to patronize exclusively these politically approved hotels, livery stables, hardware, lumber, and general stores listed for every town, village, and hamlet. Newspapers throughout the province traded support for government contracts. Voters' lists were printed in each constituency in a "friendly" office, and government advertising was similarly distributed.

The pork-barrel practice of dispensing a favor to a particular district was important in a period of growth and development. "This road work will make more Liberals," was a sentiment echoed in many letters from all parts of the province. A suggestion to transfer administration of road building to rural municipalities met with intense objection. A government supporter was quick to describe the basis of the good political organization built up in his district. He said that the local member had

been enabled to do this to a great extent by the patronage which has been in his hands, by making certain promises. If he has not the power to fulfil these promises there is absolutely no use in attempting to go to the people again or any person in this district supporting the Liberal party.[3]

The government might also guarantee bonds for railway branch lines, a matter of vital concern to residents. In an era of sharp rivalry among growing towns, courthouses and similar public buildings represented victory over a competitor as well as prizes in themselves.

This rivalry made patronage and the pork-barrel double-edged weapons. In the midst of a bitter feud between the towns of Carlyle and Arcola over location of the judicial centre, for example, Premier Scott wrote wearily:

It is discouraging to think that a thing which ought to help to strengthen the party in the District is likely to disrupt it instead. One is almost made to think the better plan would have been to place the Judge at Oxbow where we don't appear to have enough friends to fall out with each other.[4]

Road money spent in only one part of a constituency, it was charged, did more harm than "a whole army" of opponents could have done. Against the one individual who received a particular job were the several who failed to get it. The reaction even of those who were winners frequently lent weight to Sir Robert Walpole's definition of gratitude as a lively sense of future favors. "After people get all they want they feel quite free to do as they please politically," Scott cautioned a political friend.

Despite the problems the patronage system presented to the politicians who were dispensing it, it was demanded by the potential recipients. It was a system so generally accepted that one assembly member who gave his rationale for urging an appointment spoke for many: "This is purely a matter of rights and politics."

Patronage was the behind-the-scenes informal side of political organization available only to the party in power. It was cloaked by a formal organizational structure similar for both the Liberal and Conservative parties. This structure was premised on party democracy, built from the bottom up in a three-tier pyramidal structure. Polling subdivisions elected representatives to a constituency executive, which in turn was represented on the provincial council. The extent to which delegates actually were elected, in contrast to persons being designated, varied. Similarly, the jealously guarded right of the constituency to choose its own candidate for election gave way at times to more or less direct persuasion from above. A small group of party officials at the top, including variously the party organizer, the party leader, and cabinet ministers worked both through and behind the formal structure to keep a watchful eye on party processes throughout the province.

An object lesson from the negative side on the importance of organization was the fate of the Progressives. They scorned political organization as a matter of principle. Their reaction against the traditional parties was based as much on political tactics as on policy: "One of the basic principles of our organization is complete autonomy of the constituency in their [sic] choice of candidates," one official wrote. Supporters of the protest group charged that in the older parties a few dominated party activity and controlled the selection of candidates. The Progressives repudiated all such practices:

> The only attempt at organization was to call a convention. This convention then nominated whom the delegates saw fit. Thereafter the election of the candidate was the sole responsibility of his supporters, who subscribed funds, conducted the canvass, and voluntarily carried out the work of the local campaigns.[5]

In repudiating formal political organization, the Progressives failed to acknowledge their beneficial use of the province-wide organization developed by the Grain Growers' Association. This was a well-developed structure built up over the years for the Association's educational, economic, and social activities. There was consequently a significant difference between the efficiency of federal campaigns, in which the Progressives had the use of this ready-made base of operations, and provincial activity which was carried on outside the Grain Growers' Association.

One organizational device which the Progressives introduced to a limited degree was the American practice of the direct primary. By thus choosing the candidate in a preliminary unofficial election, each supporter in the constituency presumably had an equal opportunity to exercise a direct voice in the selection. This device was used in some constituencies before the 1921 federal election, but undesirable results dimmed enthusiasm for it. It developed "an army of aspirants in every constituency," and it gave "an opportunity for the growth of factional contests," it was reported to Clifford Sifton.

The major strength of the Progressives was the spontaneous and enthusiastic participation of its members. As initial exuberance subsided, the absence of any means of sustaining continued activity became evident. The party lacked any overall co-ordination of its efforts, any means of strengthening organization in constituencies where it was weak, and any machinery to initiate activity for subsequent elections. In the party's waning years a recognition of these handicaps was evident among some supporters who urged the necessity of engaging a paid organizer.

The major point of Progressive concern was for constituency control of a legislative member after election. Here they devised deliberate techniques to keep the member responsible to his constituents. The recall was the most stringent and precise. With the member's formal resignation left in the hands of a committee of the constituency nominating convention, it could be accepted at pleasure. The constituency also insisted that the member maintain close communication with it at all times, so that he might receive continuous instruction about voters' wishes. It was suggested also that the member of Parliament or of the legislature should report to an annual constituency meeting. Concentration on techniques of control to the neglect of electoral organization ran its inevitable course. Soon there was nothing to control.

A new era in party organization was launched with the CCF. The traditional parties had shown themselves well organized to win votes; internal party organization was a secondary consideration. The Progressives had exercised precise rules of internal organization for rank-and-file control of elected members; their organization for election campaigns had been casual. By combining the realism of traditional parties with the spirit of the Progressives, the CCF emerged with an organization whose effectiveness remains unmatched.

The CCF adopted the two significant principles of the Progressives, an emphasis on democratic party procedures and party control of elected representatives. A tightly knit party structure translated the principles into action, creating a party organization more pervasive and more disciplined than those of the traditional parties, and more capable of extensive and continuous activity. A secondary result of this efficiency was to stimulate other parties toward similar action in order to compete with the success of CCF techniques.

Before the CCF, the general political pattern that prevailed in Saskatchewan, as elsewhere in Canada, was for party activity to lapse after an election and to rise to a fever pitch for the succeeding contest. Both the Liberals and Conservatives soon realized the need for more sustained activity, but efforts to that end had been frustrated by lack of finances and personnel. What they envisioned was not activity different from the existing line of influence, originating at the top and extending downward to voters. As the opening quotation in this chapter indicates, their aim was simply to enhance the existing organizational structure, to have the chain of command from the centre to the periphery more readily on the alert, and to enlarge the area of support.

The CCF pattern of organization differed both in degree and in kind. It not only involved continuous party activity, but it included influence from the bottom up. The CCF achieved permanently active local units by giving them a voice both in central planning and in policy. The basic philosophy of CCF organization was the old Progressive aspiration of responsibility of the leadership to the rank and file. This responsibility operated through the familiar hierarchical structure, but the significant difference from the traditional parties was the active participation of party members at each level, a participation which provided avenues of communication in both directions. The previously moribund periods between election campaigns were used by the CCF for rank-and-file discussion of issues and party policy. Not only was interest thereby sustained, but considered views were advanced from the bottom of the hierarchy as well as from the top.

Paradoxically the CCF exercised substantial direction from the center. Explicit regulations in such matters as the holding of campaign meetings, the conduct of party affairs, and the issuing of statements of policy ensured a uniform and cohesive pattern of political activity throughout the province. Having exercised their respective voices in the policies to be pursued and in the choice of those to execute the policies, local CCF groups showed a willingness to accept considerable direction from the central office. The skill with which the CCF combined democratic procedure with a strong centralized control was undoubtedly one of its major strengths.

The Liberal and Conservative parties never achieved a similarly satisfactory relationship between central and constituency organizations. Local associations in these parties have always been suspicious of direction from the center, and guidance or suggestions have had to be advanced with tact and diplomacy. This sensitiveness probably grew out of a variety of early causes: intense local pride and isolation, lack of representation in or control over the central organization, and covert intervention by political leaders in the constituency's choice of a candidate. Interference in the constituency choice of a candidate was particularly resented. Constituency organizations occasionally rejected a candidate who had not been chosen by them, and they voiced angry charges, in the words of one Liberal supporter in 1917, of "government interference and machine politics."

Usually direct intervention was avoided, or at least not detected, and care was exercised to maintain friendly relations. "There is a wide margin to play on between dictation and doing nothing, along the line of consulting, advising, informing, and generally keeping in touch with the wishes and hopes and aspirations of our friends," the veteran politician W. R. Motherwell wrote in 1919. Some of the early causes of tension were gradually removed, and party membership became more aware of the need for unified action, but a heritage of the original feeling still requires leaders to tread cautiously.

Organizational machinery varies in detail and emphasis from time to time and from one party to another, but the basic structures have followed the general pattern evident elsewhere in Canada. At the poll level, the all-important campaign tasks are performed of personally contacting voters before election day, and then of ensuring that those who favor the party actually vote. The poll committee is small, consisting of not more than three or four persons, including a chairman or poll captain.

The zone is an intermediate level between poll and constituency. Zone organization tends to be optional, but it is more consistently used by the NDP than by other parties. How many zones should be organized and how far they are left on an informal basis are matters left to the discretion of the constituency. Zones are designed to exercise general oversight over the polls and to form an intermediate link with the constituency organization. The number of polls in a zone may vary from four or five to fifteen or twenty. In a rural area, a zone logically consists of one or two shopping centers and the surrounding district, zone divisions being determined by such factors as transportation, racial and religious groupings, and geographical divisions.

The constituency association enjoys a distinctive function in the selection of a candidate for election. Party constitutions usually allow for a delegate convention if one is desired, in which voting for a candidate is restricted to a prescribed number of delegates from each poll or zone. In practice, all three parties normally use open conventions, in which all properly certified members of the party who live in the constituency may vote in person at the nomination meeting.

NDP constituency associations meet at least annually for the election of members of a new executive (who then elect a president and vice-president from their number), for the election of delegates to the annual provincial convention, and to receive reports and perform other constituency business. An active constituency organization will meet more often, and matters from the central organization may be circulated to constituency members between meetings for information and consideration. Liberals and Conservatives have tended to hold constituency meetings less regularly, although Ross Thatcher's reorganization of the party after 1959, described later in this chapter, encouraged Liberals toward more frequent meetings. Both the Liberals and Conservatives elect their officers directly from the convention floor, to hold office until a subsequent convention.

A decline in party fortunes in the 1970s, especially the loss of two legislative members to the Conservatives within less than a year, made the Liberals introduce further techniques of organization. In 1977, hard on the heels of the second defection from the party, they appointed directors to assist constituency organization. After their stunning defeat in the 1978 election, they made organizational changes at the 1979 convention which were aimed at better grassroots participation. These changes included the provision that sixteen district representatives would be elected to the executive.

At the provincial level, the regular affairs of the party are administered by executive bodies. These include both a larger and a smaller body. The larger one, the council (or provincial council in the NDP) includes representation from each constituency as well as a number of provincial officials and ex-officio members, such as M.L.A.'s, and it meets usually every few months. The smaller body, the executive (or executive committee, as it is formally entitled by the Liberals and Conservatives), meets more frequently—in the NDP on a regular monthly basis. The NDP formerly had an even smaller body, the board of strategy, which consisted of the president and two other members elected by and from the provincial executive for the purpose of making necessary day-to-day decisions. The task of making such policy recommendations to staff has now been taken over by committees appointed by the executive. The three committees that are active on a regular basis are the education, the organization, and the communications committees. Two others, the federal and provincial strategy committees, come into more active play at election time.

The NDP also has a legislative advisory committee of five members, four appointed by and from the provincial council, and one by and from the provincial executive. The party constitution describes this committee as "advisors to and observers of the Members of the Legislature concerning the implementation of the program of the Association." The members of the committee attend caucus meetings, having a voice but no vote, and they report to the party's executive and to council. A further duty of the legislative advisory committee is to act in an advisory capacity to the premier in his choice of cabinet ministers, but with specific recognition that final responsibility rests with the premier. The NDP constitution also calls for a joint meeting at least once a year of the legislative advisory committee, the party caucus, and the provincial executive. The watchdog approach of the party, which is evident in the duties of the legislative advisory committee and in the close liaison which the party maintains with both legislators and cabinet, is a distinctive characteristic of NDP outlook and organization. The development and manifestations of this emphasis in the CCF and its continuance by the NDP, are described in chapter 11.

In early years, the provincial Liberals and Conservatives followed the general Canadian custom of calling conventions only intermittently, for particular reasons. Establishment of the province was an obvious motive for both parties to hold conventions in August of 1905 to choose their respective leaders and to organize for the forthcoming election.

During the long period in which the Liberals were subsequently in power they held one convention, in 1917, a few months after the new premier, W. M. Martin, had taken over from Walter Scott. The convention was primarily for reorganization of the party in preparation for the forthcoming election. When in opposition, the Liberals held conventions in 1931 and in 1946. They then adopted a policy of biennial conventions (although these were not always held) in halfway acknowledgement of the CCF practice of holding conventions annually. When Ross Thatcher became leader in 1959, one of the administrative changes in the party which he insisted upon was the holding of an annual convention.

Being out of power constituted an imperative reason for holding a convention. Therefore the Conservatives held more conventions than did the Liberals, although their conventions were not on a regular basis. Even during their term of office they held conventions in 1930, 1932, and 1933. Being in power during those years was more of a problem than being out, and the split in the party which further complicated the Conservative position was prominent in the conventions. The party president, Dr. D. S. Johnstone, leading the so-called "True Blue" Conservatives, attacked the Anderson government at the 1932 convention for its co-operation with other parties. The convention repudiated Dr. Johnstone's attack, but as a result of the dispute, Premier Anderson submitted his resignation as leader to a convention the following year. He was, however, re-elected to his position. Until the 1970s the general practice of the party was to hold biennial conventions, although their regularity varied with party fortunes or with the need to choose a new leader. After the rejuvenation of the party under Dick Collver, the Progressive Conservatives joined the other two parties in calling an annual meeting.

The low ebb of the Conservatives for many years was evident in the sometimes leisurely delays in finding a new head. Martin Pederson was elected leader in October of 1968, for example, to fill a vacancy that had been created by Alvin Hamilton's election to Parliament the previous year. Similarly, a gap of more than a year occurred between Pederson's resignation and the selection of Ed Nasserden to succeed him in 1970. Mr. Nasserden's resignation two years later again left the party leaderless until the election of Dick Collver in March of 1973.

Only once in Saskatchewan has a new party leader been chosen in convention when the party was in power. That was in 1961, when the CCF chose Woodrow Lloyd to succeed T. C. Douglas as party leader and premier. The Liberals changed leaders four times when in power. In 1916, 1922, 1926, and 1935, W. M. Martin, C. C. Dunning, J. G. Gardiner, and W. J. Patterson respectively were selected as leaders and succeeded to the office of premier. Each time the choice was made initially by a caucus of Liberal members and was ratified immediately afterwards by a somewhat broader Liberal group. The first three times, this group was a hastily assembled meeting of Liberals from various parts of the province, and in 1935 it was the Liberal council. The convention in 1917 confirmed the choice of Premier Martin which had been made some months earlier, although it was not a leadership convention as such.

Subsequent Liberal leaders have been chosen when the party was in opposition, at regularly constituted conventions. The 1954 selection was notable as the culmination of a long and intense contest with dramatic developments. Dispute centered around charges and denials that there had been attempts by the Rt. Hon. J. G. Gardiner to persuade certain declared candidates to withdraw. Mr. Gardiner had been noted for his political organization while in provincial politics, first as a cabinet minister and then as premier. After his move to Ottawa in 1935 as Minister of Agriculture, he remained a strong force in both federal and provincial politics in Saskatchewan, and charges of interference in the 1954 selection aroused resentment. His intervention presumably was to leave the way open for a candidate alleged to be Mr. Gardiner's choice, who was the Director of the Prairie Farm Rehabilitation Administration, a federal agency under Mr. Gardiner's jurisdiction. Adding to the interest and confusion was the circumstance that Mr. Gardiner's son, Wilfrid, was also a candidate. Tragedy was added to the situation when a candidate was killed during the last week of the campaign in the crash of his plane. Emerging from the turbulent combination of back-room wrangling and open charges which had characterized the campaign, A. H. McDonald, one of those allegedly asked to withdraw, won a decisive first ballot victory.

In 1971 Liberal leadership candidates found themselves in an unusually delicate situation. Double disaster had struck in that the resounding election defeat on June 23 had been followed by the death of Ross Thatcher from a heart attack one month later. Nothing less was required than a rejection of the approach which had lost the most recent election, without too brutally overlooking the earlier achievement of the deceased as the only leader in thirty-three years who had pulled the party across the victory line. Two of the three candidates, D. G. Steuart and Cy MacDonald, had been in Mr. Thatcher's cabinet and were clearly identified with his policies. The third, George Leith, had been a frank critic. The convention throughout emphasized the need for change, but it chose as leader the candidate most closely associated with the former regime. The victor, Dave Steuart, had been deputy leader and a senior cabinet minister, but he was also frank in admitting past mistakes in party approach.

After failing to make any gain in the 1975 election, Dave Steuart resigned to take a seat in the Senate in December, 1976, and the Liberals chose Ted Malone as their new leader. Mr. Malone was regarded as the more conventional candidate—or in NDP terms, as the establishment man—in contrast to his only opponent, the more flamboyant and unorthodox Tony Merchant. Both were Regina lawyers and MLA's. Mr. Malone was not assisted in his subsequent task of rebuilding the party by the rift evident in the convention when Mr. Merchant failed to make the customary move of unanimity. Some of Merchant's key supporters shifted from provincial to federal activity in the next few months, and Mr. Merchant himself left provincial politics to contest the 1979 federal election—a contest which was incidentally probably the longest and most intense on record and which apparently fell of its own weight.

The NDP chose Allan Blakeney in 1970 to succeed Woodrow Lloyd. Mr. Lloyd's relatively brief tenure as premier had started upon Mr. Douglas's move to the federal leadership in 1961, and it had ended with the provincial party's defeat in 1964. The inherent restlessness of opposition had been sharpened in the late 1960s by a vocal left-wing element in the party, the so-called Waffle group. After attacks upon his leadership, Mr. Lloyd made way for a new party head. In sweltering midsummer heat in 1970, delegates balloted for more than three hours to choose a new leader. Of the four candidates who had started, the two furthest to the right emerged as finalists, and the Wafflers were sufficiently disenchanted that they refused to take part at all in the choice between them. It was only in the last half of the counting of the final ballot that Allan Blakeney pulled ahead of his opponent, Roy Romanow, who until then had led all the way.

Absence of a leadership race leaves a convention with the less exciting fare of party business, reports, resolutions, inspirational speeches, and election of officers. The NDP stresses that it is the annual convention which determines the party program, and consequently resolutions are given serious and sometimes heated consideration. The CCF initiated a practice of closed panel discussions which was continued by the NDP. Delegates divided themselves among five or six panels, each dealing with a different topic, and each considering resolutions which had been submitted by constituency organizations. The respective panels then made recommendation to the convention for acceptance, rejection, or amendment of these resolutions. Early complaints were voiced because each delegate could not participate in all discussion of resolutions but the device was soon accepted as indispensable in dealing with a large number of resolutions. Even then it has not always been possible for the convention to deal with all resolutions, and some have been left for later consideration by the council.

The long-standing practice of Liberals and Conservatives was to have resolutions go to a committee before being considered by the convention, but each party has more recently experimented with other procedures. For some years the Liberals adopted the CCF practice of panel discussion, but with open rather than closed panels. In 1972 they introduced a variation that extended the consideration of resolutions over some three years before their final adoption. This system was a sort of long-term suspension, holding the platform in limbo until it was finalized before an election. Resolutions were considered in six open panels in 1972, and at the close of the convention the delegates turned in ballots which indicated their degree of agreement or disagreement on the various proposals.

The Progressive Conservatives also altered their practices in the 1970s. Conventions in 1975 and 1976 were spent mainly in policy seminars and workshops which attracted little press attention. Leader Dick Collver explained the lack of interest among reporters as the reason for changing procedures in 1977. Gearing up for an election, the 1977 convention presented resolutions to the convention for approval, but then distributed them to full party membership for a vote, presumably in order to gain the best both from press coverage and from democratic participation within the party.

In bringing policy planning before the rank and file, the Conservatives were late entrants in the contest which the NDP and the Liberals had carried on for years to out-democratize each other. The Liberals pointed out that their panel discussions were open to the press, in contrast to those of the NDP which were closed. At some conventions the Liberals also considered resolutions from outside sources such as a pensioners' association, the National Farmers Union, the Hudson Bay Route Association, and Regina Pollution Probe, all of which were heard in 1972 in panel discussions. This practice, Liberal officials noted, was in contrast to the practice in NDP conventions, where all resolutions originated within the party.

A more basic difference between NDP and Liberal efforts toward internal party democracy places the NDP squarely in front. That party's insistence on participation is grounded in the rank and file, and it is an integral element of party ideology and of well-established practice. The key here is the importance that the CCF and NDP have accorded to the annual convention, and the extensive and effective participation in the convention by the party rank and file. From the beginning, the convention has been regarded as the source of party authority. The resolutions which it adopts form the party's program and policies. Party officers report to it, and it annually elects new officers, and elects (or re-elects) the leader. The provincial convention is the culmination of earlier constituency conventions where delegates were chosen to attend the next level. Resolutions coming before the provincial convention have already been considered at the constituency level. Thus all the party machinery is brought into operation once a year, if not more often, and rank and file members have the opportunity before the provincial convention to familiarize themselves with the issues which will be raised.

The CCF and NDP constitutions always included explicit provisions to safeguard the party organization from domination by members of Parliament or by members of the legislature. Such members may not be elected as party president or vice-president, or as the constituency representative on the provincial council. These constitutional provisions have been more than paper safeguards. As discussed further in chapter 11, they have been traditionally and jealously guarded by the party membership, which asserts its voice in party and legislative matters.

In the Liberal tradition, on the other hand, influence has been from the top down. Ironically, even Liberal democratization processes have followed the same direction, in that they have generally been introduced by the leadership and resisted by the rank and file. Forms of party democracy in the Liberal party have inclined therefore to be an exterior device, a cloak to be put on or taken off, and to be much more subject to the inclinations of party leadership than corresponding institutions of the NDP.

This Liberal ambivalence towards democratic control within the party was evident in the changes introduced by Ross Thatcher. Upon becoming leader in 1959, Mr. Thatcher introduced practices which he had learned in his earlier career as a CCFer, and which many Liberals felt were imposed upon them. Paradoxically, it was Thatcher, the leader, who insisted that he come up each year for re-election as party head, and it was party members who were reluctant to provide this annual scrutiny. Many Liberals preferred their former method of determining by "osmosis" when they needed a new leader. Similarly, Liberals tended to be unhappy over the annual membership drive which Thatcher introduced. He had seen it as one of the great strengths of the CCF and as an important means of grass-roots support. The Liberal rank and file complained that it was not their way of doing things, and they were not enthusiastic about adopting what they regarded as CCF practices. On the other hand, after the Liberals came to power, protests were raised internally against too-autocratic control by Premier Thatcher and against insufficient consultation with the party.

Later efforts by Liberal officials to bring convention delegates into active participation met with only partial response. New procedures to enhance panel discussions in 1972 seemed to be well accepted but the *Leader-Post* reported that participation by the delegates had not been as general as the convention organizers had hoped, and that most of those who had used the microphones set up for the six policy committees were either prominent party members or the authors of the resolutions that were up for debate. And some of the older delegates grumbled that the openness of the convention had been taken too far in allowing resolutions from groups other than Liberal participants.

Co-ordination of provincial and federal organization in Saskatchewan presents difficulties. With a ratio of some four or five provincial constituencies to one federal district, and with boundaries cutting across one another, some kind of separate constituency organization is necessary. Accommodation within individual areas can usually be effected on an informal basis. The president of a provincial constituency association may hold the same office in the federal riding, with much the same nucleus of officials. In any event it is largely the same workers who are active, whichever the election. The problem is reduced further in Regina and Saskatoon, where the boundaries of a number of provincial constituencies and a federal city constituency are more likely to be roughly coterminous, or at least sufficiently so to enable a single organization to serve both levels.

The real problem is the overall question of whether to have one or two organizations, and the problem comes down in particular to the practical issues of which political level appoints the provincial organizer and exercises general supervision for federal contests, and to how the finances are to be apportioned and handled.

The Conservatives, with their small base of provincial support, had customarily left oversight to the federal party level. In the 1960s resentment developed among provincial Conservatives who felt that not only were their interests neglected under this arrangement but that Ottawa Conservatives interfered in arranging saw-offs in the 1967 election. The Saskatchewan Conservatives consequently established separate organizations in 1970 for provincial and for federal activity. Not only were party fortunes at a low ebb at that time, but independence from the national party also cut the provincial party off from sorely needed funds for the payment of its leader, its debts, and other expenses. The separate existence of the two levels as organizational units continued throughout the period of Mr. Collver's leadership, but there was mutual assistance and co-operation.

As the only party which over the years had any real chance for success at both levels, the Liberals have had particular difficulty in reconciling provincial and federal organizations. A sharp dispute over the issue flared in the early 1960s, and it smoldered for long afterwards. When Saskatchewan, under provincial party direction, returned only one Liberal member of Parliament in 1962, the federal party set up its own organization in the province. It appointed as federal campaign chairman Dean Otto Lang of the University's College of Law. The move was robustly opposed by provincial Liberal leader Ross Thatcher. The failure of the federal Liberals to retain even their single Saskatchewan seat in the 1963 election, followed by Ross Thatcher's provincial victory in 1964, gave the new Liberal premier obvious advantages in his dispute with Ottawa. It was, moreover, only one of the areas of well-publicized disagreement which characterized the premier's relations with Ottawa. The breach over party organization was one that the federal minority government could ill afford to see continue. Peace was declared in 1964 when agreement was reached on an organizer to be appointed, and the provincial Liberals regained effective control.

Despite this agreement, federal-provincial organization remained an area of disgruntlement, and it was the subject of resolutions and of considerable corridor talk at provincial Liberal conventions. After Mr. Steuart became leader in 1971, a compromise was worked out for joint effort. There was to be a federal affairs committee of the provincial organization, with a chairman who should be selected by Otto Lang (by now Saskatchewan's representative in the federal cabinet), with the selection to be agreeable to the provincial Liberals.

This compromise agreement proved to be a truce rather than a solution, and problems flared anew in the 1970s. In this decade the provincial Liberals came to nurse two grievances against their federal counterparts: they complained publicly of the burden cast upon provincial campaigning by deep voter antagonism to the federal Liberals, and they complained that the federal organization held too tightly to the strings of a consolidated purse. In the 1976 leadership convention, federal-provincial organization was a point of division between the two candidates. Tony Merchant, rather surprisingly as Otto Lang's brother-in-law, argued for a separation of federal and provincial organizations to encourage provincial Liberal voting. Ted Malone said that the convention was an inappropriate place to discuss so divisive an issue. He also disagreed that a split should be made, pointing out that the provincial organization would lose federal funds.

Financial relations had been affected by the federal legislation of 1974 which made donations to federal political parties tax-deductible. As a result of this legislation, Liberals agreed that all donations should be made to the federal organization and then be divided between the two levels. The formula for distribution created the problem. Controversy became open in 1977, with newspaper headlines such as "Provincial Liberals haggling with Lang for money," and conflicting reports over control of the money and about distrust between Otto Lang and provincial Liberal president John Embury.

The two Liberal MLAs who defected to the Conservatives in 1976 and 1977 each pointed to aspects of the federal Liberal presence as either a contributing or a major reason for their abandonment of the provincial party. Friction between the two levels of the party was a subject of discussion in the provincial Liberal convention in March of 1979, in which staunch determination to revive party fortunes was expressed. One of the convention hopes was that the newly elected party president, Jack Wiebe, might ease the tension between the two sections of the party.

The NDP escapes such a problem, since its only real prospects for office are provincial, and its organization is therefore provincially based. Each federal constituency draws its support from the various provincial ridings included within it, and they swing into action to concentrate effort in the federal field at election time.

Each party has the usual associated youth and women's organizations, and at times there are local clubs which may be as much social as political. Young men's associations were features of the Liberal and Conservative parties from the earliest years of provincial politics, but after its formation the CCF gave special emphasis to its youth groups. The names and the relationships of the respective youth organizations to the main party have varied, and so has the degree of control which the party attempts to exercise or which the various groups will tolerate. The movement for equality for women sparked debate on whether women should continue with their separate organizations or should merge all participation in the main association, but they have continued their identity in one form or another.

The NDP and Liberal parties both had active splinter groups in the early 1970s—the Waffle in the NDP and the 171 in the Liberals. The Waffle group, as elsewhere in Canada, showed its strong left-wing leaning in urging broad nationalization policies. In Saskatchewan it was sharply critical of the NDP government for its failure to move more strongly towards nationalization. After considerable agitation within the party for the implementation of more radical policies, in 1973 the Waffle group voted to leave the NDP to form what they described as a true socialist movement. They decided to concentrate on organization and on public education at that time. Their one member in the legislature, John Richards, who did not approve the split, left the NDP caucus to sit as an independent for the remainder of his term. The Waffle gradually was lost to the political scene as a visible organization, although a left wing which has always existed in the CCF and NDP still continues.

Group 171, a reform movement in the Liberal party, developed out of the leadership convention of 1971. The name represented the number of votes received by George Leith, the candidate who most strongly advocated change in party policies but who ran last in convention balloting. Members of the group organized formally in February, 1972, and in subsequent months they held their own meetings for discussion and preparation of resolutions to present to the next party convention. Unlike the Wafflers, Group 171 refrained from press releases and was much less vocal. Eventually it merged its activities again within the regular party structure.

The sources of party funds in Saskatchewan, as elsewhere, provide a subject for charges and denials while few facts are available. Even with the emphasis the NDP has always placed on party membership, which was copied by the Liberals and in the 1970s by the Progressive Conservatives, membership fees can supply but a small proportion of party requirements. The remainder must be secured in the normal political manner through contributions from individuals, from associations and business, and, for the NDP, from labor unions, which may affiliate with the party and pay prescribed dues on behalf of their union membership.

Constituency associations also contribute to the central office fund for the party as well as providing for their own activity in the constituency. The NDP uses a precise method for distribution of the funds coming from each constituency. Membership fees are divided three ways among national, provincial, and constituency organizations. Other funds raised in the constituency go first to meet an annual quota set by the central office; of the additional moneys over the quota, forty per cent goes to each of the constituency and provincial organizations, and ten per cent goes to the federal organization.

Liberal and Conservative arrangements have varied, and these two parties have held less consistently to a prescribed system. Mr. Thatcher, for example, again using CCF precedent, established a distribution formula as a part of his reorganization of the party. Membership fees were sent to the central office and one-half was placed in a trust fund for the constituency, the full amount being returned to the constituency if the portion in the trust fund was left intact until election time. A constituency might keep other money which it raised, except for a levy to go to the central office. Despite the theoretically precise nature of this arrangement, some complaints were voiced about its actual operation and about the ability of a constituency to get its full amount back. More recent financial arrangements in the Liberal party have been affected by its federal-provincial organization, as described earlier in this chapter.

Financial assistance has been provided by the government under legislation passed in 1974, with later amendments increasing the amounts. At the time of the 1978 election, each candidate who received at least fifteen per cent of the vote was reimbursed by the government at a rate of fifty cents a voter (increased from a previous fifteen cents), to a maximum of half his election expenses. The 1978 legislative change also included a payment to the party itself of $75,000 if it should get fifteen per cent of the total vote cast. The Liberals just missed this grant in the election later in 1978, when they received not quite fourteen per cent of the vote.

The CCF led the way in Saskatchewan in instituting systematic training procedures for party workers to supplement traditional campaign devices. These training procedures included schools and conferences for instruction in effective campaign methods and for discussion of public issues. The Liberals were slow in meeting this competition. In the 1950s, after almost a decade in oppositon, an enumeration of Liberal shortcomings was set forth by the *Leader-Post,* itself sympathetic to the Liberals:

... in many constituencies CCF campaign offices were open weeks ahead of the Liberals, having an important psychological effect; CCF central staff in Regina was large; CCYM was stronger than the young Liberals, with a camp for study and meetings, which the Liberals did not have; the examination of public issues was carried on more vigorously by the CCF under education directors; the CCF held picnics and barbecues to a considerably greater extent than the Liberals: CCF made effective use of slogans such as "Humanity First".[6]

In 1964, by contrast, it was the Liberals who showed a new dimension in Saskatchewan electioneering. Directed by an eastern public relations firm, the Liberal campaign featured bands and lively entertainment at party rallies. Despite the CCF disparagement of "PR boys and dancing girls," that party in turn felt the need to liven meetings with folksingers and with popular as well as party songs.

All parties employ advertising firms in joint effort with their own organizations. Usually the professional services are kept more in the background than in the Liberal import of 1964, so as to preserve the illusion of a completely home-grown campaign. Despite a reluctance to publicize the use of such services, professionals are regarded by party leaders as indispensable for handling such areas as advertising and publicity.

Among all the devices of party campaigning, one basic ingredient for election success remains unaltered. That is individual contact. Other techniques remain secondary. The early practice of joint political meetings gave way to separate gatherings which now have diminished in importance. Radio and television have taken over as the dominant means of mass communication. Rudimentary mail service and sparser newspaper publication saved the early voter from the barrage of literature and advertisements with which his modern counterpart is deluged. To enlarge the comment of one early organizer, all these are customary but they don't change votes.

It is significant that during the two periods of prolonged political success in Saskatchewan, the organization of the successful party was directed particularly toward personal attention to voters. The so-called Liberal machine before 1929, by the very term applied to it, gave an incorrect impression of the impersonal synchronization of levers and gears. The reality was no such thing. Its purpose was simply to maximize personal communication between Liberal workers and the voter: "According to the organizers, it was this man-to-man argument which determined the result of the election. . . ."[7]

The organization and training techniques of the CCF similarly were directed to increasing the effectiveness of personal contact. Using a strong body of volunteer workers, the CCF gave paramount importance to household canvassing, which they relied on as their particular, even if not as their infallible strength. The comeback of the NDP in 1971 was based on four rounds of party canvassing that were carried out, first to diagnose the individual situation, then to sign up members and get workers if possible, and finally to talk to people and to listen.

All parties in Saskatchewan recognize the paramount importance of ringing doorbells over all other means of persuasion; a party neglects this direct approach to its own peril and regret.

6　　　　　　　　　　　　Voters and Elections

For most voters, election day means only marking a ballot and waiting, with varying degrees of interest, for election results. For candidates and their workers it means the end of frenzied weeks of activity. For those in the provincial electoral office, election day also means the culmination of demanding weeks, but for them the work has been behind-the-scenes activities of preparing a list of qualified voters and of establishing the places and arrangements for voting. Election day also means the beginning of new rounds of duties, including not only the checking and tabulating of election results but also a post-mortem check to see that campaign rules were followed in such matters as candidate- and party-spending limits.

All election processes are, ideally, routine and neutral procedures to register the vote without influencing it. In practice, of course, the ideal is not always achieved. To the extent that political forces may bend or attempt to bend procedures to their advantage, it is the duty of the electoral office to remedy administrative oversights and to report violations to the attorney general. It is the function of the judiciary to decide on charges of specific violation referred to it. The legislature's role is to lay down policies for the electoral process, such as the qualifications for candidates and voters. The legislature also decides how many members it should have, what method should be used to determine the constituency boundaries, and, in the final analysis, which individuals may or may not be seated as members.

The number of members in the assembly has been affected on the one hand by the need to represent a scattered population, and on the other, by considerations of economy. The original House of twenty-five members in 1905 increased rapidly in the first three redistributions to keep pace with expanding settlement. A further argument advanced in the first redistribution in 1908 was that the existing membership was too small for effective organization of legislative duties. The general elections of 1908, 1912, and 1917 were each preceded by a redistribution which reduced the size of constituencies in newly settled areas and increased the legislative membership to fifty-nine. The 1920 redistribution reflected a change in the settlement pattern, with only one new rural seat added, but with Regina, Saskatoon, and Moose Jaw each having their representation doubled by becoming two-member constituencies instead of electing only one member each. This change brought the assembly membership to a peak of sixty-three, where it remained until the drought and depression years of the 1930s.

Economic pressures, a drop in population, and movement from the southern dust bowl to northern areas, resulted in changes to constituencies and to a reduction in their number. Improved transportation facilities also enabled members to cover larger areas. Partly offsetting these factors were the steadily increasing duties falling on members. This increase in duties meant the number of members could not be too sharply reduced, as Premier Patterson warned in 1938, when the total was decreased to fifty-two. Gradual but steady increases in recent decades have been characterized by relatively greater numbers of urban members. Of the sixty-one constituencies mapped out in 1973, the number of entirely urban constituencies increased by seven for a total of twenty-two, which included nine in Regina and eight in Saskatoon.

Until 1973, all redistribution bills in Saskatchewan were prepared by the government and were passed through the legislature like any other bills. Procedure for the first such bill, in 1908, included consideration by a select committee in which controversy and near deadlock resulted, despite Premier Scott's sanguine comment in the House as to the harmony which had prevailed. A different interpretation given by the leader of the opposition was that "The courtesy with which ... [our] suggestions were met was equalled by the courtesy with which they were unanimously and regularly refused." Subsequent redistribution bills followed the more common pattern for Saskatchewan legislation of consideration in Committee of the Whole instead of by a select committee. The Liberals in opposition moved on more than one occasion to have redistribution referred to a legislative committee. The key to the obvious reluctance shown by all parties when in power to trust the matter to a committee was evident in the reply of the provincial treasurer to one such Liberal motion: "this is something that affects the rights and privileges of every member of the House."

The first electoral map drawn up outside the legislature was in 1973 by an independent electoral boundaries commission which had been established the previous year. Minority NDP recommendation for such a commission had accompanied the report of a Special Legislative Committee on Election Procedures tabled in 1970. The redistribution by the Liberal government later that year, which outdid all previous examples of gerrymander in the province, was accompanied by bitter NDP criticism and by demands for an independent commission. The provisions brought in by the NDP government in

1972 did not remove redistribution from all possibility of politics, since final approval of commission recommendations rests with the legislature.

The legislation of 1972 requires a commission of three members to be established within thirty days of receipt of the decennial census statistics. One commission member is named by the chief justice of the province from the Court of Appeal or the Court of Queen's Bench; the clerk of the legislative assembly is an ex officio member; and the third member is appointed by the speaker of the assembly, after consultation with the premier and the leader of the opposition. The commission is required to make an interim report to cabinet within nine months of receipt of the census figures; it then holds public hearings, and within twelve months after receipt of the census figures, the commission is to submit its final report for approval by the legislature.

A second commission was set up in 1979 without waiting for the next decennial census. This action was taken in the belief that sufficient population changes had occurred to justify another redistribution at that time. If the legislature continues for the customary four years, it is unlikely that a commission could complete work before another election if its establishment were to be delayed until after the 1881 census figures became available.

When the new method was first used in 1973, the commission gave foremost consideration to the legislative requirement for roughly equal population in each constituency. Except for two northern ridings which were to be established regardless of the number of residents, it was specified that the population of each seat might not vary by more than fifteen per cent above or below a quotient obtained by dividing the population of the province by the number of seats. With this fifteen per cent leeway, only scant preference was given to rural in contrast to urban constituencies. Greater attention centered on areas of probable growth, both rural and urban, within the subsequent ten years.

The factor which appeared in the public hearings to be of greatest concern to residents was the preservation of their local community of interests. This preservation of locality required attention not only to the particular marketing centre, but in some instances to adjoining centres which shared a close community spirit and to local services which complemented one another, all of which might contribute to the wish to be represented by the same assembly member. Roads were significant elements in this concern, with the actual number of miles being less important than the location of a good grid road. This preoccupation with roads replaces the prime importance accorded to railway lines in early redistributions.

Historic interest was evident, particularly in the choice of constituency names. There was reluctance to have a name with historic significance disappear, or similarly to lose that of a major trading centre. The result of this attachment to significant names of places has been an increase in the number of hyphenated constituency names, even in a province as relatively young as Saskatchewan.

A particular consideration of earlier redistributions, which an independent commission was designed to avoid, was gerrymandering. This practice had been evident from the first redistribution in 1908, when one newspaper bluntly stated, "It is well known that in framing a redistribution measure, party advantage is the prime consideration,"[1] to the 1970 gerrymander, which surpassed all others in magnitude. The subtlety and the extent of manipulation varied.

Premier Scott's private assessment of his government's redistribution in 1908 was that "it was about as fair as it could be made." That included agreeing to changes which "gave away a safe seat," which the premier concluded was worth the price, since it tied opposition leader Haultain "hand and foot, and absolutely prohibited [him] from opening his mouth against any feature of the map." The 1908 redistribution also included a devious plot to introduce two new seats which had been specifically mapped out for Premier Scott and Attorney General Turgeon. These two seats were left out of the map that was taken to the committee, but "a little engineering" aroused opposition agitation, with the result, Scott wrote to a friend, that "sometimes it was difficult to keep a straight face while Haultain was making his arguments in favour of what we were going to do in any event."[2]

Such refinement of technique was missing in Scott's successor almost three score years later. Premier Thatcher's redistribution in 1970 similarly included the creation of two new "safe" Liberal seats, as well as the adjustment of existing constituencies. His was a gerrymander so blatant as to defeat its own purpose and to become one of the factors that put the government in a bad odour in the 1971 election.

A variation of the usual gerrymander approach was evident in the CCF handling of multi-member city constituencies. The custom of leaving the three larger cities each as a single multi-member constituency was altered, inconsistently, before the 1964 election. Saskatoon with its five members and Moose Jaw with its two continued undivided, with each voter having five and two choices respectively. In contrast, Regina with its six members was divided into two two-member constituencies and two one-member constituencies. Before the 1967 election, all three cities were divided into single-member constituencies.

Curiously, in gerrymandering both government and opposition made the one assumption which, if valid, would give to the practice any meaning or success—that voting strength in a given area will remain relatively unchanged from one election to the next. While this assumption may be true in particular areas, so that undoubtedly gerrymandering has bolstered the government upon occasion, the extent of losses when governments have been defeated on the basis of their respective redistributions suggests that gerrymandering is an unreliable safeguard. The *Leader-Post* noted this editorially in 1932:

The remarkable thing about the redistribution debate was the assurance with which every speaker took for granted that party advantage was the basis of the new map, and that the vote in the last election was to be the vote in the next election, that the vote in the last election can be divided up by including a few here and dropping a few there to insure the election of any particular candidate in a constituency. The tremendous turnover in the last election, it would seem, would have taught Saskatchewan politicians that the electorate is largely an unknown quantity until the ballots are in the box.

Saskatchewan has used single-member constituencies, except for the three cities that had multiple seats from the 1921 to 1964 elections. Proportional representation has been rejected by each of the three parties when in power, although it has been advocated by each party when in opposition. Each of the other western provinces has used the system in varying degrees in provincial elections, but Saskatchewan has not gone beyond permissive legislation passed in 1920 to give cities the option to use proportional representation in civic elections. Saskatchewan election results show in full measure the inequities in representation and the election by minorities which proportional representation is designed to correct. In 1934, for example, the Conservatives received twenty-seven per cent of the total vote but no seats, while the Farmer-Labour (CCF), with twenty-four per cent of the vote, won five seats, and the Liberals, with less than half of the vote, took fifty out of fifty-five seats. In 1971, the NDP won seventy-five per cent of the seats with fifty-five per cent of the votes. In three-cornered fights in 1956, only five out of forty-six members elected from single-member ridings received a clear majority.

On the other side of the coin, however, it is only the disproportion of seats to votes, which has invariably favored the winning party, that has provided sufficient legislative majorities for stable government. A mathematical correlation of seats to total vote would have given Saskatchewan not only the minority government it had in 1929, but minority governments in 1934, 1938, 1948, 1956, and in every election since except for that of 1971. In 1908, furthermore, the victorious Liberals would have found themselves on a precarious perch with fifty per cent of the vote, against the Conservative total of forty-nine per cent.

A candidate for election must be a Canadian citizen or other British subject, eighteen years of age, and resident in Saskatchewan. Residence in the constituency is not required. Senators and members of the House of Commons are not eligible to stand. No similar exclusion applies to elected civic officials, with the result that for several years the Mayor of Regina was able to combine his mayoralty position with duties as an assembly member. His staunch denial of conflict between the two positions must be tempered by his cautious references in the mayoralty campaign to certain matters beneficial to the city, toward which he had exerted legislative effort.

A voter must be a Canadian citizen, or a British subject qualified as a voter on June 23, 1971, eighteen years of age, ordinarily resident in the constituency in which he seeks to vote, and resident in

Saskatchewan six months before the issue of election writs. Earlier exclusion of various groups from voting has been removed over the years. Women received the vote in 1916, but they were not eligible to run as candidates until the following year. Chinese were enfranchised in 1944, and in 1946 the first step was taken towards enfranchising Indians by including those who had served in either World War. This enfranchisement was extended in 1951 to include the spouse of the Indian who had served and those Indians who were not resident on a reservation and were not drawing treaty money. In 1960 the franchise was made available to all Indians who meet normal voting requirements. Persons excluded from voting include judges, constituency returning officers, patients in mental hospitals, persons serving jail sentences for a criminal offence, and any persons disqualified because of corrupt practices.

Since 1920, voters' lists have been prepared by enumeration for each election. Any qualified voter whose name does not appear on the list for a provincial election may vote upon signing a statement. The former requirement of taking an oath in order to vote was abolished in 1956. The tortuous history leading to this simple and straightforward method of establishing voter qualifications illustrates the problems of adapting procedures to the requirements of a developing area. It shows, moreover, the political implications inherent in what is theoretically a routine process.

Voters' lists had not been used in Territorial elections. Any person claiming qualifications was permitted to vote, subject to the right of the scrutineer of a candidate to challenge his eligibility. If challenged, the ballot was sealed in an envelope containing the voter's name and address before it was deposited in the ballot box, and it was counted only after a court of revision had determined the right of the person to vote, a question which hinged most frequently on the voter's naturalization.

This system was continued for the first Saskatchewan election in 1905. What had worked satisfactorily for Territorial elections fought on a personal basis was not designed to withstand the rigors of a keenly fought partisan contest. Long before the election on December 13, each party was preparing its own list of voters. That this was more than a casual process is evident in the instructions which Premier Scott gave to the secretary of the Liberal party:

An arrangement should be made with some person at Moosomin to wire to the Candidates or Secretaries in the various outlying districts in that end of the province the names of the voters whose naturalization may be complete from time to time from this [time] on. The mails are very uncertain and unless the names are wired it might be that information might not reach the localities before the 13th.[3]

On election day the zeal of party scrutineers became so great that at some polls as many as twenty-five per cent of the voters were challenged, including those long resident and well-known in the community, so that their votes were "tied up" until they could be considered later by courts of revision. This high number of challenged votes made voting day, as Premier Scott pointed out later, "only the halfway stage in an election under our law."

In 1908 the legislature provided for closed lists, whereby only persons whose names appeared on the list would be allowed to vote. In rural areas registrars were to compile lists, but in towns and cities responsibility was left to the voter to present himself at registration meetings to have his name placed on the list. Adjustments might be made at courts of revision before the lists finally were closed. The election in 1908 was held before this process could be completed, and enumerators therefore drew up lists for immediate use, voters not on the list being allowed to be sworn in on polling day and to vote. Confusion naturally resulted from the closed lists' being still in the course of preparation when it was necessary to turn to the preparation of another list for the imminent election.

It was not until 1912, therefore, that closed lists were used. Inevitably, the adoption of a rigid system, after the confusion of different methods in previous elections, found many people on election day without a vote, especially since communication was difficult and responsibility was left to the voter. "The greatest factor featuring in the election had been the voters' list," J. E. Bradshaw, a Conservative member, said bluntly.[4] Even allowing for political overstatement, those on the government side admitted privately that unqualified voters were placed on the list and that a number of qualified voters were left off.

In replying to a friend whose name had been left off the list, Premier Scott outlined the variety of difficulties which the situation presented:

I am driven to the conclusion that while our opponents are howling a great deal about unfairness, in reality the Liberal Party lost more heavily than did the Opposition through the faults existing in the Lists. I am satisfied that such was the case in my own constituency and Turgeon tells me that he is prepared to swear that in his district we were the net losers to the extent of about 200 votes through omissions from the List. What is to be done? Personal registration in rural districts is not practicable as yet. I do not know whether the Opposition will change their attitude as regards closed Lists. Last term you remember they were insistent upon it. The three days and nights sitting we had two years ago arose from their demand that the closed Lists would be ready for use in the next campaign. Last session Calder tells me he made a distinct proposition to the Opposition to abandon the printed Lists idea. This proposal they resolutely refused to listen to. Perhaps before another election, knowledge of the system will become more widespread and lead to the possibility of a less imperfect list. If such cannot be hoped for my own inclination would be strongly in favor of abandoning the printed Lists regardless of any stand which may held by the Opposition. It is extremely expensive and does not permit of as fair and complete a poll as the system we used in 1908, the same as was used in the Dominion election last year. My own view is that the existing system is much worse for the party in power than the party in opposition. Nothing else stirs the resentment in the public mind more than a suspicion of unfairness in matters governing the electoral franchise and with the imperfections inevitable with printed lists under our conditions such suspicion cannot be avoided.[5]

Annual revisions of permanent lists were then tried, but there were no fewer problems. The failure of people to see that their names were included and the carelessness of those preparing the lists meant that local government assessment rolls sometimes were used almost *in toto* as voters' lists instead of merely as a guide to their preparation. The closed feature of the lists was discarded for rural areas in 1916 and was abandoned entirely in 1920 with general agreement on both sides of the assembly, and the change was then made to the present system of enumeration for each election.

Elections in Saskatchewan usually have been held at four-year intervals, allowing the government the year's leeway which they customarily like to leave themselves before the maximum five-year term expires. Exceptions have occurred both for longer and shorter durations of a legislature. Twice, in 1908 and in 1967, the government seized favorable circumstances to renew its mandate within three years. An earlier than normal election in October of 1978 was called to avoid conflict with an expected federal election the next spring. On two occasions the legislature ran the full five years, in 1917 during war time, and in 1934 when local circumstances caused by drought were even more desperate than in the war years and were openly reflected in a critical attitude to the government. During World World II, the life of the assembly was extended an extra year by a faltering Liberal government, to last from 1938 until 1944. This extension was made by the simple expedient of passing legislation in 1943 entitled "An Act to extend the Duration of the present Legislative Assembly." The legislation permitted the government to continue until July 10, 1944, without the members having to seek re-election. The election was then held on June 15, 1944.

In a province in which seeding and harvest and winter conditions have particular significance, June has been the most popular election month. The elections that were called early were all in autumn: 1908 in August, and 1967 and 1978 in October. The only July election was in 1912. The first election, in 1905, was pushed into December, with the interim government which had assumed office in September impatiently waiting for announcements to come from Ottawa about railway construction which would help in the provincial campaign. In 1964 the CCF broke a pattern of eleven successive June elections to go down to defeat in April. Since 1951, Wednesday has been the statutory election day in Saskatchewan.

The customary election officials assume responsibility after the assembly has been dissolved and writs have been issued for an election. A returning officer in each constituency appoints enumerators to prepare voters' lists, to establish polls, and to appoint deputy returning officers. The location of polls is now of less political significance than it was in early days, when transportation often was an acute problem and when voters attached great importance to the laying out of polling divisions.

Candidates must file nomination papers, signed by at least four voters, between twelve noon and two o'clock on nomination day, which is the Monday of the week three weeks before election day. Since most candidates by that time are well into the campaign, nomination day usually brings few surprises. A deposit of one hundred dollars is required of each candidate, and this deposit is returned if a vote equal to one-half that of the winning candidate is polled.

The Election Act was amended in 1971 to reduce the length of the election campaign by four days, providing for a minimum of twenty-eight to a maximum of thirty-four days. An earlier change in 1965 virtually eliminated the absentee ballot which had been in effect since 1951 and had enabled residents who were elsewhere in the province on election day to vote for candidates in their home constituencies, the ballots then being sent back for counting. In 1964, close election results in several constituencies gave unusual significance to absentee ballots, so that there was a highly uncertain situation during the month's delay which was legally required for forwarding and counting these votes. The only remnant of that system is provision for a mail-in ballot for those who are totally incapacitated. Advance polls are held for those who expect to be away from their home on election day.

Legislation to control election expenses was passed in 1974, at the same time that financial assistance was provided for candidates. Under this legislation limits apply both to the party and to individual candidates. An individual candidate has a limit of $15,000 or $1.00 per name on the voters' list. Because of greater transportation and related costs in northern constituencies, the limit for them is $20,000 or $2.00 per name on the voters' lists.

The limits for a party in general elections have not been closely restrictive. With the NDP and Liberal parties estimating their expenditures at $100,000 and $125,000 respectively in the 1971 election, before there were any restrictions, the limit set in 1974 was $125,000, but this figure was raised to $175,000 before the 1975 election. Again the limit was raised, to $250,000, before the 1978 election, even though the parties had not pushed hard on the existing limits in 1975, when all three parties reported total expenditures between $164,000 and $170,000.

Expenditures in by-elections have proved a different matter. In a keenly contested by-election in Pelly in June of 1977, each of the three parties violated the restrictions or regulations in one way or another. The Liberals spent more than three times the $10,000 legal limit for a by-election; the Progressive Conservatives were a day late in filing, and questions were also raised as to whether all expenditures had been included; and the NDP filed a second return, making changes from the original one. Despite considerable controversy there were no prosecutions. The report of the chief electoral officer to the attorney general, and of the attorney general to the legislature, included recommendations for revision to eliminate ambiguities, on such questions as whether receipts and invoices had to be submitted with a return. The by-election limit was raised to $12,500, or $1.00 per name, in the general increases which were made in 1978.

While legislators struggled in early years for a satisfactory method for voters' lists, in the 1970s they tried to fill loopholes and to forestall evasion of the spending limits introduced in the election act. The two assumptions behind the restrictions are that politics should not be controlled by big money, and that large amounts of money will unduly increase the candidate's chances of winning. To prevent control by large donors, candidates are required to list the names of individuals and organizations that contribute more than $100.00 to their campaign. A loophole which has been pointed out in this respect is that the contribution may be made to the constituency organization, which does not have to report it, for transfer to the candidate. The other assumption, that a candidate's chances for victory are in direct proportion to his expenditure, is only partly true. While a candidate undoubtedly is hampered by a tight budget, at the other end, excessive spending may have a reverse effect of alienating voters.

Limiting of election expenditure seems to have been tackled exclusively on a cost basis. Limits which are too generous are meaningless. Those which are genuinely restrictive invite increased ingenuity in evading them and the need of legislative vigilance to forestall such evasions. There is little evidence of a move to what might be a more effective control, and certainly one more merciful for the voters—that of genuinely restricting the number of times and the total length of time that a candidate or party might appear on radio or TV.

Veering slightly in that direction, however, is the prohibition since 1976 of any but emergency advertising by the government or any of its departments or agencies during an election campaign. This prohibition can result in planned announcements or programs by a government agency which are entirely related to its own activities having to be scrapped or postponed on short notice if an election is called.

The form of the ballot used in Saskatchewan has varied somewhat. A blank piece of paper served in the first election. In subsequent voting the name, address (recently dropped), and occupation of the candidate were included on the ballot. Political affiliation has been included since 1948, although in 1975 it was to be included only at the wish of the candidate.

The unique ballot of 1905, like various other early practices, was carried over from Territorial days. Replacing open voting in 1892, the ballot was a rectangular paper, one inch by two, with mucilage on one end so that it could be folded and glued. The voter used colored pencils to mark his ballot, according to the color assigned to the candidate of his choice. The reason originally advanced for this type of ballot was that it enabled those who could not read to vote, although economy also has been suggested as a reason since the use of plain paper eliminated the necessity for printing ballots.[6]

The use of this ballot in 1905 required certain adjustments by candidates to accommodate newly introduced party divisions. The law specified that the first candidate nominated in a constituency should be assigned blue; the second, red; the third, yellow; and so on, through a rainbow of allocation. In Territorial elections each constituency was in effect an individual contest, in contrast to the link provided by parties in 1905. As a result the two party leaders agreed before the 1905 election that Haultain's candidates should each nominate first in order to be assigned blue pencils, while Scott advised Liberal candidates to hold back for red ones. He explained to one of his candidates, "Red, you know, is the Liberal color and it was for this reason that I expressed a preference for Red. It would be confusing for our candidates to have different colors in adjoining districts."[7] In 1905 the resulting campaign slogan to "Vote Red" held no sinister implications.

There was unease, however, among some of the Liberal candidates over the arrangement that they should nominate second, although Scott assured his followers they need fear no trickery, "all of the Returning Officers being our own friends." In Battleford constituency, however, concern about nominating second led the Liberal party to put up another hundred dollar deposit. As closing time for nominations drew near and the Conservative candidate had not appeared, the Liberals had the janitor at their headquarters file nomination papers (and later withdraw). Having thus got "blue" out of the way, the Liberal candidate filed immediately afterwards for red, and the Conservative candidate had to accept yellow as his color when he arrived.

Until 1952, elections in northern constituencies were held a few weeks later than elsewhere in order to allow for transportation difficulties. With voting results elsewhere in the province already known, northern balloting was usually reduced to an unexciting postscript. In 1929, by contrast, when the two main parties were almost evenly balanced on election day, the north came into its own. Premier, cabinet ministers, leader of the opposition, and other politicians swarmed into the two northern constituencies to fight for the 427 and 1,270 votes which Cumberland and Ile à la Crosse respectively had to offer. Frenzied political activity was halted, on the surface at least, only for the annual stampede at Meadow Lake which occurred in the midst of the campaign. Similar activity again was evident in 1948 in deferred elections in the north after CCF strength showed a sharp drop on the regular polling day, after harsh criticism of government policy in northern areas.

Controverted elections, involving corrupt or illegal practices, have created post-election excitement upon occasion. Formal action is less frequent than threats of it, dark mutterings frequently being heard from a defeated camp, alleging that unqualified people have voted.

A relatively unsophisticated incident which subsequently led to more sophisticated legal complications occurred in three northern polls in the 1905 election. Suspicions prompted an investigation which revealed that the three deputy returning officers in charge had simply retired to the bush for an appropriate length of time and had then returned with an appropriate number of ballots to tip the election in favor of the government candidate. Unfortunately for their scheme, the hundred and fifty-one Liberal votes presented exceeded the number of voters in the three polls.

Events arising from this revelation included the resignation of the Liberal candidate and a petition to the Saskatchewan Supreme Court by the Provincial Rights candidate, S. J. Donaldson, contesting his opponent's election. Before a decision was reached, a judge in another case concluded that the courts had no jurisdiction in controverted elections, since the Saskatchewan Act had not provided for continuation of the relevant Territorial legislation. All election cases pending in the province were consequently dismissed for want of jurisdicton. Donaldson subsequently petitioned the assembly that he be declared elected, and his petition was granted on April 2, 1907. Commenting on the matter later, Premier Scott said, "I believe I am right in stating that a precedent was made. There is no precedent in the Parliament of Canada, or in the legislature of any of the provinces, for the dominant party seating a member of the opposite party without forcing him to fight for his seat." It must be a matter for speculation whether Donaldson, reviewing the events from December of 1905 until April of 1907, would be as deeply impressed by the conclusion that technically he had not had "to fight for his seat."

This incident was used as a precedent in 1931 when the legislature again seated a member; this time there was a Conservative government in power and it was a Liberal, Norman McLeod, who was seated. In a by-election in Estevan constituency on December 23, 1930, election results gave Mr. McLeod a small majority. A judicial recount gave the majority to his Conservative opponent, but a subsequent investigation established that ballots had been tampered with between the original count and the recount. As the simplest way to resolve the situation and to avoid another by-election, the assembly exercised its right to unseat or seat a member, and Mr. McLeod was accordingly seated. As it happened, he held the seat for less than two years, being unseated late in 1932, after a series of court cases, because unqualified persons had voted in the by-election.[8]

Other disputes have arisen from time to time, although infrequently. These disputes have not been confined to the north, although that region seems to have offered broader scope for unusual developments. Modern technology also has shown itself capable of adding new complications while solving others. A by-election in the vast northern area of Athabasca constituency in September of 1972 was plagued by a succession of mishaps. The by-election followed the overturning of the 1971 election because twenty-five ballots had been cast by persons who were not eligible to vote. Preparations for the by-election balloting were beset successively by a mistake in the voters' list which appeared to permit 350 people to vote four times; by the need to reprint the ballots because of incorrect listing of the names; by a controversy as to whether citizens of the Irish Republic living in the constituency were eligible to vote; and finally by a rain and snow storm which caused the crash of the plane which was carrying the reprinted ballots, the acting chief electoral officer, and some officials of the Liberal party. No fatalities resulted, one advance poll was opened only a few minute late, another was postponed, and a third one was cancelled. After the election count came a recount. The victor was Allan Guy. He had held the seat for the Liberals since 1960, and he had originally come out ahead in the 1971 voting.

7   The Legislative Assembly

The legislature of Saskatchewan consists of the lieutenant governor and the elected House, the legislative assembly. Because the lieutenant governor's role is expected to be ceremonial and the elected members form the effective body, the terms assembly and legislature are often used interchangeably in ordinary usage. Although some of the older provinces had started with a second chamber, the idea had lost its popularity before Saskatchewan became a province, and no thought was given to anything but a unicameral system.

Members have met in the present legislative chamber since 1912. The move to the newly constructed legislative building had been made during the previous year, but the chamber was not yet complete, so the first session in the new building was held in the reading room of the library. Before moving to its permanent home, the assembly had temporarily used two humbler buildings. The first assemblies met in the old Territorial government building on Dewdney Avenue, which was then deserted in favor of the post office building, used on an interim basis until the move to the new building in 1911.

As might be expected, agriculture has always been heavily represented in the legislative membership. Equally unsurprising, in view of the steady shift from rural to urban residence, is the gradual decline in the number of members with agricultural occupations. In contrast to earlier assemblies with more than one-half of the members engaged in farming, one-third of the members who assembled after the 1971 election listed farming as an occupation; farmers made up more than forty per cent of the NDP legislators and twenty-six per cent of the Liberal side of the House. The Progressive Conservative strength in rural areas in the 1978 election was shown in nine out of its seventeen members being engaged in farming or ranching, compared with one-third of the NDP members who listed these occupations.

The significance of the number of farmers in the legislature must be examined with two precautions, however. First, farming interests are not homogeneous. Divergence in outlook between the big and the small farmer may be less marked with the general trend towards larger-scale farming, but the difference has not disappeared. The extent to which farmer members of the legislature cultivate their own land varies widely, even among those who are not listed with a double occupation, but who are nevertheless carrying on another full-time business. Even among those who devote their full time (outside assembly duties) to farming, the increasing diversification and specialization in agriculture means divergent and sometimes conflicting interests. Second, and in a broader sense, no member of the legislature in Saskatchewan can overlook the central position of agriculture generally. It was opposition leader Blakeney, a lawyer and government administrator, with a Nova Scotia background, not a farmer and not even raised on a Saskatchewan farm, who led the successful election campaign of 1971 on the theme of preservation of the family farm.

In early legislatures the Conservative party traditionally had a higher proportion of professional occupations among its membership than the Liberals had. Conversely, the proportion of professionals in the CCF-NDP membership has been less than that among the Liberals. The professional groups differ in kind, with teachers the predominant professional group in the CCF-NDP parties, in contrast to lawyers, who have been more evident among Liberal and Conservative professionals. In 1971, for example, the fifteen members on the Liberal side of the legislature included two teachers and three lawyers; the NDP, with forty-five members, also had three lawyers, but it had twelve teachers, too. A marked gap in the professions has been created by the lack of any medical doctors since 1944.

Women were conspicuously absent in the Saskatchewan legislature from 1967 until 1975, when the Liberals elected two women, each of whom served a single term. One woman, a Conservative, was elected in 1978. The number of women legislators has been small at any time, a total of nine having been elected since they became eligible as candidates in 1917. The first woman member was Mrs. Sarah Ramsland, elected in a by-election in Pelly in 1919 to continue in the seat held by her husband until his death. She was re-elected in the 1921 general election, and then defeated in 1925 by a Progressive. Marjorie Cooper is the only woman who was a member for more than two terms, sitting for the CCF for fifteen years from 1952 to 1967. Only during a single session has the number of women in the House at one time reached a total of three. In the 1960-64 legislature Mrs. Cooper was joined on the CCF side by Gladys Strum, and on the other side of the House, Mary Batten of Humboldt served her second term as a Liberal member, after being first elected in 1956.

Consistent with the province's mixed ethnic population, legislative membership over the years has represented a variety of ethnic groups and religions. Although those of Anglo-Saxon background have dominated, and in the early years were over-represented in proportion to their part in the province's population, by 1964 they were for the first time under-represented. The Conservative party always showed a high proportion of Anglo-Saxon legislative membership, but the Liberal side of the House from the beginning included French, German, and Scandinavian members, to whom were added Ukrainian and Dutch. The CCF soon expanded its representation of various ethnic groups in the legislature, so that two parties on the Saskatchewan political scene were integrating diverse elements, where only one had done so in the province's earlier history.[1]

This diversification includes religion as well as ethnic origin. The Liberal party has always embraced a variety of religions, having included a higher proportion of Roman Catholics than any other party in its legislative membership, although the CCF-NDP has gradually shown increased variation in this respect. In 1971 the NDP legislative membership, in addition to being thirty-eight per cent United Church and twenty-three per cent Roman Catholic, included representatives of the Ukrainian Greek Catholic, Greek Orthodox, Lutheran, Baptist, Mennonite, Anglican, Jesus Christ of Latter Day Saints, and Pentecostal denominations. Despite the Liberal party's traditionally strong support by Roman Catholics, a bias that the leader should be Protestant held until the selection of Dave Steuart in 1971. When a new choice was made in 1976, it seemed to attract little notice that both of the contenders were Roman Catholic.

The Saskatchewan legislative assembly has traditionally met for approximately two months each year, until recent years usually starting in February and proroguing in April, with the conclusion of business frequently expedited by a determined spring thaw across the farmlands. Extra sessions, short in duration, have been called from time to time for special purposes. After the uncertain election results of 1929, Premier Gardiner called the legislature into session in September to determine its support of his administration. In 1944 the newly elected CCF government called a fall session to establish new departments and to put initial aspects of its program into effect. In December of 1951, a three-day session implemented an agreement with the federal government on old age pensions, and in October of 1961 Saskatchewan, along with other provinces, had to pass provincial tax legislation hastily in the wake of the federal government's unexpected abandonment of the former tax rental system. At the same time, the Saskatchewan government introduced provisions for its medical care program. In 1970 Premier Thatcher assembled the legislature in midsummer to enact the so-called Bill 2, the Essential Services Emergency Act, under which the government could invoke compulsory binding arbitration to terminate labor strikes; in August of the following year the new NDP premier brought the new legislature together to repeal that legislation and to give immediate effect to other NDP election promises.

A divided session, beginning in the fall and then adjourning until the customary February date, was an innovation in 1973-74. The purpose of dividing the session was to adjust to increasingly heavy legislative programs, not only by the provision of additional sitting days, but also by having the adjournment interval to provide time both for consideration of legislative proposals by M.L.A.'s and for reaction from the public. With opening ceremonies and the throne speech debate concluded, and with some legislation having been introduced in the pre-Christmas period (in 1973 almost three weeks), the legislature presumably could settle more purposefully into its duties upon re-assembling in the new year. In practice the value of the fall sitting remains to be seen, especially since the re-assembling in the new year tends to be pushed back, with the same rush at closing time in the spring as occurred previously. No fall sitting was held after the election in October of 1978, and Premier Blakeney said the government did not have enough legislation prepared to make the calling of a fall session feasible. The opposition took the occasion to question whether fall sessions were needed at all. They charged that the stated intention of introducing legislation in the fall to get public reaction had simply not happened.

The traditional forms and ceremonies of the British parliamentary system are followed in Saskatchewan, with adaptation only in detail. Neither the fairly extensive changes in legislative procedures at Ottawa nor administrative transformations in Regina have been as evident in the Saskatchewan assembly. Attention to protocol has decreased, however, with less formality evident in recent years.

The main feature of the opening ceremonies of a session is the Speech from the Throne, read by the lieutenant governor. Any members who have been elected since the previous session are presented to the speaker, and permission is asked and given to be seated. The time-honoured assertion of the independence of the assembly and the right to deal with its own business before that presented by the Crown is observed in the introduction and first reading of the *pro forma* bill respecting the Administration of Oaths of Office, which is then not heard of again. Routine housekeeping duties include a motion for the printing of assembly proceedings, and the appointment of a select special committee to choose members for the assembly's standing committees.

In the first session after an election, the House must choose a speaker. Immediately after the entry of the lieutenant governor into the legislative chamber, therefore, the provincial secretary informs the members that the lieutenant governor "does not see fit to declare the causes of the summoning of the ... Legislature" until they have elected a speaker, and the lieutenant governor then retires from the chamber. Upon his return, the newly-elected speaker makes the ancient claim, on behalf of the assembly, of "all their undoubted rights and privileges, especially that they may have freedom of speech in their debates, access to your person at all reasonable times, and that their proceedings may receive from you the most favorable consideration."

The opening of the assembly normally is a social as well as an official occasion. Visitors seated on the floor of the House include members' wives, justices of the superior courts, Saskatchewan senators and members of Parliament, high ranking officials of the public service, representatives of the clergy and the university, and of various local, provincial, and national organizations. The galleries are crowded with spectators, and a speakers' reception is held for all immediately after adjournment. Before 1944, cabinet ministers appeared in morning dress for the opening, but this custom was not continued by members of the CCF government, nor was it renewed later by the Liberals.

The Speech from the Throne serves the customary purpose of outlining in general terms the areas of legislation which the government intends to deal with. Acknowledgments may be made of royal visits, or mention made of notable events which have occurred in the province. The importance of weather, crop, and market conditions to the province is evident in the frequency with which notice of these is included in the Throne Speech, along with any other factors which have significantly affected the province's welfare.

The mover and seconder of the Address in Reply to the Speech from the Throne are often recently elected members, who are thus provided with an initiation in the House without being restricted to a particular subject. Other criteria for choosing mover and seconder have prevailed from time to time, with the order of precedence reversed upon occasion and senior members chosen. Consideration may also be given to northern and southern representation, and the CCF upon occasion chose from labor and farming respectively to represent the party's two elements of support.

Careful advice offered by Premier Scott in 1910 for the preparation of speeches by the mover and seconder illustrates some of the conventions which still prevail in these speeches, and also the way in which they may be used to complement the Throne Speech itself. In writing to the mover Scott said:

You should, of course, make congratulatory reference to the new Lieutenant-Governor and make some comment on his long and useful record in the West and also pay tribute to our former Governor. Then devote a few sentences to the late King's death, etc. Some figures might well be quoted regarding the great expansion of business generally, agriculture, etc. If you wish I could have the Agriculture Department make a few figures on this line.
Referring to the University and Agricultural College, would it not be found in place to quote some figures showing the great growth of our school system generally and as a medical man you might well expand a little of the subject of the proposed Institution for Insane Persons and also regarding the new Public Health Bureau. Without referring to Haultain at all you might very well in a sentence or two emphasize the arguments in favor of the Agricultural College. I think it is well on such an occasion to keep away from controversial references as much as possible. In the Speech itself we have tried to keep out everything inviting contention. Of course when the Leader of the Opposition comes to speak he naturally begins to criticize and it always furnishes the Leader of the Government an invitation and opportunity to strike back. It is of course quite in order for the Mover to make comment on the generally satisfactory conduct of business by the Government and the splendid advancement being made throughout the Province under good administration.

As the most important legislation of the session will be that concerning Elevators, I think that at least one-third of your speech should be on the Elevator question, and the Commission's Report. The Report will be printed probably at the end of the year and just as soon as possible I shall send you a printed copy.

I think perhaps you might leave reference to municipal development and the new Provincial Building to Mr. Stevenson who will second the motion.

Beyond the above I should like you to touch very briefly on Laurier's western trip and it might be possible to bring in an inoffensive reference to the Navy question and the Opposition's attitude last session.

Now these are only suggestions. You may wish to touch on other questions, for instance, some mention of the general railways situation and of the question of the Hudson's Bay road would be quite in order. On such an occasion, a thirty-minute speech is better than an hour speech and probably once you get down to it your main difficulty will be too much material.[2]

The seconder's speech was to serve in part to fill gaps of things not mentioned in the Throne Speech. In his suggestions the premier spoke of the need for certain changes in the judicial system, and he advised the seconder:

We have had many representations within the past year and while we will make no announcement or do anything at this session, I do not think it is a matter in which action can be staved off very long and there will be no harm in your touching the subject and taking the ground that the matter calls for the serious attention of the Government without delay.

I think too that ... you might as well dwell on the question of roads .... I think that everything which will help to educate the people of Saskatchewan into a realization of the loss they are sustaining by the absence of reasonably good roads is good work.[3]

The Throne Speech debate and the budget debate later in the session are limited to six and seven days respectively (counting the days the speeches themselves are given), with the budget debate divided into two parts of five and two days each. Each debate provides opportunity for wide-ranging discussion by assembly members. General defense and criticism of government policy abound in the Throne Speech debate, and the opportunity may be seized for the opening shots of an expected election campaign or for recriminations following a recently concluded contest. Members laud their respective constituencies and their constituencies' inhabitants, and they air pet theories and projects. An opposition member may move an amendment to emphasize alleged deficiencies in the Throne Speech or to provide an opportunity for a second round of speech-making. Although such an amendment constitutes a confidence motion, there is scarcely hope or fear on either side of the House of its passing.

The budget speech follows without great delay after the conclusion of the Throne Speech debate. The Minister of Finance first presents the estimates of expenditures for the coming year, and in his speech he reveals the means by which the money is to be raised. In the debate that follows, cabinet ministers normally review the activities of their respective departments for the past year. Other members use the broad umbrella which the debate provides to discuss matters which they did not manage to work into the Throne Speech debate.

Legislation, and the examination of spending estimates, become the major areas of consideration once the Throne Speech and budget speech debates have ended. Basic legislative processes have changed little in the province's history. After prior notice, move for leave to introduce a bill and the first reading are combined; after a time lapse of at least two days, adoption on second reading gives approval in principle; detailed consideration normally occurs in Committee of the Whole and is followed by report and third reading, and then by assent by the lieutenant governor. For private bills, dealing with matters of private rather than public concern, second reading merely passes the bill on to committee and does not commit the House in any way. It is the adoption of a favorable report by the committee which indicates approval of the bill, which then goes to Committee of the Whole. Money bills, resulting in a charge upon public funds, require recommendation from the lieutenant governor before they are introduced as government bills.

Changes in committee structure and operation have resulted in a combination of long-standing practices with later innovations. The Committee of the Whole retains its pre-eminent position in legislative proceedings. The major changes have been in certain standing committees, in the establishment of a Special Select Committee on Regulations, and in the use of intersessional committees.

Committee of the Whole continues to be used with little exception for clause by clause examination of bills which have received approval in principle on second reading. Change in the working of this committee has been made only in detail by substituting the reading of marginal titles for the complete reading of clauses in order to save time. The committee operates as Committee of Finance in the substantial duty of detailed consideration of spending estimates.

The extensive use made of Committee of the Whole reveals the reluctance of the assembly to entrust discussion to standing committees. Arguments that the entire House is not too unwieldy a body for committee discussion and that standing committees would take too much time away from the House are advanced by members as reasons in favor of using the Committee of the Whole. Less specific is simply the expressed feeling that the House is where debate should take place. Not so readily voiced, but undoubtedly a basic reason for use of Committee of the Whole, is the reluctance of each member to have significant matters referred to a body in which he may not be able to participate. A further reason is a relative lack of publicity for committee proceedings.

The select standing committees, twelve in number, vary widely in activity. Those on agriculture, education, and municipal law rarely if ever meet. Paradoxically, their subject matter is too important to trust to them. Few members would agree to have matters in these areas removed from their individual purview through consideration in a standing committee on which they might not sit, instead of dealing with them in Committee of the Whole. Matters of general party rather than individual constituency concern, or those that have slight public interest, are more readily allowed to go to standing committees. Immediately after the session begins, the Radio Broadcasting Committee allocates radio time for the two sides of the House. The Library Committee also meets each session to consider recommendations for disposal of public documents. Both the Private Bills Committee and the Committee on Law Amendments and Delegated Powers, which considers public bills by a private member, can expect work during the session, while for the Committee on Privileges and Elections, and on Rules and Procedures, the provision of work is more uncertain.

The Non-Controversial Bills Committee established in 1971 represents an effort to streamline assembly work by removing routine and minor amendments from consideration of the full House. Bills that are agreed by both sides to be non-controversial are referred to this committee after second reading instead of to Committee of the Whole. The committee cannot modify the bill, and if discussion reveals disagreement the committee will return the bill to the House so that it can go through the normal channels. This committee, composed of five opposition and three government members, is the only one with an opposition majority and it is also one of the smallest, the membership of most committees varying from a dozen to well over twenty members.

The two major standing committees are the Public Accounts Committee and the Crown Corporations Committee. Both are hard-working, meeting three or four times a week over a five- or six-week period. Since committees do not meet at the same time that the House is sitting, whenever House sittings are extended into the morning and evening in addition to the normal afternoon time, the committees have to adapt their customary schedule of morning meetings to whatever time can be found.

After a period in which the Public Accounts Committee had degenerated into little more than a forum for partisan debate, a special intra-sessional committee in 1963–64 carried out a broad and careful examination directed toward improvement of the committee's role and functions. For various reasons, including a change in government, the recommendations of the special committee were not put into effect until 1967. In that year the Public Accounts Committee was re-organized, its size was reduced from thirty to eleven members, and a member of the opposition was selected as chairman. In 1968 the committee started to hold its meetings in camera, submitting a verbatim report of proceedings upon conclusion of its activities. The committee receives the annual report of the provincial auditor, whose emphasis is on proper procedures in government spending. Appointed by the cabinet, the auditor can be dismissed only with the approval of the legislature.

An unresolved problem of the Public Accounts Committee is that the accounts referred to it for examination are at least a year old. This delay is the result of a combination of two factors: the time required to prepare the accounts after the end of the fiscal year, and the necessity for their being tabled in the legislature before being referred to the committee. Commencement of the legislative session in the fall allows for at least somewhat earlier work by this committee.

The Crown Corporations Committee arose out of the early emphasis of the CCF government on the public ownership and operation of industries. The committee has been pointed to with pride by its founders as a model for similar bodies established elsewhere and for the development of new techniques of procedure. The reports and financial statements of crown corporations are automatically referred by the House to the committee in the same manner as public accounts are referred to their committee. The Crown Corporations Committee also deals with other matters specifically referred to it, effecting a wide review of government-operated enterprises and providing information on past operations as well as on those of the year under review. All requests in the assembly for information relating to crown corporations are referred to the committee, and the answers are made available there, to be tabled in the House later as sessional papers.

The Select Special Committee on Regulations is set up during the last week or two of the legislative session to carry out its work between sessions. This committee has a majority of government members with an opposition chairman. The duty of the committee is to review regulations passed by departments and other government agencies as delegated legislation. Legal counsel examines the regulations for consistency in wording, to see that they have no retroactive effect, and that they are within legislative authority. Normally any problems which arise can be resolved by consultation with the department concerned, but as a final resort the committee can always recommend action by the legislature. The function of the Regulations Committee is similar to that of the Public Accounts Committee in that each is a post-mortem, watchdog committee. The Public Accounts Committee ensures that money is spent as directed by legislation, while the Regulations Committee sees that regulations conform to legislation.

In 1972 a Special Committee on Statutory Instruments was set up to look at the possibility of broader scrutiny that would include, in addition to regulations, other instruments such as ministerial orders and orders in council and the by-laws of professional associations. This task proved too broad, and the Regulations Committee continues its more restricted area of scrutiny.

Use of special committees on an intersessional basis has greatly increased since 1972. Subject matter and approach have changed. Formerly, intersessional committees tended to be used for those relatively complex or technical matters which required more or less intensive study, such as the methods to be used for the scrutiny of public accounts, noted above, or a Committee on Standing Orders and Procedures of the assembly in 1969. By contrast, in 1972 and 1973 special intersessional committees were set up on welfare, land ownership, small businesses, liquor, and highway safety. The intersessional nature of the committees not only provided more time, but permitted the practice adopted by these committees of holding hearings in various parts of the province during the summer months for public reaction and views. The extent of interest and of attendance at hearings varied, but the hearings gave the committees and the subjects under consideration greater publicity than they would normally receive in committee work during the session. Later in the 1970s, the areas dealt with by intersessional committees again tended to be technical and internal and therefore unsuited to public hearings. An intersessional committee on rules and procedures, for example, continued work for several years, and after being terminated by the 1978 election, it was set up again by the new legislature.

A standing committee which received unparalleled attention was the Crown Corporations Committee in its investigation during March and April of 1953 into the so-called Rawluk kickback charges. In bare statistics the committee reported forty-one meetings held, examination of twenty-six witnesses under oath, oral testimony amounting to 1700 pages of typescript, and some 115 marked exhibits.

The main charges were that Mr. M. F. Allore, the manager of the Saskatchewan Government Insurance Office, was getting a kickback of forty per cent on all commissions which he was responsible for turning over to the firm Financial Agencies Ltd., and that the Honorable C. M. Fines, the provincial treasurer, was sharing in these kickbacks. The charges, which were brought to the legislature by Walter Tucker, the leader of the opposition, were based on what was termed a copy of an affidavit sworn some nine months previously, on May 23, 1952, by J. O. Rawluk, the managing director of Financial Agencies.

Out of the maze of witnesses and conflicting testimony, the committee concluded that "much depends on the weight that can be attached to the evidence of Mr. Rawluk, the maker of these charges." Its conclusion in this respect was that it was "unhesitatingly of the opinion that Mr. Rawluk must be regarded as wholly unworthy of belief. He is not honest or reliable, either in his own everyday business affairs or in his evidence before the committee." Among evidence cited in support of this opinion was Mr. Rawluk's own admission of forging three cheques while he was manager of Financial Agencies, of continued issuance of n.s.f. cheques over a two-year period, and of the payment of trust funds of clients into the general bank account of Financial Agencies. The committee's verdict was that the charges against Mr. Fines and Mr. Allore were wholly unwarranted and unfounded.[4]

A carnival atmosphere prevailed among the press and the public during the committee sittings. Crowds were so large that proceedings were moved from the committee room to the legislative chamber, where the galleries were packed. The proceedings became a favorite topic for newspaper coverage, which extended from factual reporting to humorous speculation on whether the legislative drama might win an Oscar.

An irony of the whole exercise was the amount of money involved.

The total alleged to have been turned over to Mr. Allore was some $1,100, of which Mr. Fines had allegedly received $100 or $200 (Mr. Rawluk was uncertain which). Although the amount of course was immaterial so far as the seriousness of the alleged offence was concerned, it did put the credibility of the charge in another category. An astute cabinet minister who was willing to risk his reputation could certainly have found an arrangement more financially promising than the one described, even in 1952 monetary terms.

Oral questions to cabinet ministers have traditionally been permitted even though assembly rules have made no provision for such questions. In 1975 the assembly decided that the practice should be officially sanctioned. The intersessional committee on rules and procedures, referred to above, was given as one of its specific tasks the provision for an oral question period similar to that in the House of Commons. The result was the recommendation in its report the following year that questions might be put to ministers relating to public affairs, or to other members relating to matters of assembly business with which those members were concerned. Daily proceedings include certain routines, among them the introduction of guests in the galleries, before the oral question period, which is to begin not later than five minutes after the start of the sitting and to conclude not later than thirty minutes after it.

The speaker has a particular task during question period to try to keep the questions short and to the point. The questioner frequently has a contrary objective since he may attempt to use the query as an excuse for a partisan statement under the guise of background to the question.

Rather than being a genuine search for information, a question may be a challenge to a minister, a hope of catching him in an awkward spot, or an attempt at making him reveal information he does not wish to reveal. Consequently, questions almost always come from the opposition. Only on rare occasions will a maverick on the government side ask questions. The NDP have had two such members since they came to office. John Richards, elected in 1971, whose sympathies were with the left-wing Waffle group, frequently challenged ministers in the two years he sat with the NDP before he became an independent member. NDP member Peter Prebble, who was elected in 1978 and is an open critic of his party's development of uranium followed Richards' example, and in the 1979 session he used the question period to seek assurance of stricter safety standards for Canadian uranium development.

Aside from the informal questioning which is allowed, assembly rules provide for information to be requested of ministers either through written questions or by returns.[5] Questions require forty-eight hours' notice, and the answer must then be tabled in the assembly. Returns, which normally deal with a broader area of information, do not have a time limit. Upon occasion, returns have been delayed by cabinet ministers for notoriously long periods, sometimes from one session to another. Questions and motions for returns have been refused from time to time on the grounds that the information might be found in regularly printed government documents or that a far-reaching inquiry would involve an unreasonable amount of work. Ministers also refuse questions involving government opinion, those that concern information about the private affairs of a citizen, or those which violate the broad safeguard ministers frequently rely on, that to reveal the information asked for would not be in the public interest.

Rules, or as they are termed, the standing orders of the assembly, under which day-to-day proceedings are regulated, have been continued in the main from Territorial days. Since they are based upon the rules of the Canadian House of Commons, the usages of that body are to be followed in any instances that are not provided for in the assembly regulations. As noted above, the whole question of rules and proceeding has been under study in recent years by intersessional committees.

As in other legislative bodies, the amount of time consumed in lengthy speeches has presented a problem in the Saskatchewan assembly. In early years speeches of two, three, or even four hours' duration were reported upon occasion. In 1932 new rules limited speeches to forty minutes, with certain exceptions. The rule proved ineffective since members adopted forty minutes as a minimum rather than a maximum, and since it was not enforced the rule was dropped two years later.

Defense of speech-making has occurred from time to time in reminders that the legislature is a place for discussion. Premier Scott said in 1911, "My view is that in the past we have done our work with too little discussion, so much so that the people have not become really aware of the amount and importance of the work done."[6] As a result, at the start of that year's session, the premier informed members on the government side of the House that they had not been doing enough speaking. Forty years later, the speaker of the House reprimanded members for referring to debates and proceedings in disparaging terms, and reminded them that the House was a deliberative and legislative body, and not an administrative or executive one.[7]

The quantity of speech-making has been affected less by admonition or rules than by pragmatism, and since 1946, the length of speeches has conformed to the realities of legislative broadcasting. With "radio time" eagerly sought and carefully apportioned, members' speeches have become skillfully tailored to the air time allotted them. Broadcasting also has increased the number of members who wish to speak, with the result at first of increasingly longer throne and budget speech debates. When time limits were placed on these debates, evening sittings became necessary to accommodate all the speakers within the allotted number of days. Previously evening and morning sittings normally occurred only toward the end of a session.

Official recording of assembly debates began in 1947. Before that, newspaper reports served as an unofficial Hansard, with the *Leader* in

Regina early establishing a tradition of full newspaper reporting of assembly debate, which was continued by its successors, the *Morning Leader* and the *Leader-Post*. This reporting was supplemented by limited official recording from 1919 of important speeches, such as the budget speech. The present recording includes proceedings of the House in session and, since 1976, proceedings in Committee of the Whole and in the Finance Committee. This last change corrected an anomaly of many years in which the speeches of legislative members welcoming the visits of numerous groups of school children to the assembly were recorded, for example, while the considerably more significant discussion of proposed departmental spending in the Committee of Finance was omitted.

The powers and privileges of the assembly are defined by statute, and they include the customary double prerogative relating to the House as a body, and also to individual members. Complaints of infringement upon the dignity of the House have been directed most often against government members for publishing reports or information in the press before informing the assembly, or against newspaper accounts of assembly happenings. The latter was particularly true when rival political newspapers in Regina used greater vigor and less restraint than had been evident in the assembly itself, and the premier on at least one occasion warned the press that it could be excluded from the House.

Legislative galleries, both public and press, were in fact ordered cleared by the speaker in a brief but unique circumstance in 1965. The incident was sparked by an opposition member who, noticing a minister's executive assistant on the floor of the House, interrupted his own comments in debate to call the attention of the speaker: ". . . there is a stranger in the House." The speaker's resulting order for the withdrawal of strangers included all galleries, under assembly rules, and the public and press galleries therefore were cleared. The offending "stranger" not surprisingly had quickly disappeared from the floor of the House. After the ejection of press members, however, the president of the press gallery took a stand by entering the press gallery in defiance of the speaker's order and refusing to leave. Brief but confused debate in the assembly included the admission by the acting opposition leader that there had been no intention to get into the existing situation, and discussion by members as to how to get themselves out of it. They solved their problem by rescinding the motion to eject strangers, and both press and public galleries were re-opened some fifteen minutes after they had been cleared.

In exercising discipline against individual members, the speaker upon rare occasions has named a member and suspended him from the House for refusing to retract an unparliamentary reference or statement. In 1948 A. T. Proctor, a former Liberal cabinet minister; in 1963 Ross Thatcher, a future premier; and in 1974 C. P. MacDonald, who had served in Premier Thatcher's cabinet, each was expelled for the remainder of the day's sitting. In an earlier incident in 1942 J. L. Phelps, a future CCF cabinet minister, had been escorted from the

House by the sergeant-at-arms for refusing to accept the chairman's ruling in Committee of Supply. By the time it was noted that the chairman of the committee had authority only to report the incident to the House, Mr. Phelps had left the building. He did not return to his seat for the remainder of the session, but that was through his own choice.

In the fall session of 1977–78, three Progressive Conservative members were each suspended for five days for breaching parliamentary privilege. The incident arose because the Liberal and Progressive Conservative parties each had eleven members after the defection of Colin Thatcher from the Liberals to the Conservatives in the previous June. Speaker John Brockelbank took the position that in this circumstance there was no official opposition. In preparation for the session, meetings were held between the speaker, the legislative clerk Gordon Barnhart, and representatives of each of the three parties, in order to work out procedural details for the sharing of opposition duties by the Liberals and the Progressive Conservatives.

On the day the house opened, on November 16, Progressive Conservative whip Eric Berntson in a letter to the speaker charged a "political deal" between the NDP and the Liberals to deprive the Conservatives of what they referred to as their rightful place as the official opposition. The Conservative claim to official opposition status was made in anticipation of the resignation of two Liberal M.L.A.'s who had declared their intention of running in the federal election whenever it was called. All others who had been present at the preparatory meetings denied any kind of a deal, and Berntson agreed to withdraw his letter, but on the same day he repeated his charge in a radio news report.

The Standing Committee on Privileges and Elections met for the first time in thirty years, the Progressive Conservative members refused to sit on it, and Colin Thatcher and Gary Lane were each suspended from the legislature for five days for referring to the committee as a kangaroo court. These were, incidentally, the two recent recruits from the Liberal party. After a letter had been sent requesting party leader Dick Collver to appear before the committee and he had made a statement to the press that he would not do so unless subpoenaed, the committee took the unusual step of communicating with him through an open-line radio program on which Collver was the guest. The request of the committee chairman and Mr. Collver's reply reaffirmed their original positions. Neither Collver nor Berntson would appear before the committee, and the committee decided not to subpoena them. It apparently was not particularly anxious to re-establish long disused historical practice, noting that the process had not been used in the British parliamentary system since 1741.

In its report tabled on January 3, 1978, the committee ruled Bernston's letter a "flagrant breach of privilege", and the House laid down four conditions that the offender must comply with. Mr. Berntson went only halfway. He honored the order to withdraw the letter and to apologize to Speaker John Brockelbank, but he refused to admit the allegation was unfounded and to apologize to the assembly. As a result he became the third Progressive Conservative in the session to receive a five-day suspension.

The most serious exercise of discipline against an assembly member was in 1917, when Charles H. Cawthorpe was expelled from the House and his seat declared vacant. This action was the outcome of the investigation of bribery and corruption charges in connection with liquor administration and graft in road work in 1916, discussed in the next chapter, in which four assembly members were found guilty of charges. One was sentenced to the penitentiary, two resigned from the House, and it was upon Mr. Cawthorpe's refusal to resign that he was expelled.

The earlier investigation of these charges by a committee of the legislature had led to the calling of a witness to the bar of the House who was subsequently committed to the custody of the sergeant-at-arms. During committee investigation in February, 1916, of the charges of bribery in liquor administration, Fred Brunner, treasurer of the Licensed Victuallers of Saskatchewan, refused to answer questions on the ground that he might incriminate himself. The assembly committed him to the custody of the sergeant-at-arms, who delivered him over to the care of the Mounted Police until, a week later, he testified before the committee as required, craved the pardon of the House for the contempt of its authority, and was released. There is no evidence whether the standing order was complied with that "No stranger who has been committed by order of the House to the custody of the Sergeant-at-Arms, shall be released from such custody, until he has paid a fee of four dollars to the Sergeant-at-Arms."[8]

Mr. Brunner's detention apparently was not onerous, and the circumstances were light-heartedly described by a local newspaper. The *Evening Province* reported on February 23, 1916, on Mr. Brunner's situation under the guard of a Mounted Police escort:

He seems to be fully enjoying his forced retirement from the affairs of the day. His headquarters during his confinement is at the Wascana Hotel. He is, however, not so much a prisoner as the rest of the people of this city, for he is free from business cares and is permitted to move where he wishes, so long as he is accompanied by his guard.

Although he may be seen greeting his friends on the streets of the city he is not allowed by his watchful guard to communicate too freely with the outside world. When visited this morning by a reporter of the *Evening Province,* Mr. Brunner was not allowed to make a statement.

A new speaker normally was chosen for each legislature before 1944, but speakers since then have tended to be re-elected if the same party is in power. Tom Johnson, elected speaker in 1944 when the CCF came to power and continuing until 1956, is the only incumbent to serve for more than two legislatures. Fred Dewhurst's situation was unique in that he held the post on separate occasions, from 1962 to 1964 under the CCF, and then after the return of the NDP, when he was re-elected as speaker in 1971.

Since 1977 a speaker's procession occurs at the opening of each legislative sitting, with the speaker preceded by the sergeant-at-arms and followed by the legislative clerks and two of the assembly pages. The reason for introducing this daily practice, which is similar to that in the House of Commons, is to emphasize the continued observance of parliamentary procedure, and to reiterate the independence of the legislative assembly through the speaker, its elected head.

The difficulties a speaker may face in the dual role of an elected party member as well as of an impartial arbiter in the House were sharply illustrated in the spring of 1974, when Mr. Dewhurst's constituency nominating convention was called while the assembly was still in session, and while he was carrying on his duties as speaker. Contrary to the practice in recent conventions, other contenders were seeking the nomination, and the situation was complicated by the disappearance of the previous constituency, as such, through redistribution. Mr. Dewhurst informed his constituents that he could not be a candidate in a convention while the House was in session, because the role of speaker demanded that he remain as politically neutral as possible. He did not attend the convention, and another candidate was chosen.

Longer sessions, intersessional committee work, and increasing demands from constituents now make an M.L.A.'s work almost a full-time job. It is in fact at present in an awkward midway position, not quite recognized as eligible for full-time remuneration, yet requiring members in some occupations to drop their regular jobs—a factor frequently cited in justifying pay increases for members.

Increases in the members' indemnity usually have been brought in at the end of the session and pushed through hastily in an effort to lessen the embarrassment of increasing their own pay and to avoid discussion of it as much as possible. This was the situation in the last hours of the 1979 session when increases were approved. The outstanding difference this time was that in addition to the increases which it made, the legislation tried to forestall the need for such future action. It provided for subsequent increases to come into effect automatically according to the industrial composite, a scale of average weekly earnings by Canadians.

The remuneration of M.L.A.'s is not simply stated, being divided into indemnity, sessional and sitting allowances, expense allowance, and other perquisites which, especially since the 1979 changes, tend to be on a complicated formula basis. The basic annual indemnity of a member in 1979 was $9,250.00, plus an allowance per session of $5,000, an expense allowance of $8,250.00, and a per diem allowance for each day's attendance at a session of $55.00 ($35.00 for members residing in Regina). Greater expenses of the northern members in Athabasca and Cumberland constituencies is recognized in higher indemnity and expense allowances, of $10,450 and $8,530 respectively, plus two return air trips to each community in the constituency.

Each member also has telephone and mailing privileges and travel and office allowances. The telephone allowance is $800 annually, or the total amount of phone bills for M.L.A. business if the requirements of receipts or credit card use are complied with. The mailing allowance is the equivalent of three first-class mailings to each voter in the constituency. This amount may be used at the member's discretion for postage, advertising, or other forms of communication to the constituents. A member also receives travel expenses, as well as reimbursement to a maximum of $500 a month for a constituency office and secretarial expenses.

In addition, the premier receives $27,250 annually, cabinet ministers and the leader of the opposition $20,500, legislative secretaries $5,000, the speaker of the house $8,000, the deputy speaker $4,750, and party whips and deputy whips $1,500 and $750 respectively. A sum of $50,000 is provided for the office of the leader of the opposition. Each party caucus receives an allowance equivalent to $2,500 per member (excluding cabinet ministers, other party leaders and the speaker), as well as an allowance of $15,000 per annum for secretarial services. Members on intersessional committees are paid at the rate of $65.00 a day, plus expenses, for time spent in committee work or attending meetings.

Conflict of interest provisions, to ensure that a member does not use his position, or information gained by it, for his own personal advantage has received considerable attention in Saskatchewan and elsewhere. Saskatchewan legislation in 1979 dealt with participation by members in government contracts and with disclosure of assets. With various exceptions, the general position is that any person participating in a government contract as a shareholder, director, manager, or other officer of a corporation would not be eligible to serve as an M.L.A. Each member is required to file a statement, to be updated annually, setting out various areas of personal financial interests including land holdings; disclosing whether there is participation in government contracts; identifying corporations in which the member is a shareholder, director, or other officer; and acknowledging grants and subsidies received when there is any discretion in whether such payments should be made. This statement by the M.L.A. includes the interests of spouse and dependent children.

Guidance for legislative enactments has been sought by the assembly both from outside and within the province. It is not surprising that in early years especially, legislators relied extensively on experience elsewhere. Strong influence from Ontario was evident in Territorial ordinances, many of which were continued under provincial administration. Early debate in the provincial legislature included frequent reference to the legislation in other provinces, to federal legislation, and to the enactments of various states to the south. The railway bill of 1906 was modelled upon a dominion act of 1903; in discussing a seed grain bill in 1908 the attorney general referred to similar provisions in "Upper Canada", Manitoba, and Alberta. Negatively, examination of government-owned telephone systems in various states and provinces resulted in different action in Saskatchewan. A comprehensive study of Manitoba liquor legislation was made in 1916 before the introduction of Saskatchewan legislation on the subject. In 1914 Premier Scott's visits abroad for health reasons were combined with a study of experimental legislation in New Zealand and Australia which might be useful in prairie development.

Borrowings from outside were combined with experience growing out of local needs and inclination. It is significant that fields in which distinctive local imprints were evident during the first two decades included farm implement purchase and mortgage loans. The ideological basis of the CCF in later years was evident in pioneer legislation in such areas as collective bargaining for civil servants, in a government insurance plan, and in hospitalization and medical care insurance, with NDP enactments in succeeding years following the same pattern in drug and dental care programs, a land bank plan, and an oil and gas crown corporation. The content of Saskatchewan legislation, like its machinery of government, thus represents a combination of adoptions from outside with a recognition of the unique needs of the province, and a blend of CCF-NDP ideology.

8   The Lieutenant Governor

The lieutenant governor of a province has a double role. He is best known as the representative of the sovereign, but he is also a federal officer. His role as a federal officer has decreased in importance and now is evident mainly in his appointment. It is the Governor General in council—in practice the Prime Minister of Canada—who appoints the lieutenant governor. The federal government pays him and could dismiss him. As a federal appointee, the lieutenant governor gives assent to bills passed by the provincial assembly. Legally he can withhold assent (thus killing the bill) or he can reserve it, thus passing it on to Ottawa for a final decision. The right to withhold assent has never been used in Saskatchewan and the power to reserve only once, in 1961. As described later in this chapter, the 1961 incident took both levels of government by surprise as both withholding and reserving assent had long been considered obsolete. Despite this proof that exceptions can occur, they are powers which a lieutenant governor no longer is expected to exercise.

The lieutenant governor's position as a representative of the sovereign is the one clearly seen by the public. Constitutionally, however, it is ambiguous, and in the early years of Confederation it was a point of debate whether the lieutenant governor was really a representative of the sovereign at all. This was because he was seen originally as a federal officer, as one of the means of keeping the provinces in line. Less attention was paid to the constitutional relationship between lieutenant governor and Queen. Certainly the lieutenant governor's position in the province does not parallel the Governor General's position in Canada. The Queen is the head of state in Canada, and the B.N.A. Act vests her with executive authority and designates her and the two Houses as forming Parliament. The Governor General then acts for the sovereign in the necessary executive duties.

In a province the Queen is not given similar executive authority (even in theory), and she is not designated as part of the legislature. Instead, the provincial legislature is composed of the lieutenant governor and the elected assembly. The B.N.A. Act further directs that the lieutenant governor's powers of assent, disallowance, or reservation of legislation are to be exercised in the name of the Governor General, and not in that of the Queen. That is the constitutional directive, but this is one of the areas where practice has overridden the written constitution. In most of the provinces, including Saskatchewan, lieutenant governors do give assent in the name of the Queen.

Although that constitutional difference has been blurred by practice, other developments have sharpened the difference between the positions at the federal and the provincial level, at least theoretically. Originally the Governor General also had a double role, being in a sense an officer of the British government as well as the representative of the Queen. Full Canadian autonomy having been formally granted in 1931, any authority of Britain over Canada was officially removed (except for Canada's request that amendment of the B.N.A. Act remain with the British Parliament). The Governor General henceforth has had a single clear-cut role; he unambiguously represents the Queen in her position as Queen of Canada. The lieutenant governor nevertheless continues in the role of a federal officer and he cannot exclusively be the Queen's representative. The result has been the pragmatic and flexible solution that the lieutenant governor continues in a double role and is regarded as the representative of the Queen in duties which require that role.

The lieutenant governor's main duty is to see that there is always a government in office. This duty is normally performed routinely, by his choosing as premier the leader of the party which has majority support in the House. In unusual circumstances of particular uncertainty, the lieutenant governor might have to make a discretionary choice. He has never had to do so in Saskatchewan, unless the 1905 appointment of Walter Scott, described later in this chapter, is regarded as such an instance. Once a government is installed, the lieutenant governor carries out his normal constitutional duties on the advice of his responsible ministers. Summoning, proroguing, and dissolving the legislature, giving approval for the introduction of money bills, and making appointments are routinely performed.

The lieutenant governor receives his power from the double sources of statute and of prerogative, which reflect his double role as federal agent and as representative of the Queen. The statutory powers are mainly those in the B.N.A. Act which deal with the overall position of lieutenant governors in the provinces, and those in the Saskatchewan Act which apply these provisions to Saskatchewan. Prerogative powers are the residue of powers customarily exercised by the sovereign, and they are delegated by the Governor General in council to the lieutenant governor. Some of these powers, such as the summoning of the legislature, are expressly recognized in the B.N.A.

Act, and executive powers are implied to the extent necessary to carry legislative powers into effect.

Like his statutory powers, the lieutenant governor's prerogative powers normally are exercised on the advice of his ministers. The prerogative powers, however, do contain a narrow and vaguely established area of reserve or emergency power which the lieutenant governor can exercise on his own initiative in rare cases of constitutional impropriety or possible disaster too unusual to predict.

Actions in the lieutenant governor's name are expected to be carried out by the executive council, but it is possible for some other body to perform a particular function nominally assigned to him. In 1920, for example, controversy in the university resulted in a request for the lieutenant governor to exercise the powers of Visitor given to him by the University Act. No machinery existed for this purpose, so the King's Bench Act was amended to give power to the court, under direction of the lieutenant governor, to represent the Crown as Visitor of corporations, a power which meant that it could carry out investigations.

A new lieutenant governor coming into office is given scant assistance in learning his duties. The official instructions issued with his commission appointing him to the office do little more than specify the oaths to be taken or administered; tell the lieutenant governor that he is to abstract bills in the margin to be sent to Ottawa; and order him to proclaim federal disallowance of bills (which has never happened) and to receive permission before leaving the province. A guide to precedence is available for formal occasions. Even on those sparse occasions when policy has been issued by the federal government, little effort apparently is made to communicate established practice to succeeding lieutenant governors. This lack of instruction in carrying out his duties was evident in the reservation case in 1961, when the lieutenant governor of Saskatchewan acted in direct contravention of federal policy that had been in effect since 1882. Thus the lieutenant governor is left largely to his own devices to find out as he can from his secretary, his aide, or other officials what duties he is expected to perform and how he is to perform them.

This neglect undoubtedly comes from the lieutenant governor's major functions being regarded as social rather than constitutional. Even social demands now have greatly diminished, but for early incumbents they were important. The tradition of Government House, the official residence, as a social center was established in Territorial days and the tradition was carried over into the early years of the province. Government House was the scene of annual functions such as the New Year's Levee and the entertainment of assembly members. Dinners were given on numerous occasions, garden parties and other social gatherings were held for distinguished guests, and Government House might also be lent for various purposes. The lieutenant governor's wife held her weekly afternoon "at home", entertained members of women's organizations, and in other similar ways was expected to be a social leader.

Whatever claims might be made upon the lieutenant governor for appearances in other parts of the province, in those early years Reginans regarded Government House functions as peculiarly their own. Failure to carry out these duties was not lightly regarded, either in public or in official circles. This attitude was particularly evident with the first change of lieutenant governor in the province. The Hon. A. E. Forget, who had been lieutenant governor of the Territories, had continued for a term in the new province. He had become withdrawn and so he initiated fewer and fewer social functions, to the chagrin of Regina residents. Hope for a renewal of social activity was an important consideration in the choice of a successor in 1910. Upon the eve of G. W. Brown's appointment to the office, Premier Scott was warned by a political friend, Senator J. H. Ross, to advise Brown "to go in for some good splurging at the opening," and to have two or three good functions the first month and some luncheons: "You know the Regina people are sore in respect to the social functions which have been held or haven't been held during the last few years. I am afraid people will say that the same thing will happen with the new people," he admonished.[1] Since Brown's appointment would be credited to Scott, Ross pointed out further that a good start would mean much for both Brown and the premier. Scott took the advice seriously, and in helping Brown to find a suitable secretary he stressed the management of social functions as an important part of the secretary's duties.

Both Ross's fears and the wisdom of his advice apparently were well grounded. Early objections to the appointment were reported to Scott as being "mostly along the lines that it was a mistake owing to the probability that Brown would not entertain, I think this is the great kick and most of this comes from members of your own government."[2] Fortunately for those concerned, these forebodings were not borne out, as may be seen by a newspaper report that appeared two years after Lieutenant Governor Brown's appointment:

With the opening of the Legislature and the holding of the big reception at Government House last evening the busy winter social season may be said to be now in full swing, and for the next few months no one in the social world of Saskatchewan will be busier than the popular wife of the Lieutenant-Governor, Mrs. G. W. Brown.

A general decline in social demands in later years was accelerated by particular circumstances. During the thirties any lavish display would have been deeply resented in a drought-stricken province. War conditions similarly dampened activity. Then the closing of Government House by the new CCF government in 1945 prevented any revival of earlier social patterns. Subsequent entertaining has been at the Hotel Saskatchewan, and in line with society's generally more casual approach, the number of formal functions has declined. In 1973, for example, the long-standing tradition of the New Year Levee was quietly dropped.

The emphasis has shifted from the former almost mandatory duties of playing host to the less conspicuous lending of patronage and presence to various associations and events. Occasions such as the province's Jubilee celebrations bring the lieutenant governor in demand to attend and extend congratulations to a wide variety of functions throughout the province. There may also be Canada-wide encouragement of enterprises in which the Governor General wishes his provincial counterparts to assist. In general, however, the extent and direction of activity of the modern lieutenant governor is left to his own initiative to make of his job largely what he wishes. He may take the direction of his own personal interests or provide encouragement in areas which he feels have been overlooked or neglected.

The term of office of a lieutenant governor is normally five years. With no mandatory limits either of age or length of tenure, lieutenant governors have sometimes continued in office for some months or even years longer before a new appointment has been made. Re-appointment has occurred only once, when the Hon. H. W. Newlands was in office from 1921 to 1931.

The appointment [of a lieutenant governor] is one of the things wholly in the gift of the Prime Minister, but, as we are a friendly government, we may naturally expect to be taken into previous confidence. Owing to the relationship which must exist between the appointee and myself, I consider myself precluded from giving any expression on the question except to the Prime Minister and then only in the event of his inviting me to do so.[3]

This reply by Premier Scott in 1910 to an enquiry respecting the lieutenant governor's job sums up the established procedure for appointment. Prime Minister Laurier confirmed the practice in responding to urgent representations which certain Liberals in Saskatchewan made to him respecting a new appointment:

I have consulted only one man with reference to the appointment which is to be made for that province and that man is Walter Scott. I do not realize what objection there could be to that course. Walter Scott is as good a Grit as you or I, and has more interest in the question than any one else, much more than you or I, and if there is one man who above every other has the right to advise in such matters, it is certainly he.
. . . I do not mean to imply that I abdicate my judgment, and if he were to offer some advice which would not be suitable, I would do as I do under all circumstances—take my own course.
I will receive with great respect the memorial which you say the Members from the Province are preparing for me, but here again, I must say that I reserve to myself the right to judge and determine.[4]

It is to be noted that the tradition of consultation exists only when there are "friendly" governments at Regina and Ottawa. This tradition led to misunderstanding in the first appointment to be made after the CCF came to power. The immediately previous appointments in the province had been made with the Liberals in power at both levels of government, and Premier Douglas expected the same consultation which had previously occurred. He met firm refusal from

Prime Minister King, who pointed out that consultation was a matter of choice on the part of the Prime Minister, not one of necessity.[5]

Unlike some provinces in which a substantial private income has been necessary to meet heavy social obligations, in Saskatchewan the salary of the lieutenant governor has in some instances provided a much needed means of livelihood. Although the private means possessed by some incumbents have been of real advantage in entertaining, and lack of entertainment has caused unpopularity in other instances, appointments have not gone necessarily to the well-to-do.

The swearing-in of a new lieutenant governor usually is a simple ceremony. Earlier it was carried out at Government House, but in later years it has been held either in the court house, the executive council chamber, or in the lieutenant governor's office in the Hotel Saskatchewan. The Commission to appoint the new official is read by the clerk of the executive council, and the oath is administered by the chief justice of the province, with cabinet ministers, government officials, and the family and close friends of the lieutenant governor usually present. It was an entirely different occasion in 1905 when the swearing-in of the lieutenant governor was conducted before a huge crowd as part of the inaugural ceremonies of the province. There was also an exception to the usual pattern in 1921, when the new appointee was sworn in at Ottawa while returning to Regina from a trip outside the country.

As might be expected, all fifteen appointees have been long-time residents of the province, and in early years especially they tended to be prominent political supporters of the party appointing them. After A. E. Forget and George W. Brown, Richard S. Lake became lieutenant governor in 1915, the first appointee of a Conservative government at Ottawa. A pioneer farmer in the Territories, Mr. Lake had sat in the Territorial assembly before he became a Conservative member of Parliament from 1904 to 1911. Judge H. W. Newlands, in office from 1921 to 1931, had been a judge of the Supreme Court of the Territories and later of Saskatchewan. Judge Newlands, and Dr. H. E. Munroe who followed him in 1931, were among the few earlier appointees who had not previously been elected members at either Regina or Ottawa.

Archie McNab, lieutenant governor from 1936 to 1945, spanned the depression and war years. A miller and grain merchant, Mr. McNab had a political career that included nineteen years as a Liberal member of the Saskatchewan legislature. Sixteen of these years were in the cabinet, where he served from 1910 to 1926, under the first three premiers of the province.

"Archie of Saskatchewan", as he was dubbed by Governor General Tweedsmuir, undoubtedly gave the sprightliest performance of all lieutenant governors, and he left behind a host of tales of his informality and unpretentiousness. One of his first acts after becoming lieutenant governor was to throw open the gates of Government House to provide a short cut for children on their way to school. He had a particular fondness for old cars and for picking up passengers on his daily trips to the legislative building, and he carried this informality into official duties by smiling and acknowledging the greetings of friends as he entered and left the legislative chamber when opening the House. He cheerily invited the King and Queen, during their 1939 royal tour, to come again "when you can bring the kids."

A visiting newspaperman who was in Regina to cover commission sittings in 1938 was intrigued by the lieutenant governor's "smiling gnome's face", and even more so by an incident he saw during the hearings. The lieutenant governor had tiptoed in to observe, and he unwittingly took the chair of a local official who was concerned with the proceedings. When that person returned he casually requested the lieutenant governor, "Move over, Archie." And, reported the fascinated observer, "Archie moved over."[6]

Thomas Miller, a newspaperman appointed in 1945, was the first of three successive lieutenant governors to die in office. When Mr. Miller died only a few months after his appointment, he was succeeded by R. J. M. Parker, who died in 1948 toward the end of the legislative session. His death created an urgent situation, with bills to be assented to and a House to prorogue. An administrator, usually the chief justice of the province, carries out the duties of the lieutenant governor if he is out of the province or ill, or for some other reason unable to act. An administrator cannot act, however, if the office is vacant, so a new lieutenant governor had to be chosen quickly. This choice was made on the day of Mr. Parker's death, when Dr. J. M. Uhrich was appointed, despite a reluctance on his part, accentuated in these circumstances by a close personal friendship with Mr. Parker, who previously had been his desk-mate in the assembly.

W. J. Patterson, appointed in 1951 upon Dr. Uhrich's death, has been the only former premier to hold the post, and he was also the first provincial-born lieutenant governor. Mr. Patterson was succeeded in 1958 by Frank L. Bastedo, a Regina lawyer who treated his new position with as much formality as McNab had greeted it with informality. Robert L. Hanbidge, who held the office from 1963 until 1970, had roots in the early history of the province which included articling in 1909 in the law firm of Frederick Haultain, the Territorial premier and later the chief justice of Saskatchewan. Mr. Hanbidge had a particular interest in sports, and in his official duties he not only encouraged sports activities but at the same time acquired a reputation as a friendly and informal raconteur.

Appointments in the 1970s showed a departure from the long-standing practice of appointing senior or retired politicians. There has been a shift to those with more varied backgrounds and even to some who are still pursuing their own careers. In the appointment of Dr. Stephen Worobetz in 1970, the influence of a provincial Liberal premier with a Liberal government at Ottawa was evident, even though the relationship of the two levels of government was not so cordial on all matters. Premier Thatcher thought that the contribution made by Ukrainians in the development of Saskatchewan had long been overlooked and might be recognized in this way. Dr. Worobetz, a Saskatoon physician, also broke with tradition by continuing his profession for a time, carrying out his duties as a part-time lieutenant governor during the first years of his appointment.

George Porteous, appointed in 1976, was a survivor of a Hong Kong prisoner of war camp who had been active in community affairs, especially among senior citizens. Although he was seventy-two years of age when he was appointed, he established a high profile in the office, travelling widely, keeping many speaking engagements, and taking particular pleasure in visiting schools wherever he went. His sudden death in February, 1978, shortly before the legislative session was to open, required the quick appointment of a successor, although the appointment was not so urgent as when Mr. Parker had died thirty years earlier.

Irwin McIntosh, who succeeded Mr. Porteous in February, 1978, at fifty-two years of age was the youngest appointee since 1910. His appointment required him to interrupt his career as a publisher in North Battleford in order to carry out the rounds of travelling and visiting imposed by his new job.

None of the last three lieutenant governors took up residence in Regina. Dr. Worobetz and Mr. Porteous kept their respective homes in Saskatoon, and Mr. McIntosh has kept his in North Battleford, each spending time in the office in Regina as necessary, when not carrying out duties in other parts of the province.

A private status for the lieutenant governor, separate from his official position, was confirmed in the early years of the Saskatchewan legislature. In 1912 Lieutenant Governor Brown, as "a barrister of Regina," with two others petitioned the legislature to be incorporated as a trust company. The opposition in the House protested the impropriety in the lieutenant governor, as one portion of the legislature, petitioning the other portion for private legislation to which he would have to give assent in his official capacity. The attorney general in debate upheld a distinction between Mr. Brown as a representative of the Crown and Mr. Brown as a private citizen, and the legislation was passed. This action conformed to a tradition from colonial days that "a Governor can legally take a benefit under a statute of the colony . . . though he is himself a necessary party to it, as in fact he is to all legislation in the colony."[7]

This tradition of private status does not mean that the lieutenant governor has freedom to speak out on political or controversial topics. A comment by Mr. McIntosh in 1978 favouring reinstitution of the death penalty in certain instances did not go unnoticed. The press reported Premier Blakeney's reference to the precedent that governor generals and lieutenant governors do not make statements on matters of active political debate and his remark that the lieutenant governor's comment was probably unwise.

The need for a lieutenant governor has been publicly questioned from time to time. During the 1930s, assembly members on more than one occasion moved to eliminate the office as an economy measure, leaving the duties to be performed by the chief justice. The CCF objected on principle to the office and would have liked to abolish it when they came to power, but the most they could do was to close Government House, which they saw as an unnecessary expense and a relic of a bygone age. Any suggestion to eliminate the office has foundered on the reality that the office is safeguarded in the B.N.A. Act. Whatever may be done about expenditures or residence, the position itself remains.

There is no set relationship between a lieutenant governor and the premier. The extent of consultation between the two and the degree to which the lieutenant governor has been informed of government business has varied widely, depending upon the personal relationship between the two officials and their respective attitudes. This varying degree of communication is well illustrated in the relations of Premier Scott with the first three lieutenant governors. Although the premier had been a political as well as a personal friend of each of the first two incumbents, he had markedly different relations with each of them in office. Scott noted that Mr. Forget had become almost a recluse, and his own practice was to send recommendations for the lieutenant governor's signature, but to see him personally very seldom.

Relations between Scott and Lieutenant Governor Brown were unusually close, and the personal relationship overshadowed the official one. Their earlier friendship continued after Brown's appointment, and they travelled together on occasion as they had done before. Scott sometimes spent a few days at a time at Government House, the lieutenant governor lent Scott money on at least one occasion, and at times when the premier was absent from the province, the lieutenant governor kept him informed in a general way of government activity.

After the appointment in 1915 of Richard Lake, the extent of regular consultation evidently was limited. Aside from their differing political affiliations, this return to limited communication with the lieutenant governor may be explained in part by Scott's continuing as premier only a little more than a year after Lake's appointment, during which time he was not well and was away from Regina a great deal. And, as noted later in this chapter, discussions between the two at a time of government crisis early in 1916 strained relations. Premier Martin, who succeeded Scott in October of 1916, took care to keep the lieutenant governor informed about proposed legislation and other government matters, and there was frequent consultation between the two. In 1935 Premier Gardiner pointed to the office of lieutenant governor as a necessary link between outgoing and incoming governments, and said that the lieutenant governor had been of real service to him upon occasion when he had sought advice. In recent administrations the relationship has been formal and routine, without consultation on government business and with no additional information provided to the lieutenant governor beyond that contained in documents presented for his signature.

The lieutenant governor has been charged with partisanship upon occasion. In at least two instances, charges that he favored the government through inaction were completely unjustified. In 1908, when the Liberal government called a snap election after being in office for less than three years, the opposition press suggested that if the lieutenant governor had not been a part of the party machine he would have prevented the surprise dissolution.

After the 1929 election, when no party emerged with a majority, the incumbent Liberals decided to meet the House instead of resigning immediately. The opposition demanded that the lieutenant governor dismiss the government. Because the Conservatives had won more seats than the Liberals, the Conservative press took up the cry and bitterly criticized the lieutenant governor for failure to act. In each of these instances the government action was not in violation of any constitutional principle and no crisis existed to justify intervention. Opposition outrage arose in fact from their unhappiness over the particular political circumstances rather than over any constitutional impropriety. Action by the lieutenant governor was not only unnecessary but would have been improper in either instance.

More genuine questions arose on three other occasions. The first of these was the first official act of a lieutenant governor of the province, when he appointed Walter Scott as the new premier in 1905. Since F. W. G. Haultain had headed the Territorial government, it was widely expected that he would continue as the first provincial premier. Many considered it shabby treatment for him to be by-passed in view of the prominent part which he had played in constitutional struggles.

Criticism of the choice of Scott instead of Haultain included mention that Scott had not even been a member of the Territorial legislature. As noted earlier, Scott had been a member of the House of Commons until he resigned to accept the leadership of the newly formed provincial Liberal party in August, 1905, whereupon he had been chosen premier of the new province. It was charged that federal Liberals had intervened in the choice in order to secure control in the province and in order to prevent a judicial appeal to the Privy Council on the clauses in the new constitution which related to schools and lands.

There can be little doubt that these charges were true. During the last two years of Territorial government, the earlier confidence which the Liberals had placed in Haultain had turned to distrust, as described in chapter 2. By the time a choice of premier had to be made, members of the federal government and western Liberal M.P.'s were seriously concerned over Haultain's expressed determination to submit the Alberta and Saskatchewan Acts to the courts in order to test their constitutionality.

Whatever the extent to which Liberal concern was for the welfare of the new provinces or for party fortunes, Prime Minister Laurier reluctantly became persuaded that Haultain could not be appointed premier of Saskatchewan. It was clear that the real decision lay with the Prime Minister and not with Lieutenant Governor Forget, whose constitutional duty it was to make the appointment. When charged later in the House of Commons with interference, Laurier denied, incorrectly, that he had had any correspondence with the lieutenant governor on the matter. Even if the crudity of a direct order was not required, the choice was made in accordance with the Prime Minister's express wishes.

For those interested in greater detail, an account of the course of events and correspondence involved in this matter is included in the supplement on page 203.

The second incident of controversy was in 1916, after the appointment in the previous October of the former Conservative member of Parliament, R. S. Lake, as lieutenant governor. Early in 1916 rumors circulated that the new lieutenant governor was part of a plot to oust the provincial Liberal government of Walter Scott. These rumors were accompanied by Conservative press reports of impending scandal in the Scott government.

Events in Manitoba in 1915 formed a backdrop for the rumors in Saskatchewan. In Manitoba the reverse political situation had existed: that province had had a provincial Conservative government while the lieutenant governor was a Liberal appointee of Prime Minister Laurier. At issue were charges of corruption in the construction of the Manitoba legislative building. The Conservative government of the province so steadfastly resisted any investigation that the Liberal opposition finally presented a petition to the lieutenant governor. The lieutenant governor agreed there was sufficient need for an enquiry to justify his intervention and, by threat of dismissal, he forced the government to appoint a commission of investigation. The results of the investigation showed that the Manitoba government had been deeply involved in corruption and spelled the end of their Conservative administration.

Saskatchewan now presented an opportunity for political retaliation, according to rumor. Premier Walter Scott gave official notice to the rumors when he referred to them in the throne speech debate in the Saskatchewan legislature early in 1916. He spoke of Conservative newspaper reports of disclosures to be made against his government and of the suggestion that the Conservative opposition in the legislature would demand a royal commission into aspects of his administration. If the government refused, Scott explained, the newspaper reports said an appeal would be made over his head to the lieutenant governor, as had happened in Manitoba.

On February 10 it appeared that the script was being played out. J. E. Bradshaw, a Conservative member of the assembly, charged fraud among Liberal members in road contracts, and bribery and improper conduct over liquor administration. He asked for a royal commission investigation. Bradshaw declined to name members but left the charges general, and the government refused a royal commission. Instead, it set up legislative committees to investigate. The Conservative opposition refused to serve on the committees, and on February 21 Mr. Bradshaw brought specific charges of corruption against four members of the government. The sequel included appointment of three royal commissions of investigation which cleared all cabinet ministers, although four members of the legislature and certain civil servants were shown to be implicated.

Although controversial, these events did not lead to any constitutional crisis. Unlike that of Manitoba, the Saskatchewan government did set up royal commissions to investigate when specific charges were made. None of the charges against cabinet ministers were established, and the government took immediate action against the private members and civil servants who were found to be implicated, with the result that some were sent to jail. Not only was the lieutenant governor not pushed to the necessity of exercising any reserve or emergency power, but there was no evidence to show his participation in any way in a plan to discredit the government, participation which, if it had been proved, would have been a serious breach of responsibility.

During the unfolding of these events, however, behind-the-scenes relations between the premier and the lieutenant governor deteriorated as a result of their conflicting views of the role of lieutenant governor, which were revealed during a week of frequent private discussions between the two men. In general, the lieutenant governor thought he had greater freedom to seek advice outside his responsible ministers than Premier Scott thought he might properly take under the existing circumstances. The discussions played no significant part in the events themselves and were never made public. They are mainly of academic interest in revealing the gropings of both premier and lieutenant governor in unfamiliar constitutional fields. Further description of the precise nature of their discussions is included in the supplement on page 203.

The third incident of controversy was in 1961, when Lieutenant Governor Bastedo unexpectedly reserved a bill passed by the assembly. This action startled both levels of government and embarrassed mainly the federal Conservative government which had appointed Mr. Bastedo. The lieutenant governor's action meant that the federal government now was brought into the picture, either to reject the provincial legislation or to assent to it.

The bill in question was the Alteration of Certain Mineral Contracts. It concerned the terms under which oil companies had secured mineral rights from farmers, and the legislation had a long and uneasy background. The oil companies had contracted for the mineral rights of many farmers before the discovery of oil in certain areas of the province in the 1950s. Farmers had not realized the potential value of their oil rights, and, as the Hon. A. E. Blakeney now explained in the legislature, many of those who had signed their mineral rights away had not understood the nature of the contracts. In some instances the terms were so unfair to the farmer as to be, as Blakeney expressed it, unconscionable.

Attempts that were made in the 1950s to correct the inequities were only partly successful. Legal action had been tried, but it was a slow and expensive process for farmers, who were ill-matched in contests against the oil companies. In 1959 the government set up a Mineral Contracts Renegotiation Board which had succeeded in renegotiating a large number of the contracts. One oil company, however, held out and refused to negotiate. Thus the purpose behind the 1961 legislation was to require this company to renegotiate its contracts along the same lines as those agreed to by the other oil companies.

A bill to renegotiate existing contracts was not the sort of legislation that any government likes to pass. It was, in starkest terms, wielding a big stick over the oil company. It is significant, however, that even though the government admitted its legislation was distasteful, there was support for it from the other side of the House. Liberal opposition leader Ross Thatcher agreed with the objective of the bill and frankly admitted that his party found itself in a quandary. This quandary was reflected in opposition voting. Of a total of seventeen Liberal opposition members only six voted against the bill, including the leader. Four joined the government in supporting it, and the other seven did not vote. The bill therefore had not aroused any sharp difference of opinion in the legislature but had been accepted, in the main, as unpleasant but necessary.

Mr. Bastedo acted on his own initiative in reserving the bill, apparently being unaware that the lieutenant governor's power of reservation was regarded as obsolete. He also apparently did not know that since a federal directive of 1882 it was understood that in any event lieutenant governors would not act without prior consultation with Ottawa.

Prime Minister Diefenbaker emphatically denied that there had been any instructions from Ottawa. Had he been consulted, the Prime Minister said, he would have told the lieutenant governor not to reserve the bill. There is every reason to believe Mr. Diefenbaker. The lieutenant governor's action placed the federal government in too awkward a situation for the Prime Minister to have in any way contributed to it.

Lieutenant Governor Bastedo based his action on the double grounds of doubt as to the legislation's validity and doubt of its being in the public interest. Ottawa rejected both arguments. The federal Minister of Justice held that the province had the right to pass the legislation and that it was therefore valid. And the federal government did not agree that it conflicted with the public interest, saying that merely a "difference of opinion or point of view" did not mean conflict with national policy or interest. Mr. Bastedo apparently did not realize that even if either of his objections had substance, the remedy more properly lay through means other than his reservation of the bill. If the legislation was not valid, the question was for the courts to decide; if it was a matter of public interest, the federal cabinet could act on its own by using disallowance.

With the federal government's assent the bill became law as passed by the legislative assembly. The only practical effect of the lieutenant governor's action was that the federal government now would have to share the blame, if there was to be any, for legislation which even its originators had considered unpalatable.

Political reaction varied. The national leader of the CCF, Hazen Argue, called for the lieutenant governor's resignation. The former leader of the party, Mr. Coldwell, revived the CCF demand for abolition of the office. In Saskatchewan, the leader of the opposition, Ross Thatcher, gave cautious approval to the reservation. He reiterated Liberal party approval of the purpose of the legislation but said that he was afraid it gave the government sweeping and arbitrary power. There were rumors of federal dismissal of the lieutenant governor, but it was unclear if these had any greater substance than curiosity as to whether the action was possible. The lieutenant governor served out his term, although it is notable that at its conclusion a successor was named with somewhat more dispatch than usual.

9   The Cabinet

The cabinet is the center of government activity and administration. That the terms *cabinet* and *government* are interchangeable indicates the reality of its authority, which contrasts with its theoretical position. In the unreality of constitutional language it acts as an advisory body to, or in conjunction with the lieutenant governor, in whose name all action is carried out. Theoretically the lieutenant governor selects the cabinet. In reality he makes the formal appointment of the premier who then chooses his colleagues. Even the cabinet name is unofficial, a substitute for the official title of executive council.

An increase in the number of cabinet ministers in Saskatchewan from the original four in 1905 to twenty in 1979 represents the ever widening extent and scope of government administration. Originally Clifford Sifton advised the new premier that a cabinet of three would be sufficient, admonishing Scott that "any larger number would look like unnecessarily multiplying portfolios." More recent increases have elicited similar comment from the opposition, who frequently charge unnecessary proliferation in the number of ministers.

The first addition to the original four was made in 1908, with an increase to seven in 1913. This number continued as the customary size of the cabinet to the end of the Liberal regime in 1929. Premier Anderson raised the total to ten, including two ministers without portfolio. In the course of the CCF administration the number grew from eleven to fifteen and then dropped to thirteen under the Liberals. Upon assuming office in 1971, Premier Blakeney proceeded slowly with cabinet appointments. He began with nine members, several of whom held double portfolios. He soon increased the number to relieve ministers of their extra duties, and the cabinet eventually reached the peak size of twenty.

The choice of cabinet ministers in the province is beset by substantially fewer problems than at Ottawa, but it is not without difficulty. The merit of the prospective appointee is a foremost consideration, but a cabinet which includes between one-third and one-half of the government side of the House inevitably extends through widely varying areas of ability. There has been a firm tradition of choosing only elected members in forming a new administration, and in only a few instances has a premier subsequently gone outside the House for a ministerial appointment. In such instances the requirement has been scrupulously observed that the appointee find a seat without delay.

Geographical demands were particularly important in early days, and they sometimes proved difficult in a small cabinet. Even the relatively uncomplicated north–south division that had to be satisfied in the first cabinet caused grief. J. H. Lamont, a prominent Prince Albert lawyer, was chosen attorney general, both as an able man and as one who could be looked upon as a suitable representative for the north. The choice caused the defection of an equally able lawyer from the south, J. T. Brown, to the Provincial Rights party, where Premier Scott regarded him as the government's ablest opponent. In later years maintaining a rural-urban balance and paying proper attention to the respective cities developed as refinements of geographical considerations.

Attention to religion has varied. Despite a provincial population approaching one-third Roman Catholic, cabinets have been predominantly Protestant, and some have been exclusively so. In reply to a complaint that Roman Catholics were being overlooked in the first cabinet, Premier Scott stated that it had been formed without regard to sectarian distinction: "Geographical considerations had to be remembered," he explained, but with that exception "nothing but fitness for the work was considered. . . ."[1]

Whether or not this prodding was among the reasons for the selection of W. F. A. Turgeon as attorney general in 1907, Scott came to find Roman Catholic representation a useful defense in matters such as separate schools. When Laurier later proposed the appointment of Turgeon to the Supreme Court, Scott protested that with no other Roman Catholic lawyer qualified, he would be compelled to select a Protestant as Turgeon's successor.

Scott's precedent was not always followed, although there has been greater Catholic representation in recent administrations than in some earlier ones. When J. E. Burton was appointed to the CCF cabinet in 1952, his standing with the Catholic church and with the German population were factors in his favor. Premier Thatcher considered both Catholic and ethnic representation essential, and the NDP similarly has cabinet representation in both areas.

Previous cabinet experience is a qualification difficult for a premier to overlook. After a relatively short period out of office, as when the Liberals returned to power in 1934 or when the NDP came back in 1971, former cabinet ministers still remain among the legislative membership. This carry-over may open the way to a welcome balance of experience among newcomers. It may, on the other hand, restrict a premier's effective freedom of choice. Unlike a Canadian Prime Minister, a Saskatchewan premier has no senate to which he may graduate either the senior party faithful or the political embarrassments.

Particular skills or experience that match an appointee to his portfolio frequently are pointed to as necessary or desirable. Such thinking ignores the reality that specialized knowledge will be supplied by departmental officials. For the minister, the qualities of "intelligence, integrity, and common sense head the list of requirements," at the provincial as well as at the federal level.

Of course there is always the possibility that the occupation of the minister may be relevant in particular circumstances so as to retain public confidence. This consideration was evident in the agriculture department in 1920–21. In the midst of farmer unrest the premier went to considerable pains to find convincing leadership for that department. Agriculture Minister C. A. Dunning, although he was active in farmers' organizations, was not actually a farmer, and he was shifted out of the post in 1920. The attempt to shore up the government's situation was described to the former premier of Saskatchewan, Walter Scott, by his secretary of those earlier days:

The Government here has made one more effort to stem the rising tide of farmer feeling against them by appointing a bona fide farmer to the Cabinet in the person of Hon. C. M. Hamilton. Mr. Hamilton has loudly announced that he will still retain his home on his farm and only spend such time in Regina as his official duties make necessary. Personally, I think they might as well save their wind to cool their porridge.[2]

Premier Martin obviously concluded that this appointment left something to be desired. After the 1921 election J. A. Maharg, president of the Saskatchewan Grain Growers' Association, assumed the post of Minister of Agriculture. The appointment involved an ambiguous alliance, and it was short-lived. Before entering provincial politics Mr. Maharg had sat with the Progressives in the House of Commons, and he had been elected to the Saskatchewan legislature as "Independent pro-Government." He entered the provincial cabinet on the understanding that he could continue his support of the Progressive party federally, and in doing so, as he understood it, he would have "more or less the sympathy of the different members of ... Government."[3] Maharg subsequently objected that Premier Martin's support of the Liberal candidate, W. R. Motherwell, against a Progressive in a federal election late in 1921 violated their agreement. Mr. Maharg consequently resigned his cabinet position, six months after assuming it. Mr. Hamilton then returned to the post for the remainder of the Liberal tenure of office.

Some decades later the CCF government similarly found itself faced with an urgent need to strengthen a vulnerable cabinet post. Walter Erb had held the public health portfolio from 1956, and his performance even in normal circumstances inspired little confidence in leaving him to occupy a key position in the looming medicare battle. Accordingly he was moved to a less vital portfolio late in 1961. Again, the emergency shift resulted in defection, this time of the minister who had been moved. Six months after the change, with the medicare crisis at a peak, Mr. Erb made a sudden announcement that he would leave his new post as well as the NDP caucus to sit as an independent. Shortly afterwards he moved to the Liberal benches.

The executive duties of a minister are twofold. Individually he is head of his department; collectively he shares with his colleagues general cabinet oversight. As head of a department he is ultimately responsible for all its activities, is its spokesman, and provides liaison between it and the public, the legislature, and the cabinet. As a member of the cabinet he participates in broad policy decisions and jointly assumes responsibility for overall government performance. Saskatchewan has had few ministers without portfolio—involved only in general cabinet duties and without a department to administer. Premier Anderson included two such ministers from 1929 to 1934, one from his own Conservative party and one matching member from the Progressives. Otherwise such appointments have been used only for exceptional circumstances. In 1941 the Hon. E. M. Culliton left his cabinet duties for military service, and in 1956 the Hon. J. H. Sturdy relinquished long departmental service to assume a newly created post as assistant to the premier. Each was designated Minister without Portfolio.

The legislative duties of a cabinet minister include preparing and piloting through the house all legislation concerning his department or related areas of jurisdiction. And, like other members, the minister owes allegiance to his constituents and must respond to their needs and requests.

Demands upon a cabinet minister extend in a less official way, and in varying degrees, into two other areas—the representation of a region, and performance of party functions. Both of these responsibilities overlap his duties as a legislative member, but they extend further. To the extent that cabinet posts represent a geographical region, each minister, in a general and informal way, may be expected to keep a watchful eye on the interests of his area. Party activity similarly is an integral part of legislative life, but a cabinet minister usually finds himself with substantially heavier political responsibilities than his backbencher colleague.

As noted in chapter 7, the salary rate for cabinet ministers in 1979 was $43,000 annually, and for the premier, $49,750, in addition to the sessional indemnity and other allowances which each receives as a legislative member. Increases from the salary of $5,000 which ministers originally received in 1905 ($6,000 for the premier) have not progressed in a straight line. The level of $7,200 ($9,000 for the premier) reached by 1928 was reduced in the drought years of the 1930s to $6,000 ($7,500), where it remained until 1944. One of the first acts of the new CCF government upon assuming office was to reduce ministers' salaries to the 1905 level of $5,000. As a result, Saskatchewan cabinet ministers' salaries were the lowest in Canada, except for those in Prince Edward Island, until there was an increase in 1953 to $7,000 for ministers and $8,500 for the premier, with further subsequent increases.

Legislative secretaries, chosen from M.L.A.'s to assist cabinet ministers, were first provided for in 1965. Debate in the legislature on establishment of the office centered on the Liberal government's claim that economy would result, since legislative secretaries would make a smaller cabinet possible. Secretaries would work part-time in departmental duties, and they initially received $2,000 (by 1979 raised to $5,000) in addition to their legislative indemnity. The unsuccessful opposition objection was that the government would be better advised to appoint more cabinet ministers instead. Legislative secretaries held office for a one-year term, and one-half of the six original Liberal appointees subsequently were appointed to the cabinet. The NDP made some initial appointments upon coming to power, but they have used the office less than did their Liberal predecessors, although three members held the office when the legislature was dissolved in 1978 for an election. In general, however, the NDP have followed the approach that they argued for as the opposition in 1965, of enlarging the cabinet rather than using legislative secretaries.

Good administration remains a primary duty of a CCF Government, and must begin at the top. There can be no real advance toward a planned economy or an integrated administration unless the Cabinet operates as a supreme and continuing entity. It is therefore of prime importance to establish a Cabinet secretariat which will give the Cabinet permanent existence and undisputed authority by clear directives and good organization of its business.[4]

This statement of purpose in 1948 represented a start toward orderly cabinet procedures which at the time was unique among provincial governments. In Britain and at Ottawa the respective demands of the first and second world wars had led to establishment of a cabinet secretariat. In Saskatchewan, along with the CCF ideological emphasis on structured processes, there was a genuine concern to affirm the "undisputed authority" of the cabinet. The CCF emphasis on planning and the consequent importance accorded to the planning agency, combined with an aggressive personality at its head, had raised the danger that the government would come to be dominated by its own creature. This danger became evident in a power struggle between the chairman of the planning board and the provincial treasurer.

Upon assuming office in 1944 the CCF had continued the traditional practice of leaving cabinet organization and management exclusively to the premier. He kept notes of decisions arrived at and occasionally forwarded a memorandum to remind a minister about a matter requiring action. The expressed recognition in 1948 of the desirability of formal organization was shortly followed by establishment of a secretariat. It was not until 1950 that the cabinet secretary attended all cabinet meetings to record discussions and decisions. In the interval, practices moved gradually in that direction. The premier at first kept the minutes; later he dictated them in general form for purposes of record and had ministers advised respecting decisions; still later the secretary sat in at some cabinet meetings to take notes, and then he eventually assumed full responsibility for this duty at all meetings.[5]

The order in council of November 30, 1948, which outlined the objectives and functions of the secretariat, attached it to the premier's office. In addition to keeping minutes, the secretary prepared the cabinet agenda and distributed information to members concerning matters to be raised in cabinet. Ministers were to forward to the secretary notice of items they wished included on the agenda, or to give advance notice at one cabinet meeting of a matter that was to be raised at the next meeting. Last-minute items might be included, although lack of time rarely permitted discussion of items that were not on the agenda. The agenda itself was not circulated to ministers in advance, and the premier might always determine the order in which items were to be discussed. Minutes went only to ministers, and normally each minister received only those portions of the minutes that were his own concern. In practice considerable flexibility existed in cabinet procedure. Items on the agenda might be carried over successively from one meeting to the next, and advance circulation of information was not widely observed.

A new spirit in cabinet procedure became evident in 1961 under Premier Lloyd's direction. Despite a brief tenure which opened in the face of the medicare crisis and closed with the election of 1964, attention was given to a re-ordering of cabinet processes. This re-ordering included a division of duties among secretariat personnel, a tightening-up of existing procedures, and the examination of new practices that were to be introduced.

The "secretariat" established in 1948 had consisted of a cabinet secretary. His wide-ranging functions included, in addition to his secretarial duties, acting as clerk of the executive council, as executive assistant to the premier, and as press liaison. A division of duties was effected in 1961. The position of executive assistant was separated from that of a combined secretary and clerk of the executive council, and some months later a third person was appointed for press liaison.

Immediate changes in procedures consisted mainly in following more conscientiously the practices which previously had been accepted in principle. There was an effort to pre-plan cabinet discussions more, to get ministers to identify agenda items ahead of time, to provide written information, and generally to tighten up practices.[6]

In 1963 a committee on cabinet procedure, formed from among ministers and senior administrative personnel, reviewed existing methods of handling items on the cabinet agenda, orders in council, and legislation. Recommendations that were made by the committee and approved by cabinet included the elimination from cabinet

discussion of specified routine matters, the more efficient documentation of items coming to cabinet, and the grouping and arrangement of
agenda items in order to prevent duplication of discussion. Orders in
council were to be approved by a committee headed by the attorney
general and reporting in general terms to the cabinet. Any minister
could have an order referred to cabinet for consideration.

Defects identified by the committee in the cabinet handling of
legislation were the late arrival of proposed legislation, its unsystema-
tic presentation, and a lack of formal records of decisions made. It was
noted also that cabinet time was spent in performing staff duties of
checking draftsmanship, seeing that details conformed with principle,
and considering civil rights and financial implications. The cabinet
agreed that among procedures which ministers should take up with
their departments for discussion was the early preparation of minor
and non-controversial items of legislation. The ministers also agreed
that principles of legislation only should be raised in cabinet, leaving
all drafting and routine duties to be done by administrative personnel.
All draft legislation should then be submitted to a cabinet committee
on legislation for scrutiny of details and of various implications.[7]
Despite this initial consideration, the problem of efficient handling of
legislation remained unresolved when the government went out of
office a year later.

Two other bodies contributed to the performance of cabinet
functions, the Economic Advisory and Planning Board, and the
Treasury Board. These will be discussed at greater length in
succeeding chapters, but it should be noted that the Economic
Advisory and Planning Board, despite the broad planning role which
its title indicates, came increasingly to perform duties of a cabinet
secretariat. The Treasury Board was the most prominent cabinet
committee, having statutory existence and a staff which served the
cabinet in matters of finance and organization.

Increasing use was made of a variety of cabinet committees, either
more or less formally organized as ad hoc or as relatively long-term
bodies. Committees frequently included senior administrators as well
as ministers. An ad hoc committee might look into an isolated
circumstance, such as a problem arising out of proposed legislation or
a particular situation concerning a civil servant. Other committees
might deal with more general matters requiring either short- or
longer-term consideration. In 1962 a party organization committee to
prepare for the election and in 1963 a committee on the Federal
Municipal Development and Loan Fund were added to existing
committees such as those on industrial development, medical care,
publicity and emergency measures, and minority groups. The
government Labor Liaison Committee established in 1962 "to study
and discuss important problems of mutual concern, arrive at some
common understanding and resolve major differences of opinion"
went beyond a cabinet committee as such to include membership from
labor as well as cabinet representation and administrative personnel.

The development of structured cabinet organization was halted with the accession of Premier Thatcher in 1964. His personal inclinations as well as Liberal party tradition harked back to the pre-1940s method of having cabinet direction stem entirely from the premier. No formal minutes were kept of cabinet meetings. Mr. Thatcher reportedly had gained access to at least some CCF cabinet minutes, and he had no intention of providing a reciprocal opportunity. Furthermore, it was in line with his general approach to maintain personal scrutiny over areas of particular interest to him. Decisions tended to be implemented as a result of personal communication or of reminders sent to ministers from notes made by the premier or the secretary at cabinet meetings.

Little attention apparently was given to separation of duties among personnel in the premier's office, although specific titles were assigned. Part of the time, for example, the positions of secretary of the cabinet and clerk of the executive council were separate, but separate in name rather than in fact. The respective incumbents worked together without appreciable distinction of powers, with either of them preparing the cabinet agenda. At other times the jobs were combined, and perhaps other duties would be added, such as those of assistant to the clerk of the legislature. An administrative innovation was to give the clerk of the executive council the status of a permanent head. He was to act in effect as a deputy minister for the agencies which reported directly to the premier, and during Mr. Thatcher's administration such agencies became numerous.

The form of the Treasury Board was retained, although for a time Premier Thatcher, as provincial treasurer, exercised its functions by himself. The Economic Advisory and Planning Board, renamed the Economic Development Board, survived in a much reduced form under the management and protection of the premier's executive assistant, Jim Moore. The board was abolished after Mr. Moore's departure in 1969.

The contrast between the outlook of Premier Lloyd and that of Premier Thatcher in all aspects of government organization is probably nowhere better illustrated than in the short history of the Saskatchewan Public Administration Foundation. Premier Lloyd established the body in 1963 to encourage research in public administration and policy, and in related fields. The independence of the foundation was safeguarded by its manner of funding, which was the income from a million-dollar grant with which the government had established the foundation and its personnel. The chairman, political science professor Norman Ward, not only was not an NDP supporter but, as he revealed in later writing, was in fact at the time a member of the Liberal party. Establishment of the research foundation was innovative, and it was characteristic of Mr. Lloyd's approach to provide an avenue for thoughtful and comprehensive examination of broad aspects of public administration. It was equally characteristic of Mr. Thatcher, disdainful even of practical day-to-day administrative processes, to have it abolished summarily in 1966 and to put the foundation funds into the consolidated revenue fund.

After coming to power in 1971, the NDP restored and extended the earlier CCF action toward orderly cabinet procedure. This re-ordering was particularly evident in a firm division between the cabinet secretariat and the premier's staff. The secretariat was given formal legislative existence in 1972, with provision for a secretary, a clerk of the executive council, and such other employees as were required. The activities of the office were to be devoted almost exclusively to cabinet requirements, with duties, personnel, and location distinct from the premier's office.

Preparation of the agenda and arrangements for cabinet meetings also became more highly organized. All material for distribution to cabinet members, both from committees and individual ministers, was to go through the secretary's office. This material included reports to cabinet and background information for agenda items, as well as the recommended solution which a minister must submit along with the problem being raised. After any necessary consultation with the premier or a minister, the secretary would reroute matters not requiring cabinet attention, or those which needed prior consideration by Treasury Board or some other cabinet committee. The premier might exercise his discretion in determining the order in which agenda items were discussed, but items from cabinet committees usually came ahead of those from ministers. The cabinet met once a week except during the session, when meetings were held twice a week, with special ones if they were needed.

Considerable use was made of cabinet committees. A Planning and Research Committee was established in 1972 by legislative action, sharing with the Treasury Board the status accorded the two most prominent cabinet committees—and the only ones with their own staffs. A Legislative Review Committee was also set up, bringing to fulfillment the earlier intention of the CCF government. This was a committee of cabinet ministers, but it was also attended by officials of the attorney general's department, the department of finance, and the legislative council, where legislation is drafted. Proposed legislation was to go through this committee on its way to cabinet. The rather considerable problem of keeping a record of the progress of individual items of legislation, recognized earlier, was met in 1974 with the appointment of a person specifically to monitor legislation, to know what stage each legislative item had reached, and to keep each item moving. Establishment of other committees followed much the same pattern as in the former CCF administration. They were formed as needed, as ad hoc or longer-term bodies.

The cabinet's constitutional position inhibits straight-line progress in efficiency and orderliness. Since there is periodically a complete change-over of cabinet personnel, disruption inevitably occurs. This disruption affects delegation more than it affects procedures as such, as the handling of orders in council by the CCF and later by the NDP illustrates. In its latter years, the CCF delegated routine consideration of orders to a cabinet committee. The NDP reverted to the practice of considering orders-in-council in full cabinet, at least initially. This change resulted from the inevitable reluctance of new cabinet ministers to let matters out of their hands, a reluctance that had also been evident in the early years of the CCF, until experience and greater familiarity enabled ministers to distinguish between the routine and the significant.

Such limitations affecting delegation do not necessarily apply to continuity in routine procedures. The orderly handling of cabinet business enhances rather than detracts from a minister's overall comprehension. In the procedural area it is the turnover of the secretariat rather than of the cabinet which is most likely to cause disruption. So far in Saskatchewan the secretariat has changed with the government. After the establishment of the present secretariat structure in 1972, top officials were conscious of the desirability of its detachment from partisan involvement. The continuation of a secretariat from one administration to another, however, rests on more than a non-partisan performance of duties. Such continuation of personnel requires both a confidence on the part of an incoming administration that non-partisanship of the existing secretariat is a reality, and a desire for that non-partisan attitude to continue. In Saskatchewan a barrier in this respect lies in the genuine and deep suspicion felt by one party for the other, and in the tradition of change of personnel which has been established.

As a result of this tradition of change, there is little indication of a permanent secretariat's being achieved in the near future. At Ottawa a distinction was consciously made in the Privy Council Office over a number of years between political sensitivity and partisanship. This distinction acknowledged that the secretary must be attuned to the political considerations of those he serves, without being partisan in the sense of being committed to a particular party.[8] Even after being established at Ottawa, this distinction was broken down before the end of the Trudeau regime. Given the gulf to be bridged between the protagonists in Saskatchewan, the distinction is too narrow to be acceptable here.

As the pivot around which day-to-day government activity revolves, the cabinet's relationships are of prime importance, both the internal relationships with other governmental organs, and the external relationships with the public. Of overriding importance is the constitutional relationship of responsibility to the assembly. Particular relationships that have developed with the party and with administrative agencies are discussed in chapter 11. Over and above these official relationships is the cabinet's direct contact with the public.

One of the means of direct communication which the cabinet makes available is the annual reception of views from a variety of provincial associations, usually some twenty or thirty in number. Informal ad hoc committees of cabinet receive the delegations, and considerable attention is accorded to the briefs which are presented. The importance attached to this link of communication was evident in the appointment in the mid 1970s of a special assistant to the cabinet secretary who had as a prime duty the arrangement of meetings and the responsibility for follow-up consideration of the proposals.

The holding of cabinet meetings at various places throughout the province is another means the government uses to invite direct communication. The practice was started by the CCF in 1963, was continued to some extent by the Liberals, and is used increasingly by the NDP. Several meetings a year are held outside Regina, although no regular schedule has been established. The usual pattern is for a private cabinet meeting in the morning to be followed by public representations to the cabinet, such as briefs from agencies of local government, chambers of commerce, and other organizations of the area. Considerable publicity usually attends these meetings, and the government may also advertise them ahead of time, inviting briefs from individuals and organizations.

Beginning in 1972 and in most years since then, Premier Blakeney has taken a summer bus tour throughout the province in addition to holding cabinet meetings outside Regina. The tour lasts from one to two weeks and is usually broken into two sections; it is a more systematic and organized journey round the province than the occasional speaking forays of premiers which were customary in the past. One of the main purposes of the bus tour is to provide residents with a first-hand opportunity for complaints and questions. On the premier's side the tour is an occasion to explain government policies and to determine what problems are foremost among local residents. During the 1973 tour, for example, people showed a lack of interest in certain topics which had been hotly debated in the legislative session, such as a hog commission, university legislation, and teachers' salary bargaining. Instead, questions which were raised tended to be on matters more directly affecting individuals, such as care for the aged and chronically ill, local topics related to public works, and personal encounters with government bureaucracy. Similarly during the tour in 1974, after oil marketing and royalties had been a topic of considerable public discussion for some months, the matter ranked far below concern expressed for nursing homes and roads, even in the oil centers of the province. The tours inevitably provide an opportunity for the premier to meet with and strengthen the hand of local party workers. To the extent that it is possible to make a distinction, the trips seem nevertheless to be carried out primarily for him to meet the people as premier rather than as party leader.

A decentralization of cabinet activity was effected in November of 1973 with the opening of a cabinet office in Saskatoon which was intended as a means of communication between the government and the people of Saskatoon and surrounding areas. The office was organized to open during regular government hours with cabinet ministers attending twice a week in rotation, except that each week one was from Saskatoon. Newspaper advertisements announced the schedule of ministers and invited the public to meet the ministers, to advance suggestions or criticism, and to ask questions.

Royal commissions are appointed in Saskatchewan, as elsewhere, to secure for the cabinet information on a particular question—information which usually includes both the views of the public and the results of professional study. Widely varying commissions have been set up for guidance in government action and in drafting legislation. In 1913 a commission on agricultural credit investigated legislative needs in that field, and a new workmen's compensation act that was passed in the 1928–29 session was based on the report of a recent royal commission. Agriculture and rural life was the subject of a comprehensive survey begun in 1952, and a taxation commission was established in 1963 to complement at the provincial level the taxation study which was under way federally. In 1964 a commission on government administration was established to examine ways to streamline government operations. These and other commissions have suffered the customary fate of such bodies—varying from substantial action on some reports to an almost complete ignoring of others.

Two other major purposes of royal commissions have been evident in those conducted in Saskatchewan: to avoid immediate action, and to carry out an investigation. A commission appointed ostensibly to seek out information may be useful in circumventing pressure. The delay itself may dull enthusiasm, new factors may intervene, action may be less embarrassing at a later date, or the commission may recommend alternative action. An early and highly successful use of this technique occurred in 1910 when, unwilling to accede to strong popular demand for public ownership of grain elevators, the government appointed a royal commission. Its usefulness, even before it had completed its duties, was evident in Premier Scott's comments that "the Commission meetings, the evidence taken, and the general discussion resulting, has done a great deal already to clear the situation and so remove dangers, so far as we are concerned."[9] The government was subsequently further gratified by the commission's recommendation encouraging co-operative action by the farmers instead of government ownership.

Commissions of investigation have been fewer, but they have been set up from time to time to investigate charges against government members or administration, when a more objective body than a legislative committee was required. Prominent among these investigatory commissions were the three established in 1916 to enquire into the charges of bribery and corruption in road building and liquor administration which are referred to in chapter 8.

Cabinet solidarity and cabinet secrecy are the prime elements of that body's internal relationships. Both have been carefully maintained in Saskatchewan. Occasional lapses in secrecy have not gone unchecked, and reprimands have been administered by early as well as by more recent premiers. After the appointment of the irrepressible George Langley to the cabinet in 1912, fellow members of the assembly waited in gleeful anticipation to see whether cabinet restraints would be sufficient to subdue this member's well-known independence. They were not. Premier Scott finally chided his willful colleague about a newspaper report which had appeared:

... I exceedingly regret to have to say that you have brought about a condition threatening grave consequences to the Government. The intimation given by you at Saskatoon is one which no member of Council was free to give out. How am I to justify the position to our colleagues? Men sitting in Cabinet Council must be able to freely exchange views in full confidence that until Council's decision has been arrived at, and mutually agreeable arrangements made for public announcement, the rule for Cabinet secrecy shall be held inviolate.

Were the present the first occasion of complaint of identical nature I should take it less to heart. I should deem it merely a more or less serious inadvertance. In ten years' record the only times there have been any approach towards friction amongst members of Council here were due to premature public statements by you upon questions of equal moment to each member of Council. The Saskatoon report, which I have just now seen gives me grave concern.[10]

Premier Lloyd similarly found it necessary to reprimand a colleague for an announcement which he had made on a matter not yet approved by cabinet. In an admonition to the erring Eiling Kramer the premier wrote:

Statements which have a tendency to commit the government before they have been approved can only produce difficulties and problems for everybody and for yourself most of all. As a result, I must urge you to exercise a greater degree of caution with regard to such commitments.[11]

The principle of cabinet solidarity leaves resignation as the only alternative for a minister who is unable to accept a policy decision. Such resignations have been rare in Saskatchewan, and those which have occurred have been clouded by side issues.

The first break was the resignation in 1918 of W. R. Motherwell, who was one of the original four ministers and who had served continuously from 1905 as Minister of Agriculture. He gave a double reason for his resignation. He deplored Premier Martin's failure to take a stand condemning the Union Government at Ottawa, and he disagreed with the introduction of provincial legislation that would curtail the teaching of French in the schools. The language question was the immediate cause of the break, although Motherwell made only indirect reference to it when he resigned, as the terms of the legislation had not yet been made public. "There were a number of other questions upon which I did not agree with my leader," Motherwell wrote to Laurier after his resignation, "particularly his refusal to take a stand for or against Union Government."[12]

It seems quite possible that this issue was the key to the entire episode, and furthermore that there was truth in the suspicions that Martin had "jockeyed" Motherwell out of his cabinet.[13] Motherwell was earnest and straightforward and little inclined to political ambiguity or compromise. Premier Martin had to maneuver in a precarious situation in which a split in the federal Liberal party in 1917 was reflected provincially. Motherwell himself noted that his objections to language provisions had been remedied twenty-four hours after his resignation, and every difference he had with the premier, "with the exception of him taking a stand one way or another on Federal politics, has been complied with and even that is almost on the verge of being done."

The delicacy of the political path which Premier Martin had to tread is evident in his loss of two Ministers of Agriculture within three years. These represented the two chasms of political instability which opened before the premier in quick succession, the federal Liberal split, and the threatening Progressive movement. In part at least, Motherwell resigned because Martin refused to take a stand against the federal Union government. Maharg resigned the same post in 1921 as a direct result of Premier Martin's support of Motherwell as a federal Liberal candidate opposing a Progressive.

The departure of Walter Erb from the cabinet in 1962 also resulted, it appeared, from more than what he described as "disagreement with . . . fundamental issues." The issues to which the minister referred in his letter of resignation included one of the principles of the medical care program, and an objection to the position of labor within the NDP party. The purity of his protest was clouded by a failure to resign while he held the public health portfolio and by a delay of any action until six months after his removal from the post. Premier Lloyd pointed out that no change had occurred on either of the points raised since the minister's earlier acceptance of them, and he concluded that "the only changed factor . . . is that Mr. Erb is no longer minister of public health."[14]

In the Canadian House of Commons cabinet secrecy is relaxed somewhat when a minister's resignation is under discussion, but in Saskatchewan such revelations are considered violations of the secrecy rule. This disapproval has not prevented cabinet revelations from occurring in ministers' attempts to justify their resignation. When Motherwell resigned he made only indirect reference to the legislation against which he protested, since it had not been presented to the House. When it later came up for debate with the changes he had urged, he read to the legislature the original draft to which he had objected. The premier interrupted and asked the former minister "whether he should not consider his position before he divulge what took place in the executive council where he was a member thereof?" Motherwell's response, as he continued, was that he had fully considered his position and was "quite prepared to take the consequences." Again, in 1921, the premier ineffectually reminded a former minister of his oath of office. George Langley, whose resignation had been required because of his attempt to influence a magistrate, had quoted from alleged personal incidents in cabinet to prove a point against the premier, a course of conduct to which the premier "took grave exception."

The premier's official position gives him a place of dominance in the cabinet but normally not a dictatorial one. The post itself affords prestige, and in practical terms it is the premier who chooses his ministers and who may call for their resignations. The extent to which the premier emphasizes general cabinet responsibility or instead assumes a high degree of individual direction depends largely upon his own personality. The relationship is affected further by the ability and the political sophistication and experience of the other ministers as well as by those of the premier.

Considerable contrast in this respect has been evident in recent administrations. Premier Thatcher's seven-year rule represents the most notable departure from the approach shown by earlier Liberal premiers as well as by the CCF and NDP incumbents who preceded and succeeded him.

Mr. Thatcher dominated his cabinet from the day he assumed office. Aggressive and distrustful of others, he was little inclined to share responsibility. His view of government was the business outlook of a boss at the top. From a practical point of view, cabinet ministers were keenly aware they would continue in office only on the premier's terms. Psychologically, they feared confrontation with him. On the positive side, they tended gradually to come to the view not only that the premier's method was the way they must accept, but that it was in fact the right way, and that a government had to be run essentially by one man at the top. Without assuming uniformity of views among the ministers or their complete subjection to the premier, these attitudes appeared to be the basic elements of the relationships in the Thatcher cabinet. It was in every sense a Thatcher government.

The positions taken by the CCF and NDP premiers with their respective cabinets showed a much greater inclination towards a team approach. A distinctive party philosophy emphasizing the diffusion of authority was a common factor impelling all three towards teamwork. Differing personalities and circumstances naturally made for differing performances within that framework.

A dynamic personality gave Premier Douglas a considerable appearance of running a one-man government. Just as he overshadowed his colleagues in public, in private discussion also, as one associate described it, "the head of the table was always where Douglas sat." At the same time he gathered a strong team around him. Two ministers who were prominent in cabinet counsel and who served throughout the twenty years of the CCF administration were J. H. Brockelbank and Woodrow Lloyd, who moved from minister to premier in 1961. In particular, however, Premier Douglas shared top direction with J. W. Corman, who was attorney general until he retired in 1956, and with C. M. Fines, who was provincial treasurer until 1960. These three complemented and supplemented each other's strengths and weaknesses in a remarkable combination of effort and effectiveness. Corman, who was content to stay in the background, was the party strategist and realist; Fines had the administrative and financial expertise; and Douglas was the publicist. "Corman planned them, Fines made the spitballs, and Douglas fired them," observers quipped. It has been noted that it was no accident that the government's most serious miscalculation, its underestimation of the extent of doctor resistance to medicare, occurred after both Corman and Fines had retired. To the extent therefore that power in the Douglas cabinet was concentrated, it was, behind the scenes, less that of one man than of a triumvirate.

A lower profile appeared in the approach of Premier Lloyd and later in that of Premier Blakeney. Mr. Lloyd's tenure was brief, and through inheriting the medicare upheaval from his predecessor, it was turbulent. And, as noted above, Mr. Lloyd devoted considerable effort in the direction of orderly and systematic processes, which are areas that attract little public attention. Mr. Blakeney, although he has proven himself outspoken in relations with the federal government, has gained a reputation for keeping his head down when controversy has resulted from government action or inaction, and for letting the appropriate minister make the public explanations. Moreover, as an administrator himself, he has like Lloyd given substantial attention to administrative processes, and he has carried out extensive re-organization within the government over the years.

The team approach which was so successful in the Douglas years has been evident also in the Blakeney administration. Here, however, it is rather a partnership, with Attorney General Roy Romanow sharing the spotlight with the premier to a greater extent than occurred in the Douglas era. As an extremely close runner-up to Blakeney in the leadership race, the more aggressive and colorful Romanow has supplemented the lower-key approach of the premier, which was especially evident in his earlier years in the office.

A basic fact of cabinet government nevertheless prevails: whatever the direction or desire of party policy or personal inclination toward mutual participation, it is the premier who assumes the ultimate responsibility, and it is his stamp which will be the distinguishing feature of the cabinet which he heads.

10   The Public Service:
Its Organization and Personnel

Government services have featured prominently in the life of Saskatchewan residents. The nature and emphasis of requirements have varied over the years but "the department" has always been a significant factor, whether to a farmer seeking assistance in insect control, to an isolated student taking high school by correspondence course, or to municipal officials requiring engineering services in road construction.

The modern resident who experiences bewilderment in locating the proper channels of assistance, or who feels bedevilled by a complex of official regulation, may look with nostalgia to the simple beginnings of Saskatchewan's public service. The province started with four ministers, six departments, and some 120 civil servants. In reply to opposition criticism in 1907 that "the government had gone to the extreme in employing officials to run the machine," a government spokesman in the assembly required only a few minutes to explain the changes in each department which had resulted in an increase in the number of civil servants from 115 in 1904 to a total of 123 in 1906.

The rapid expansion in civil service organization generally evident in the twentieth century has been intensified in Saskatchewan by two particular factors. These have been first, the opening up and rapid settlement of the province, with the consequent need for increased services for more people, and second, the impetus toward expansion which was accelerated after 1944 by an administration ideologically committed to the positive role of government.

The original departments, Agriculture, Attorney General, Education, Provincial Secretary, Public Works, and Treasury were carried over from Territorial jurisdiction with little immediate change. Their number increased rapidly in the first decade after 1905, usually by means of a branch which dealt with a specific activity that was being elevated to departmental status. The broad scope which Public Works originally covered became contracted, for example, when its Local

Improvement Branch became the Department of Municipal Affairs in 1908, and when road building duties were removed in 1912. Over the years other departments came into existence through a variety of reasons. When natural resources were transferred to the province in 1930, a department was required to look after the new duties which were now under provincial jurisdicton. Departments which resulted from the particular emphasis of the CCF were established in 1944 as Co-operation and Co-operative Development, Social Welfare, and Labor. The Department of Indian and Metis Affairs, established in 1969, reflected a contemporary area of concern. The next government replaced this department by the Department of Northern Saskatchewan, in a new concept of geographical decentralization and co-ordination of services.

Not only has there been an increase in the number of departments and in the scope of departmental activity, but their relative importance has altered as the province has developed and as social emphasis has changed. This change in departments' relative importance is most dramatically illustrated in the areas of public works and of public health. The role played by the Department of Public Works during the process of settlement was sufficiently important that the shift of a cabinet minister from Agriculture to Public Works in 1903 was referred to as a promotion. In 1972, however, Public Works was re-organized as a branch within a newly created Department of Public Services.

Health services, in contrast, were originally provided by a single employee who was lodged within the Department of Agriculture. Dr. Seymour, who served as this pioneer medical administrator, described early health services in a report to Premier Scott in 1914:

Previous to the formation of the province ... any public health work was chiefly under the care of the Royal North-West Mounted Police, who administered the provisions of the Public Health Ordinance of 1902, under the Government of the North West Territories.

The Executive Council of the newly elected Legislative Assembly placed the administration of public health work under the Minister of Agriculture, and on the 10th of April, 1906, Dr. M. M. Seymour was officially appointed Provincial Medical Health Officer.

A start was at once made in the development of a Public Health Service, which the rapid increase in the population of the new province rendered absolutely necessary and indispensable.

For the first two years of office Dr. Seymour carried out all the work himself, unaided, using one of the rooms in his private residence as an office, and personally travelling the length and breadth of the province to visit and deal with outbreaks of infectious diseases. [This travel included] ... a trip of one hundred and fifty miles with horses to the lumber camps north of Prince Albert to deal with an outbreak of small-pox, with the thermometer averaging fifty degrees below zero.[1]

Some seventy years later, the provision of various types of health services within the province was a major area of government activity, employing in 1974 more than 3000 persons. Health services held a record for many years as the largest single area of government expenditure, constituting approximately one-fourth of the provincial budget with the 1974–75 estimates totalling almost 224 million dollars.

The growth in the number and size of departments has been paralleled by the establishment of a variety of other types of government agencies, including boards and commissions, crown corporations, and a less readily classified miscellany. In mid-1974 the count was twenty-one departments, sixteen crown corporations, more than thirty boards and commissions, and a dozen or more authorities, services, offices, and similar special purpose agencies. Personnel numbers have expanded even more rapidly within these administrative structures. More than 18,000 persons filled permanent positions in 1974, of whom more than 11,000 came under the direct public service category, with some 7,000 employed by crown corporations, boards, and agencies outside the purview of the Public Service Commission. As well as these, there were various categories of temporary employees whose numbers at times reach a peak of several thousand, and some order-in-council appointments in the upper levels of the administration.

Organization within departments follows the traditional straight-line responsibility to the minister. Advisory councils composed of citizens who are knowledgeable within the area or are representative of interest groups are frequently attached to departments such as Agriculture, Education, or Health, but they are outside the normal operating structure of the department. They are intended to give the viewpoint of those using or affected by the activities of the department, although in some instances the real intent has been for the council to serve as a protection from public criticism. Because of this double purpose, appointees may include those with political views known to be contrary to those of the government.

Boards and commissions in Saskatchewan operate under the customary varying patterns of owing responsibility to a minister or reporting to a minister, and of functioning under the immediate supervision of a chairman or under other administrative organization. Size and clientele also differ markedly, depending on the agency's area of activities and duties. The Saskatchewan Medical Care Insurance Commission serves the entire population of the province in administering the medical care insurance plan. The duties of the Board of Examiners are restricted to determining the qualifications of candidates who apply for jobs as rural municipal secretary-treasurers and town clerks. The Saskatchewan Archives Board is a joint university-government agency, and the Saskatchewan Arts Board makes broad use of part-time consultative specialists in different aspects of the arts. The predominance of agriculture in the province is evident in a wide range of such agencies as the Saskatchewan Crop Insurance Board, the Land Bank Commission, the Hog Marketing Commission, the Sheep and Wool Marketing Commission, and the Feed Grain Marketing Commission.

Among the agencies which do not fit into the normal departmental or commission structure are those offices or authorities which perform duties of a very specific or limited scope, those which may be closely related to a department but not part of it, and those which provide inter-departmental services. These agencies may be directly responsible to a minister in the same manner as a department, or they may operate under a committee of ministers. The Municipal Road Assistance Authority, for example, is responsible to the Minister of Municipal Affairs, but it has charge of a particular program for grid roads. The Wascana Center Authority, in which the government, the university, and the city of Regina participate, is responsible for the development and administration of a specific territory within the city which includes government and university buildings and grounds and adjoining park and recreational facilities. Core Services Administration was to perform a co-ordinating function for the mental retardation and disabled persons programs. It reported to a committee consisting of the Ministers and Deputy Ministers of Health, Education, and Social Services, under the chairmanship of the Minister of Social Services.

As a result of innovations introduced by the CCF, crown corporations in Saskatchewan show a departure from the administrative practices used elsewhere in Canada. Because this was an area of particular interest to the new government in 1944, an organizational system for crown corporations was established which differs from their previous structure in Saskatchewan and from the general pattern outside Saskatchewan. Government ownership and operation of commercial enterprises existed in the province from the beginning, hail insurance and the creamery business having been inherited from the Territories. Other areas of activity which the government entered in early provincial days included agricultural credit, liquor, and even coal mining for a brief time during an emergency situation in 1907. These enterprises were undertaken pragmatically, with the government acting, sometimes reluctantly, where need arose, and then discontinuing its participation when the service was no longer necessary or when other alternatives were available. Before 1944, the main government enterprises were the two utilities of telephones, entered into in 1908, and power, which dated from 1928.

New crown corporations mushroomed quickly after the CCF came to power. They included insurance; corporations dealing with the northern resources of fur, fish and timber; a northern air service; industrial enterprises producing brick and tile, wool, leather products, and later sodium sulfate; and a bus company. The number of such enterprises, the success of some and the failure and eventual abandonment of others, such as the brick, wool, and leather plants, is of less permanent interest than their administrative pattern.

Two specific principles guided administrative experimentation in the CCF establishment of crown corporations. First, the CCF government held that ministerial responsibility must prevail here as elsewhere in the government. Second, they believed government activities must operate as a whole, so that each agency was "part of a total organization directed toward a total concept of governmental responsibilities."[2] These two principles were complementary, and both denied the possibility of the customary independence of corporations.

Direct ministerial responsibility for crown corporations was effected by appointing as chairman of the board of directors the minister through whom the corporation reported. Inclusion of the corporations in overall government planning was achieved in an equally simple and direct manner, by the cabinet's exercising ultimate control over corporation policy. Crown corporations established under these provisions were in reality only a modification of the traditional departmental structure.

The board of directors was in a curiously ambiguous position within this administrative system. With the cabinet as the effective governing body, the directors were cast in the dual role of advisers and boards of management.[3] The cabinet recognized the need for carefully selected boards to avoid conflict and strain within this particular structure, and it reserved to itself the right to make appointments to boards. It was agreed, however, that the respective boards should be consulted for their views on proposed new appointments, and that they could make recommendations through their responsible minister on appointments or dismissals.[4] The boards normally consisted of government supporters chosen from among cabinet ministers and senior civil servants, with some representation from the public. The practice was to exclude members of the management of a corporation from its board.

Officially, boards of directors were to deal with matters of policy, but they were not to participate in the management of the corporation's operations. In practice, although the board might "deal" with them, final decisions in significant matters of policy were reserved to the cabinet. In this way the board's role was an advisory one in those matters of policy which were to be decided by the cabinet. These matters included key financial controls such as capital advances or authorization for borrowing, the creation of reserves and disposition of surpluses, major purchases, and pricing policy. The appointment and salaries of general managers of corporations, as well as the limits within which negotiations for staff salaries and other benefits might proceed also were decided by cabinet. As Dr. McLeod says in his study of Saskatchewan crown corporations:

The effective board of directors of the various governmental business enterprises in Saskatchewan is the cabinet itself. The scheme of administration and control, so it would seem, can best be characterized by depicting the cabinet as a supreme board of directors advised and assisted in the mechanics of administration by a cluster of auxiliary boards or committees fulfilling the dual role of boards of management and advisory committees.[5]

To relieve the cabinet of obviously oppressive duties which the supervision of crown corporations added to its normal work load, the

Government Finance Office was established. It was intended that the office be in effect a committee of cabinet to exercise rather close control over the crown corporations. Unfortunately for this purpose, the agency was set up as another crown corporation. As such, it had difficulty in asserting authority over other crown corporations, and in preventing their by-passing the Office to go directly to cabinet. It was not sufficiently clearly established that the GFO was not simply "another one of us," but that it did in fact act for and represent cabinet authority. It was, "in effect, to sit between the government and the operating corporations, guiding and controlling on behalf of the former, while through day-to-day contacts of its staff officers, being fully conversant with and sympathetic to the problems of the latter."[6]

The main control the Office exerted was financial, since it operated as a holding company for crown corporations. All funds from the provincial treasury for crown corporations, except those for the Power Corporation and Government Telephones, were voted as a lump sum to GFO, and all surpluses from corporations went to the GFO. In addition to exerting financial control, the GFO was empowered to enquire into the affairs of any corporation. Rather than intervening directly, a more conciliatory approach obviously was to exercise its powers of consultation and advice. It was, unfortunately for the Office, this power of moral suasion which was most seriously affected by the lack of prestige which followed from the GFO's not being clearly recognized as a committee of cabinet.

If the GFO's relations with crown corporations were clouded, there was no doubt about its direct supervision by cabinet. The cabinet not only provided the funds but made the decisions, on GFO recommendations, for their allocations. These decisions extended from such matters as expansion of physical facilities of a corporation or the purchase of shares to the limits of negotiations for wage increases.

Crown corporations and their relationships with the cabinet posed a continuing problem throughout the CCF regime. After almost twenty years in office they were still searching for a clear definition and understanding of the role of the corporation as an arm of public policy. Ideological and practical considerations were merged from the beginning in a many-sided complex. CCF philosophy placed great emphasis on this mixed form of government activity. Ideologically the aim was "a process by which we hope to establish a new pattern of operation for publicly owned enterprises which will measure up to a capitalist balance sheet, and also adopt patterns of human and financial relationships superior to those in present industry."[7] Practically there were continuing problems of adjusting authority between elected ministers and appointed officials, so that ministers could be protected against routine administrative concerns without suffering officials to establish "little empires in which the dynamics of . . . [government] policy are ineffective."

It is interesting to note that with the return of the NDP to power, one of the early problems for consideration was the continuing one of administrative relations in the field of crown corporations. The existing structure had been maintained by Liberal cabinet ministers who liked the direct control which it gave them over the corporations and who were, ironically, unaware that it was a uniquely CCF organizational structure. Crown corporations thus passed on into NDP hands with the organizational structure established by the CCF still intact.

A crown corporation which presents a different facet of activity is the Saskatchewan Economic Development Corporation, or SEDCO, which was established in 1963. In contrast to the intent of most crown corporations of carrying out business on behalf of the government, SEDCO's purpose is to provide loans to private industry to encourage their establishment or expansion in Saskatchewan. An example of such activity is aid given to the Interprovincial Steel Company, operating outside Regina. This policy of SEDCO is in accord with the continuing emphasis of the CCF and NDP on development within the province through the three-fold methods of government activity, co-operatives, and private enterprise.

In addition to crown corporations, central administrative agencies also were given special emphasis by the CCF. These agencies were designed for co-ordination of activities within the administrative service and for overall planning. Until 1944 the Treasury Board was the only central government agency, and it did not hold a particularly significant position.

The key central administrative agencies of the CCF were the Economic Advisory and Planning Board, the Budget Bureau, and the Treasury Board with enlarged authority. During the first year of the CCF government an Economic Advisory Committee of three university professors, Drs. G. E. Britnell and V. C. Fowke and Dean F. C. Cronkite, advised on economic matters referred to it by the government. The Economic Advisory and Planning Board was established on January 1, 1946, and was made responsible to the cabinet through the premier. Throughout its existence the Planning Board had wide jurisdiction and enjoyed high prestige within the CCF administration. The original structure of the Board was unusual in that a civil servant was chairman, while cabinet ministers served as members. George Cadbury, an economist from Britain, served as full-time chairman, and when he left in 1951, the premier assumed the chairmanship, direction of day-to-day activities passing to the secretary of the Board. Those composing the Board in later years included the premier as chairman, four other cabinet ministers, the deputy provincial treasurer, and the secretary of the Board.

Certain original functions of the Planning Board which were later transferred to other jurisdictions concerned the operation of crown corporations and the organization of the machinery of government. In its more basic research and planning duties, the Board saw its essential role as being "to provide objective data, technical judgement and advice to the government in the formulation of its policies and programs."[8] This role was to be carried out along three general lines:

in broad policy and program planning; in economic research and measurement; and in acting as a research secretariat to the cabinet.

The first function of policy and program planning well illustrates the scope of the Planning Board's activities and its relationships with other government agencies. Through the development of basic economic data, its aim was to help in the co-ordination and integration of programs between departments, and to assist in the setting of priorities between competing interests. To carry out its duties, it said, required "the closest possible liaison with the Cabinet and Legislature, the Treasury Board and Treasury Department and the main program agencies, including Crown Corporations." The secretary was an ex-officio member of the Treasury Board and a member of the board of directors of the Government Finance Office and of various crown corporations. He was engaged in the activities of various planning and co-ordinating agencies, and he participated in meetings of federal and provincial officials. The Board also developed new program ideas that could not conveniently be assigned to a particular department. Some departments had their own research and planning units for the analysis and planning of departmental programs; in 1962, for example, eight departments had such branches, employing a total of nineteen economists. Although the Planning Board exercised no supervision over departmental planning units, it was responsible for co-ordinating research that involved a number of different agencies.

The two other areas of Planning Board functions related to the first. General economic research into such matters as trends in the provincial economy and population studies provided a background of information for program planning. These research activities led to the Board's being pressed into service as a secretariat to the cabinet in such ad hoc duties as preparing briefs to other governments or royal commissions, preparing articles for public information, and similar duties which might be assigned to it by the cabinet or by individual ministers.

The Budget Bureau was established in November, 1946, less than a year after the creation of the Economic Advisory and Planning Board. Budgeting was regarded as an instrument both of fiscal and of economic planning.[9] For an effective analysis of budget proposals, the Budget Bureau engaged in an examination not only of the work programs and objectives which departments were required to submit with their estimates, but it also examined the efficiency of each department's administrative organization. The agency was described by Premier Douglas as "an attempt to combine the advantages of a Bureau such as many of the States have organized with our particular set-up in which the Provincial Treasurer has the budgetary responsibility. At the same time, the Bureau of the Budget is responsible for improving the efficiency of administration and has a strong section dealing with management problems."[10] Set up originally under the Economic Advisory and Planning Board, the Budget Bureau later was transferred to Treasury, but it continued in its same duties of examining departmental budget proposals before their presentation to the Treasury Board.

During the Liberal administration, only the Budget Bureau remained as the active central administrative agency, but the NDP government which followed restored essentially the same structure that the CCF had developed. Differences in the new agencies which were established were mainly in details of organization and in some shifts in duties. Overall, the system was somewhat more structured and precise than it had been under the CCF during the greater part of that government's administration.

As the two major committees serving the NDP cabinet, the Treasury Board and the Planning Committee that was established in 1972 had distinct, though complementary and sometimes overlapping areas of activity. The Treasury Board dealt with day-to-day management. Its duties in matters of personnel, program budgeting, and management were essentially with short-term concerns. The Planning Committee looked at long-term aspects, which were broader in scope but less specific. Such long-term planning was regarded not in any sense as the laying out of a definite path to be followed, but as the identification of the options that might be open. Whereas the Economic Advisory and Planning Board of the CCF focused particularly on economic programs, the Planning Committee encompassed the broad area of cabinet activity and policy covering social, economic and other affairs. The Planning Committee also had a co-ordinating role in departmental program development, but policy making itself was left largely with the departments.

It was suggested that the public image of government was not that of advocate or protector of civil rights. While government might appear as the protector of some individuals against other individuals or organizations, it was also considered to be an oppressor of civil rights itself.[11]

This self-evaluation by the CCF government in the wake of an unexpected defeat in a by-election on December 13, 1961, amounted to a recognition by the government of its neglect in an important administrative area. Increased government services had consistently received foremost attention in CCF philosophy. The CCF emphasized also the protection of the individual from other individuals or groups in the community, and it therefore attached great importance to the Bill of Rights passed in 1947. Concentrating on policies which were directed toward their concept of the welfare of the people, the government was slow to recognize and to meet the need for individual protection against the expanded bureaucracy which had been established to carry its policies into effect.

Not until late 1961 did the CCF government take active cognizance of this problem of protecting individuals against bureaucracy. The decision to single out specific areas of public criticism and to take corrective action resulted in the appointment of a committee of senior civil servants. This committee reported on three important areas for possible action to the 1962 cabinet conference (whose composition and activity is described in the next chapter). These areas for action were identified as:

1. the enacting and review of delegated legislation—i.e., regulatory orders-in-council;
2. appeal procedures open to the public which are established by legislation;
3. the redress of grievances that citizens have against government officials.

An examination of existing practices in handling delegated legislation revealed shortcomings both in drafting and in publishing regulatory orders-in-council, and a lack of any provision for legislative review of these orders-in-council. The committee reported that the few departments which had legal branches or solicitors carried out the drafting of orders meticulously. Those that were without legal services had the orders drafted by program administration, with or without the help of the attorney general's department. The committee pointed to the danger that when program administrators did the drafting, the freedom of the individual might be sacrificed for the efficiency of the program. They noted that the existing method of drafting sometimes led to bias and to orders that were inconsistent with the statute or that contradicted orders administered by other departments, or that were even illegal.

Publishing of orders-in-council in the *Saskatchewan Gazette* was inconsistent, too. Practices varied, some departments publishing virtually all orders, and others publishing only those that were specifically required by legislation. For orders of sufficient public interest, departments and agencies also used other forms of publication, such as press releases or pamphlets.

In recommending enactment of a Regulations Act, the committee noted that in 1943 the Conference of Commissioners on Uniformity of Legislation in Canada had drafted a model Regulations Act which had been adopted in British Columbia, Alberta, Manitoba, Ontario, and New Brunswick, and had passed but not been proclaimed in Newfoundland. With this example before it, the committee recommended that Saskatchewan should have a Regulations Act which would define a regulatory order to be recorded, establish a position of registrar and legal officer for regulations, and draw up a uniform policy for publishing orders.

A Regulations Act consequently was passed in 1963, although its implementation did not proceed as rapidly as planned. A change of government and administrative delay intervened, and the Act did not go into effect until 1968. Under its provisions all regulations are to be filed with the registrar, who is to publish them in the *Gazette* within one month. Copies are to be sent also to the clerk of the legislative assembly for examination by the assembly committee on regulations, described on page 106.

The second area reported on by the committee in 1962, that of appeal procedures, received attention but no action. Committee investigation showed wide variation in appeal procedures in legislation administered by the various government departments and agencies. The committee found that at least forty-four acts included sections prescribing formal appeal procedures, including twenty-two different procedures, and in at least eight acts more than one method of appeal was provided. The conditions under which an appeal might be launched varied greatly from act to act, and a number of other acts expressly prohibited appeals against decisions made under them. An inquiry about informal appeals that had no statutory base revealed that only a small number were launched each year against administrative decisions. The committee concluded that an adequate study of this area was beyond its resources, and the matter was left for future consideration.

The question of redress of the grievances of citizens led to consideration of the appointment of an ombudsman for Saskatchewan. Such an appointment was not, however, considered with any enthusiasm in government circles. The cabinet conference in 1962 expressed considerable scepticism about the idea and about its application to Saskatchewan. Little more enthusiasm was evident the following year, although it was noted that the ombudsman idea was gaining greater attention and popularity. Since there was concern to maintain and strengthen the public respect for government, it was conceded that if an ombudsman contributed to this strengthening of respect, the appointment might be considered. The only action taken, however, was to have the Planning Board prepare a report.

Establishment of the office of ombudsman was delayed until 1972, after the NDP return to power, the first appointment to the office being made in 1973. Appointment is by the legislature for a five-year term, with earlier removal only at the direction of the legislature. Substantial criticism has been directed at the provision which restricts the ombudsman from investigations of matters which concern a deputy minister, an assistant deputy minister or any person who "is explicitly or by necessary implication directly responsible to the minister." An even more restrictive provision that was originally in the bill and was removed only under sharp opposition criticism in legislative debate, would have given the attorney general power to order that no investigation be held, or to halt one that was under way, if he deemed it to be "a matter contrary to the public interest".

A dichotomy seems to be evident in the CCF-NDP outlook on safeguarding individual rights. The difference in outlook depends on whom the individual is to be protected from. CCF and NDP governments have been active in provisions to protect citizens from one another; they have been hesitant in measures to protect citizens from the government and its bureaucracy. This deficiency was specifically recognized during the late years of the CCF administration in the report quoted on pages 154-55, the terms of which, it would appear, might similarly be applied to the NDP.

The protection of minorities and the provision of safeguards against discrimination have been emphasized in human rights legislation, particularly in relation to protection from such groups as employers and landlords. But in the matter of protection from government agencies, even when the NDP did establish the office of ombudsman, it did so within the unusually restrictive framework mentioned above, excluding the deputy minister's office. The contrast of the two attitudes to the twin sources of injustice is highlighted by two circumstances in 1979. The government brought into effect revised human rights legislation which included a broader area of protection against discrimination in that it incorporated the principle of so-called "affirmative action" to require employers to hire people in roughly the same proportion as they appear in the local community. At the same time, the department of social services was engaged in challenging the power of the ombudsman to investigate prisoners' complaints against a staff member in a provincial jail. A court decision of August 30 ruled against the ombudsman, thus showing that his power of investigation into the actions of government employees was restricted.

Even in the area which has been emphasized, combating discrimination, the situation of women and their position in the public life of the province has drawn attention to the shortcomings of the CCF and NDP. Despite party statements upholding equal opportunity for all, only three women have sat on the CCF side of the legislature, and only one has been seated since the NDP came to power. One of the party stalwarts, J. H. Brockelbank, on at least one occasion took the party to task in convention discussion, pointing to the CCF practice of nominating women only in losing seats and of by-passing them in seats where the party had any real chance of winning. No woman has ever been included in the cabinet in Saskatchewan, although the CCF had a capable and experienced woman on their side of the House for twelve years while they were in power.

The composition of the public service has of necessity shown a marked change in conformity with the altered role and nature of the services demanded of the government. This change among personnel has been paralleled by equally significant changes in the conditions of public service employment.

The civil service offered neither security nor challenge in the early days of the province. The patronage system prevailed, and there were few attractive positions. Premier Scott was keenly aware of the defects of the civil service, and his implied defense of the existing system was only that it was no worse than elsewhere in Canada. Shortly after taking office he agreed with an official who was resigning his position "that the Government Service offers a very poor return and very poor prospects for any man having ability and industry." Further experience only strengthened the premier's opinion, and three years later he said to another retiring civil servant:

I am not going to try to say that I regret your step because I am sure that you will do much better for yourself and your family working on your own account than we could ever do for you in the Service. The real truth is that the Civil Service, as far as I know it—and I know it fairly well both at Ottawa and here—is not at all a desirable place for any good man. In it a man is open to criticism in a way which restricts his freedom and is constantly kept grinding away at tedious work for which the pay is niggardly. The actual state of the average person in the Service is so totally the reverse of what the general public believes it to be that I am always sorry when I see a good man enter the Service, knowing as I do, the disappointment which he is likely to meet.[12]

The premier's reply to a complaint of unfair treatment touched on other defects in the system:

I find that in the Civil Service, and the same remark applies to the Ottawa service so far as I obtained knowledge of it, fully 49 out of every 50 persons in the service are convinced that compared with others they are improperly or unjustly treated. I dare say that this is inevitable with the haphazard method of fixing duties and salaries which prevails in the Civil Service everywhere in Canada.

Appointments to the public service, according to the legislation of 1906, were to be made "by the Lieutenant-Governor in Council on the application and report of the head of the department in which the person appointed is to be employed; all such appointments shall be during pleasure." In practice, a broad area of positions came under the patronage system, by which recommendation was made by the legislative member on the government side of the assembly, or by the defeated candidate, for appointments in each constituency. This was the system in operation until the mid 1940s, with two ineffectual moves toward reform in the interval, in 1913 and in 1930.

A civil service commissioner was appointed early in 1913 and new civil service legislation was enacted later that year. The appointment of the commissioner, it was explained, was necessitated by the rapid growth of the civil service of the province. According to the legislation, appointments to the civil service henceforth were to be made by the lieutenant governor in council—in effect by the cabinet, upon the recommendation of the commissioner. Subject to the approval of the lieutenant governor in council, the commissioner might also make rules and regulations respecting classification of employees, salaries, promotions, and similar matters. Another possible duty, foreshadowing the introduction of competitive examinations, was "the examination of applicants for admission to the civil service." The commissioner later described the act as being in the middle of the road between a government patronage system and a system which would provide for a written competitive examination system and the setting of salaries for different classes in the civil service.

Civil service changes of 1913 were more in form than in substance. Real power still lay with the cabinet. The commissioner was directly responsible to cabinet and it prescribed his duties. It also continued to make important rules and regulations, and it retained final authority in appointments and in settling disputes over dismissals and requests for reinstatement. Competitive examinations were not introduced, and the patronage system still flourished, with assembly members continuing to recommend appointments from their respective constituencies. As a result of retaining old civil service tradition, the activities of the civil service commissioner were largely restricted to administrative detail and to making recommendations. In 1917 he mildly recommended that "in the not too distant future" provision might be made for examinations of certain classes, and perhaps for the setting of salaries.

Both existing practices and the condition of the civil service continued therefore with little change. Advice which Premier Martin gave to prospective employees more than a decade after formation of the province echoed Scott's earlier views: "As a matter of fact I think it would not be wise for you to enter into Government employ as you would be able to do so much better in other lines of work," he wrote to one enquirer in 1917, and to another a few months later:

In so far as your entering the Government employ is concerned it strikes me that you would be making a very grave mistake as there are only a few positions in connection with the Government service that are really worth while a man undertaking, and these positions are usually well filled.[13]

In assembly debate in 1920, the government claimed that there had been some attempt made at a gradation of the service, but apparently it was applicable only to a limited extent. In 1926 it was admitted that

the Saskatchewan government was no exception to the rule that governments did not pay handsome salaries. There was a disposition to demand service from civil servants on a minimum basis. . . . Little encouragement was given to individual initiative or resource, while promotion and increase in salaries were slow and frequently too long delayed.[14]

A Civil Service Association had been formed early as a social group, and it then became the spokesman in matters affecting working conditions and civil service policies. Despite a reported "great want of cohesion and lack of esprit-de-corps among the civil service staff," it effected improvements in some areas by 1920. Through its efforts a joint council was formed in that year from representatives of government and of the civil service, to which grievances on such questions as working conditions might be taken, and this council provided a forum where salaries might be discussed.

One area of consideration bore fruit in 1927 when provision was made for a contributory pension scheme. Before 1927, the government pursued a haphazard policy, upon the death of a civil servant, of voting a gratuity to his widow or family in case of need, each instance being determined individually. There was no provision whatever for a retirement pension. Aside from the obvious hardship for individuals, the lack of a pension was a detriment to efficient administration because civil servants tended to postpone retirement as long as possible. The 1927 legislation provided for men to retire on pension at the age of sixty-five and women at sixty, unless they were permitted by the lieutenant governor in council to continue working for a further limited period.

Civil service reform was one of the planks of the Conservative platform in the 1929 election campaign. More significantly perhaps, this reform was one of the conditions under which the Progressives and Independents agreed to support the Anderson government. Shortly after assuming office, the government appointed a commission to enquire into existing conditions in the civil service and to submit recommendations for improvement. Premier Anderson explained the commission's objectives to be economy and efficiency, and the removal of the civil service of the province entirely from the realm of partisan politics.

The Public Service Act passed in 1930 represented the second attempt to reform the civil service system, and it followed closely the recommendations of the commission of enquiry. A public service commission was to be appointed by the legislative assembly, to consist of a full-time chairman appointed for ten years and of two other members, each appointed for five years. The public service was to be graded and classified, admission was to be through competitive examinations, and promotion was to be on merit, with consideration for seniority. Civil servants were not to take part in partisan activity and they would be dismissed for doing so. The joint council of government and civil service representatives formed to hear grievances, which had operated voluntarily since 1920, was now given legislative sanction. The new legislation provided for such a council to hear appeals from decisions of the public service commission and to adjust complaints of employees.

This move to eliminate partisanship from the civil service had run a gauntlet of fierce partisan charge and counter-charge. The Liberal press claimed that the new administration was "firing Government employees right and left" and "plugging" the service with good party workers before taking it out of politics. Premier Anderson defended dismissals on the ground that former employees had been politically active and that he had no recourse but to dismiss them. The Progressives dissociated themselves from any responsibility for dismissals or new appointments and reaffirmed their advocacy of "the entire removal of the Civil Service from the sphere of party influence."

The clamor became so intense that the chairman of the commission of enquiry, M. J. Coldwell, felt obliged to point out the distinction between his commission and the government. He explained that the commission had no power or responsibility for any changes in the public service, and that any which had occurred were made by the government and had no connection with his commission of enquiry.

Despite its background of partisan controversy, the legislation gave promise of a brave new beginning in civil service administration. A commission was established with jurisdiction over a wide area of the civil service, and a partial system of competitive examinations was introduced, mainly for positions that required special training or experience.

Events denied the newly introduced system any real opportunity to become established. It lasted only for the single term of the government which created it, and it existed during the most stringent economic period the province has ever experienced. The principal matters of civil service concern soon became not the manner of recruiting new members, but how to reduce members' numbers and pay those who remained.

When the Liberals replaced the Conservatives in 1934, the civil service innovations were abandoned. Appointment of the public service commissioners was transferred from the assembly to the cabinet, and the number was changed to one or more members to be appointed for a seven-year term. In the legislature Premier Gardiner justified the action by saying that government responsibility in the administration of the civil service must be restored, that the government must have absolute control of expenditures, and that no civil service commissioner should be able to hamper a government which wanted to limit expenditure. Even the *Leader-Post,* normally sympathetic to the Liberals, referred to the changes as leaving "the patronage gate open" and spoke of charges currently being made that the government was firing civil servants to give jobs to its own supporters. After a change was made to a one-man commission, the same newspaper also condemned the appointment as a partisan one. Competitive examinations were eliminated, and the civil service reverted to the former patronage system.

The first effective move to base the public service on merit came with the CCF. The new government announced its intention in the 1945 Speech from the Throne of making the civil service non-political and of giving security of tenure. Amendments to the Public Service Act in 1945 and a new Act in 1947 provided for competitive examinations, and for a grading and classification of the civil service. The principle of equal pay for equal work was written into the legislation, with no person to be discriminated against because of sex, race, or religion. Immediate steps were taken to put these provisions into effect, a commercial public administration firm being hired in 1946 to classify the Saskatchewan civil service. A Public Service Commission of three persons to carry out civil service administration was appointed by the lieutenant governor in council in 1947. Emphasis was placed on merit and efficiency and on security of job tenure, with examinations to be used both for admittance to the civil service and for promotion, although with consideration given to seniority.

Two innovations in civil service administration were made by the CCF: legislation provided for collective bargaining between the government and the civil service, and government employees were allowed to participate in politics.

The initial step toward collective bargaining was the right which the Trade Union Act of 1944 gave to government employees to organize unions. This provision led to unionization of the civil service and to its affiliation with the Trades and Labor Congress. The right to organize a union resulted at the same time in the abandonment of the former Saskatchewan Government Services Association, which had succeeded the original Civil Service Association. Affiliation with the T.L.C. was preceded by a three-way struggle among it, the competing Canadian Congress of Labor, and the existing Government Services Association. The government ruled out the existing Association as a collective bargaining agent because it was not constituted as a trade union. Civil servants, on the other hand, rejected the C.C.L. because of its designation as the political arm of the CCF. Their reservation was not shared by the premier, who reportedly stated that he saw no impropriety in a government workers' union joining an organization affiliated with a political party.[15] Later the C.C.L. secured affiliation of employees of the Telephone Department, the mental hospitals, and the crown corporations. With the subsequent merging of the two labor unions as the Canadian Labor Congress, this difference in affiliation disappeared.

The collective bargaining agreement that was signed by the government and its employees in 1945 was pointed to as pioneer action in the field, since it contained provisions unique in North America for that type of agreement. As required by the Trade Union Act, maintenance of membership was included, whereby each member joining the civil service had to maintain his or her membership in the union as a condition of employment, and provision for check-off of union dues was also included.

A reversal of the customary attitudes of employer and employee was a notable feature of the action. The employees had not pressed for the new provisions, but on the contrary they showed reluctance to accept them. It was the government, as the employer, which had initiated the legislation allowing unionization in the civil service and which encouraged the change. The normal roles subsequently became evident, with the government over the years finding itself faced with the usual employee demands and even with strike action. The Saskatchewan situation also ceased to be unique as Quebec, following Saskatchewan's lead some twenty years later, accepted unionization of its employees and collective bargaining in 1965. There was similar action by the federal government in 1967 and subsequently by most of the other provinces, although the right to strike was not always provided for.

The Saskatchewan Government Employees Association showed increased militancy at its 1974 convention. It decided to reaffiliate with the Saskatchewan Federation of Labor and the Canadian Labor Congress, which it had left in 1961. That move had been in protest over what it regarded as a break in faith on the part of the C.L.C. which had given jurisdiction over the staff of a new training school to the Canadian Union of Public Employees. In 1974 the Association also decided, for the first time, to set up a strike fund. A new two-tier system of bargaining was agreed upon, along lines similar to that used in several other provinces. This two-tier system would include the negotiation of a master contract covering items applying to all members and a second tier of separate negotiations by occupational groups, which would deal with wages and special proposals. A further decision, in keeping with the decentralization of government administration, was to establish an office in Prince Albert and a branch at La Ronge.

Permitting civil servants to participate freely in politics was a break with previously accepted principles and one with continuing controversial overtones. Partisan activity had never been absent from the civil service, but until 1947 it had never been officially approved. Before the legislation of 1930 which specifically banned political activity, the principle of non-participation by civil servants was mutually accepted by government and opposition. In the first legislature the leader of the Opposition stated that "while of course . . . civil servants were entitled to be free in the casting of a ballot they should not become parties active in the elections."[16] In 1911 the complaint of the secretary-treasurer of the Regina Liberal Club that civil servants had monopolized most of the executive positions in the Club was poor testimony to the reality of political restraint. Premier Scott's reply indicated that the appearance if not the reality should be upheld: "It is not in harmony with proper public policy that members of the Civil Service should be in positions where they may be advertised as political partisans," he said.[17] Civic politics also came under the ban: "While no law or regulation with regard to this matter exists in the Province it is generally recognized to be unwise, if not improper, for members of the Service to engage in civic or other politics to the extent of becoming candidates," Scott admonished.

The 1930 enactment decreed that "no employee shall engage in partisan work in connection with any . . . election, or contribute, receive or in any way deal with any money for any party funds." Successive public service commissions handed down conflicting interpretations of this decree. An early ruling after the passage of the legislation permitted a civil servant to belong to a political club and to take part in its private meetings. By contrast, according to a new interpretation in August of 1935, "Employees shall have the right to vote at any Dominion or provincial election if under the laws governing the election he has the right to vote, but beyond that the liberty of political activity ceases to exist."[18] The ruling was an interesting accompaniment to the dismantling of the vanquished government's attempt toward a civil service on merit, and to an obvious return to the patronage system.

The CCF change in the Public Service Act in 1947 concerning political participation was explained as providing a protection for civil servants as well as a freedom. By providing that a public servant might not engage in any form of political activity during his working hours, the legislation afforded protection for an unwilling employee from pressure by a superior. It gave by implication the right to act freely in off-duty hours. This right was both confirmed and limited by the qualification that at no time was the civil servant to "take such part in political activities as to impair his usefulness in the position in which he is employed."

As with collective bargaining, freedom for political activity resulted from government policy rather than from initiative on the part of civil servants. Many employees feared that the legislation would undo the efforts of their organization to dissociate government jobs from politics, and that it would be a threat to their security in the public service. A sharp change in the prevailing attitude was evident by the time a new government took over in 1964. Fearing restrictions or reprisals for political activity, the Saskatchewan Government Employees Association asked for clarification of the position of a civil servant in partisan politics. The Association advocated for approval specific areas of political activity, including candidacy for election at each level of government, leave of absence to campaign on behalf of a party or candidate, and speaking, writing, and fund-raising on behalf of a party outside working hours. The Association asked for an all-party committee of the legislature to examine and make recommendations on its proposals. There was no response to these proposals, but equally there was no action by the new Liberal government to prohibit them.

An early argument in support of the right to participate politically was that it merely legalized what was already a fact. The further defense that government employees should not be denied the political rights enjoyed by other citizens gains prominence as the size of the public service increases. Despite the argument that the right, theoretically, is equal for all parties, there can be no doubt that the provision allowing civil servants to be politically active favors the party in power. The significant factor is the inevitable tendency for the party in power to attract to the government service those who believe in its policies. Equally inevitable, political activity for the opposition party is more keenly and less favorably noted than activity on behalf of the governing party.

Order-in-council appointments, outside the scope of the Public Service Commission, normally are used for positions in senior levels of the public service, as well as for a variety of temporary or other positions which are not included in regular classifications. There is provision also in the Public Service Act to permit a position to be removed from the administration of the commission by order-in-council. Information as to the number of order-in-council appointments tends to be guarded by the government, with the opposition invariably charging political patronage in this area of appointment. Substance is given to the charge when defeated party candidates are appointed to positions as ministers' executive assistants or similar offices, a practice evident in both Liberal and NDP administrations. In the 1970s increasingly vocal criticism was directed by the Liberal opposition against the NDP government for the practice of granting short leaves of absence to executive assistants and others, for a two- or three-week period immediately before an election, whether for provincial by-elections, federal elections, or for elections in other provinces.

Premier Thatcher's order-in-council appointments gained particular attention because they were frequently erratic and they showed a glaring indifference to an appointee's qualifications, the premier being guided by his own personal inclinations, of which the foremost was to keep salaries low. Mr. Thatcher's mode of operation might upon occasion incur the impotent wrath of both the Public Service Commission, because a job had been abruptly pulled from its jurisdiction, and of the party, because it was not a partisan appointment. Friends, neighbors, or a former employee in his hardware store shared appointments with party adherents. Because of scant attention given to qualifications for a position, the department or agency to which the premier made the appointment might experience greater demoralization than that suffered by either the party or the Public Service Commission.

Partisan consideration has not been entirely absent under any party, even in areas covered by the Public Service Commission. Since 1945, practices which have evaded at least the spirit if not the letter of non-partisan appointment have operated through the established machinery for merit appointment rather than in defiance of it. The CCF, for a time at least, used a political checking procedure for those who had been certified by the Public Service Commission. Certification was the selection of the three top applicants for a job through established commission processes, with the final choice from among these three to be made by the department or agency concerned. The party checking procedure occurred between certification of the three and the selection of one of them. The procedure included the referral of each of the three names to the CCF assembly member (or defeated candidate) for the constituency, as well as to a party contact in the local community who was listed for that purpose. Results of the checking were then sent to the department minister concerned. Similar checking was carried out for temporary positions, mainly in the Highways Department, and for a few out-of-scope personnel. In these instances certification was not required, and applicants' names went directly to the contacts.

This party checking procedure was a closely guarded process, and, it appeared, was one to which some top officials in the government attached less importance than did those who operated it.[19] Furthermore, the extent to which replies were received from the contacts varied. There is no indication of any attempt to influence certification as such, party activity being restricted to the final stage of selection.

Premier Thatcher's intervention in appointments was widely known even if not openly admitted, and it reached further down into the system than the CCF intervention had done. Pressure was exerted upon occasion at the certification level, and frequent direction was given as to the final selection to be made. Care was taken to retain the commission structure and processes, with the desired end achieved, technically, through established procedures. Interference at the certification level, if it was carried out to any considerable extent, obviously held graver implications for both the quality and morale of the public service through the danger of bringing in unqualified people.

It is characteristic of patronage that it is the party which urges it, not the government. "I take the stand that we must look after our friends in time of peace or we cannot expect them to line up in our ranks in time of war," was representative of the basic philosophy of the early patronage system. Throughout, premiers have found themselves harassed in this respect, especially upon first assuming office, and in proportion to the harshness of current economic conditions.

Premier Thatcher's approach differed from the traditional system of early days, both in order-in-council appointments and to the extent that he intervened in appointments under the Public Service Commission. The early patronage system was decentralized among legislative members on the government side, and it followed a well understood pattern. Mr. Thatcher's method was highly personal and centralized, and as noted earlier, it was not necessarily restricted to party supporters. His erratic and casual approach as to the nature of appointments which were made revealed his generally low opinion of the public service. His view was that anyone with merit would avoid the public service in favor of private business. His aim therefore was to deal with public service openings, by and large, in the least expensive and least bothersome way.

The CCF position on patronage showed a strange contradiction for a party which emphasized rationality. Despite a firm platform of taking the public service out of politics and an evident pride in the merit system which the government had established, the party consistently exerted pressure on the government for partisan appointments. This pressure manifested itself throughout the CCF regime in insistence on formal participation in high level appointments as described in the following chapter. In positions under the Public Service Commission, one of the measures of success of the party checking procedure was the appreciation indicated by local party members at being consulted on appointments. In 1962, after twenty-two years of CCF administration, unsuccessful pressure exerted against the government for a greater voice in appointments was followed by a resolution at the party convention that:

Whereas there are too many employees in the public service that do not believe in the philosophies and policies of the government and therefore, do not work to the best of their ability in the interest of the people of Saskatchewan,

Therefore be it resolved that the entire question of hiring of public servants be referred to the incoming council.[20]

Patronage is not the only problem of public service administration, even though it is the most publicized. Despite the imperfections of the public service in its rudimentary stages, there was an awareness of other dangers to be guarded against as reforms were initiated. A warning of the civil service commissioner to the premier in 1917, when the introduction of competitive examinations was under discussion, still possesses validity:

Too much importance should not be placed upon a literary or written competitive examination, as it is just as essential in most cases for a candidate to qualify in other ways, and only a full and careful investigation, wherein the human element is understood can cope with this, and thus be able to determine a person's business ability, temperament, disposition, etc. to fit him for the particular position to which he is to be assigned.[21]

11 Democracy, Party, and Government

The character of a government is most clearly revealed in the use which it makes of its component agencies and in the relationships existing among them. It was the nature of the relationships that were consciously developed among party, cabinet, and public service which gave the CCF government in Saskatchewan its distinctive features. Several of these features were at the time unique in Canada, and some still are. The CCF government established the pattern followed later by the NDP administration, and it provided a contrast to Liberal governments which preceded and followed it.

The Liberal party has been the most consistent political force in Saskatchewan, until 1978 forming either the government or the official opposition throughout the province's history. It held power for well over half that time, including the twenty-four-year span during the formative years of the province's institutions. As one of the "old line" parties, therefore, it has its roots in the traditional practices of Canadian politics, albeit with adaptation to the Saskatchewan scene. When the party was in power before the CCF, relationships between party and government and within the administrative structure showed little variance from contemporary Canadian practices.

The party's duty was to propel its leaders to office. Having achieved this objective the reward was, in general, the satisfaction of victory and, in particular, the spoils of victory which the patronage system offered. Assuming that the rewards were properly dispensed, the party was content to leave administrative and legislative duties to the elected members. Advice or complaints which came from individuals or groups tended to relate to specific points of concern rather than to any thought of formal or comprehensive party control over government processes and administration.

In contrast, close interrelationship between party and government was a foremost feature distinguishing the CCF regime.[1] The party's long-standing emphasis on rank-and-file control of its leaders logically extended to party control of the government when the CCF assumed office. For the CCF the achieving of power was not the sole concern, but the avenues through which power was to operate were also important. It was not simply that the right things must be done, but that they must be determined by the right people, the party members. Therefore process as well as policy was important, and internal party democracy was a firmly held tenet. Policy and process were in fact not separate aspects of CCF doctrine, but were inseparable parts of an overall approach. The necessity for established procedures to ensure rank-and-file control of policy was indelibly imprinted upon the CCF by its Progressive antecedents.

The considerable attention which the CCF directed to party organization from the time it came into existence was designed therefore to serve it in two spheres. Externally, it was to bring the party to power; internally it was to establish democratic control over its leadership. The CCF was determined that when it achieved office it should not as a party be drained of power or lose control of its leaders in the government. In the twelve years between its beginning in 1932 and its assumption of office in 1944, the CCF worked out in firm detail the relationships which were to exist between the party and the CCF members of the legislature and between the party and a CCF government.

The CCF early established the principle as well as the practice of party ascendency in the determination of both leadership and the party program. An incident which first led to the articulation of the principle and to establishment of the practice arose out of events following the June, 1934 Saskatchewan election. The party's provincial leader, M. J. Coldwell, failed to secure a seat. Little more than a week after the election, the five party members who were elected, acting upon the initiative of one of their number, George Williams, chose Mr. Williams as their House leader. This move on the part of the members-elect aroused concern within the party. The annual provincial convention a month later adopted a motion brought to it from a meeting of party officials and leaders which had met just before the convention, to accept the "generous offer" of the members-elect to rescind all actions of their earlier meeting.[2] The choice of House leader was then delegated by the convention to a group consisting of the party's directive board, M.L.A.'s, candidates, and campaign managers. This group selected Mr. Williams. Although the result was the same, the significant difference was that the party established its right over that of legislative members to choose their House leader.

The party similarly emphasized its prior place in drawing up the legislative program. The annual convention was regarded as the authoritative voice of the party, and CCF legislative members were admonished to follow the program which it set forth. The 1941 convention established machinery "to ensure the necessary collaboration between the CCF organization and the elected M.L.A.'s ...," and also "between the CCF organization and a CCF government in the formulation of legislation and in selecting a Cabinet." This machinery enabled the legislative advisory committee to provide formal liaison between party and legislators and a voice for the party in the eventual selection of cabinet ministers. The committee originally consisted of three members appointed by and from the party's provincial council and two members elected by the M.L.A.'s from their own membership. In 1949, M.L.A. representation was dropped to eliminate the awkwardness in having legislative members give advice to the premier on cabinet appointments for which they were themselves eligible.

In 1941 and 1942 the party moved to forestall future concentration of power with one person. This move was the direct result of concern which developed when the energetic and aggressive George Williams, in addition to the duties of an M.L.A., the House leader, and the president of the party, also took on the role of provincial leader after Mr. Coldwell was elected to the House of Commons in 1935. When Mr. Williams left for overseas service in 1941, the party took the opportunity to divide responsibilities. After some confusion about the positions of president and leader, the offices were separated at the 1942 convention. It was specified that the leader was to have supervision of all political and legislative matters, and that he was to head the government when the party came to power, leaving the president as a separate official to deal with party as opposed to governmental duties.

As the time for a provincial election approached, the party drew up a detailed legislative and budgetary program ready for implementation. For more than two years before the election, committees and sub-committees developed party policies and plans. The result was much more comprehensive and specific than a mere party manifesto. It represented a long-range government program.[3]

When the CCF came to power in 1944, a legislative program prepared by the party thus awaited implementation by the new government. The party was well organized, with active rank-and-file participation and with the basic relationship which was to prevail between party and government already determined. Through its annual convention the party was to maintain control of the government and to determine the program to be followed.

For the CCF party the achievement of power represented a critical juncture in its relations with the government and its legislative members. The lesson which the party inherited from the Progressives was not to be ignored. After the election of Progressives to Parliament in the 1920s it was felt that they had been seduced by the federal Liberals and had betrayed the party. That the CCF now formed the government at the provincial level was no reason for the party to relax. On the contrary it meant that care must be taken to keep government and M.L.A.'s faithful to the principle and practice of party control. Party vigilance was exercised in three areas: to safeguard the independence of its own organization; to maintain its control over legislative members and programs; and to participate in government administration.

The party had already ensured that it should not be drained either of leadership or power to a newly formed government. With the clear separation of the offices of president and leader, and the barring of an M.L.A. from the positions of president or vice-president, the party had assured the continuation of its leadership distinct from that of the government. To forestall undue influence of elected legislative members in party decision-making, an M.L.A. or M.P. could not be elected as the council member from a constituency.

Premier Douglas was an articulate ally in proclaiming party control over the elected members who provided his support in the legislature. At the 1947 convention he spoke of each M.L.A.'s dual responsibility to his own constituency and to the CCF movement as a whole. He reminded the 1953 convention of its position as the "sovereign body" to which elected members must report on the carrying out of its policies. In 1954 he stressed members' responsibility to report to and to accept instructions from their respective constituencies.

The party showed no reluctance in spelling out such details of control as it considered necessary. In 1944, in seeking to control one of the more unpredictable of its legislative members, the CCF provincial council issued instructions for M.L.A. attendance at caucus, and laid down the procedure to be followed if a member disagreed with caucus decisions. After a substantial upsurge in CCF strength in the 1952 election, the convention admonished the newly elected members to conduct themselves "in the same vigilant manner as if their member margin was near the majority line."

An individual constituency had formal potential control over its elected M.L.A. through the possibility of recall. The CCF constitution outlined the procedure whereby party members in a riding might petition for a special constituency convention to consider and vote on the recall of their member. The more extreme form of recall practiced by the Progressives, in which the candidate left his signed resignation with constituency officials, was also used to some extent by the CCF in early elections. Less rigorous than the formal provisions, the spirit of close constituency control was evident in regular association and communication. The member was expected to attend constituency meetings and to be available for questioning and information. Theoretically he was required to report at the end of each session, although this requirement was not always carried out in a formal way.

Means were devised for direct participation by party members, not only in drawing up the continuing CCF program but also in consideration of legislative enactments to carry it into effect. Provision was made for interchange between individual party members and cabinet ministers; between the CCF provincial council and cabinet and legislative members; and between the party president and the premier.

The principal arena for discussion between rank-and-file party members and cabinet ministers was the closed convention panel. It was here that party resolutions could be threshed out in camera before coming to the open convention floor for final consideration. Ministers attended the panels that dealt with subjects appropriate to their respective departments, and while party members welcomed this opportunity to express their views directly to the minister, he had the opportunity to present his own position and to explain possible difficulties in the implementation of a proposed resolution.

The party's provincial council had a formal link with legislative members through the legislative advisory committee. Appointed by and from the provincial council, this committee exercised a watch-dog function from the beginning. It sat in legislative caucus, and it reported back to council.

The council had an opportunity for earlier consideration of legislative proposals at meetings which were held with the cabinet for this purpose. Prolonged discussions took place, usually in November or December, and again in February just before the session began. Between these meetings CCF council members could, if they wished, refer proposals to the executive of their respective constituencies or even to a constituency meeting. Care was taken to see that agreement was reached between council and cabinet before proposals were acted on. It was the opportunity presented by convention proceedings as well as by cabinet-council meetings which led Premier Douglas to declare that the rank and file of the CCF approved of every piece of provincial legislation before it became law.

Reciprocal association of cabinet and council was evident in the invitation to legislative and cabinet members to attend regular party council meetings. Although legislative members were restricted from holding office in the party, their presence was welcomed for "information and advice."[4] The priority which the government gave to such attendance was evident in their changing the time of the regular cabinet meeting upon occasion to avoid conflict with a party council meeting. On at least one occasion the premier missed a cabinet meeting in order to be at council, and he admonished cabinet ministers to adjust their schedules to be able to attend the meetings of the provincial council. Morever there was not the slightest doubt as to the auspices under which party council meetings were held, with visiting M.L.A.'s, including cabinet ministers, being unmistakably regarded as guests.[5]

At the top level, it became established for the premier and the CCF president to hold frequent meetings, normally once a week but oftener if necessary. The meetings provided for an exchange of views and for general discussion of party and government matters.

These avenues of influence in policy and legislative fields were less difficult to maintain than the party's third line of endeavor, to establish an effective voice in government administration. The government's agreement with the principle but concurrent difficulties in putting the principle into practice were evident in Premier Douglas's directive to all ministers in 1948 calling for "the establishment of a more satisfactory and effective liaison between the work of each department and the CCF organization with regard to suitable personnel, local undertakings, and the initiation of new projects."

The party placed particular emphasis on having a voice in administrative appointments, an area of delicate balance between party and government. It was agreed that whenever possible the party executive should be consulted in key appointments. The executive took seriously this right of consultation and stoutly maintained its prerogative. Problems arose through repeated and insistent pressure from party groups for partisan appointments in significant positions, while the government was equally insistent that competence was requisite as well as ideology. Premier Douglas made the government position plain when he told the party convention two years after he came to power:

We know that people can't carry out a socialist program unless they believe in socialism. We want more socialists in the government service, but they must be trained and efficient.[6]

A government spokesman reportedly answered party complaints on another occasion with similar sentiments, expressed more bluntly in the aphorism, "It is easier to make a socialist out of an engineer than to make an engineer out of a socialist."

Adherence to the principle of party approval for administrative appointments did not preclude lapses in practice, as indicated by reminders or reiteration of the policy from time to time. Heads of agencies were specifically singled out in the cabinet's reaffirmation of the policy in 1962:

It was agreed that as a matter of policy no appointments should be made to positions of Deputy Minister, General Manager of Crown Corporations and Chairman of Boards and Commissions until:
(a) Such appointments have been approved by the Cabinet.
(b) The minister concerned has consulted with members of the Provincial CCF-NDP Executive.[7]

It was impossible for party members and officials to maintain such close association with the government and legislative caucus without influence being reciprocal. When convention delegates in closed panel discussion were able to express their views to the minister, they were exposed in turn to the minister's explanation of the government viewpoint. If in the consideration of legislative proposals the cabinet met with the party council, it was a two-way process. And, it may be assumed, the president-premier meetings were dialogues, not monologues.

The genuine give-and-take among party members, and between party members and cabinet ministers was nowhere better illustrated than at the annual convention. When resolutions came from the panels to the plenary session for final decision, those who had failed to carry their respective views in the panel had an opportunity to make a last stand. The 1960 convention provided examples, one of an individual delegate, and another of a cabinet minister, each making such an appeal on the convention floor for reversal of a panel recommendation, and each losing. A resolution to provide compensation for crop damage caused by big game had been defeated in panel, but its supporters attempted to have it adopted in plenary session. Two cabinet ministers, obviously with an eye on the administrative implications, joined forces and led the battle for its defeat. On the other hand, the major and contentious resolution "that when the medical plan is implemented, a deterrent fee be imposed," had also been defeated in panel. In this instance cabinet ministers, concerned with financial realities, made a strong plea on the convention floor for the resolution's adoption, but it was nevertheless defeated. A similar resolution at the convention the following year met the same fate, and the government refrained from imposing the fee, although it obviously was anxious to do so.

Such instances illustrate Premier Douglas's assertion that in both legislative and administrative matters the cabinet operated within the framework of party wishes to the extent that was constitutionally and financially possible. The degree of party participation in government planning was, as might be expected, most pronounced in the early years. Even with increased experience and the development of greater cabinet authority, the full machinery of party participation remained and operated to a remarkable degree. The reciprocal nature of party-government influence blurred clear-cut lines and permitted varying interpretations of party "control". In practice the cabinet interpreted this term with sufficient latitude to carry out its functions with all the authority and initiative necessary for the effective operation of the cabinet system of government. The cabinet prepared and accepted responsibility for legislative and budgetary programs, for making appointments, and for effective control over all other areas of administration.

The theory of party supremacy was never questioned. Any open disregard of party wishes brought quick reaction, and few such instances occurred. On one occasion a cabinet minister announced in the legislature the dropping of a tax levy, which was directly contrary to expressed party policy. In that instance, however, the minister had upstaged the cabinet as well as the party, since the change had not yet been approved by the minister's colleagues. Under the circumstances, neither group had much alternative but to accept the public pronouncement. The cabinet preserved its dignity and a show of solidarity by a discreet silence. The party spoke out. At the next convention it passed the strongly worded resolution:

Whereas the Provincial Convention of the CCF is our policy-formulating body, and a directive body to our Legislature, this Convention feels that the action of our Minister of Municipal Affairs in stating on the floor of the Legislature that the Public Revenue Tax was to be removed and thus committing the Government to a policy directly contradictory to that agreed to by the Provincial Convention of 1951, was an unwarranted breach of faith on his part and deserving of severe censure.[8]

The convention recognized this as the unilateral action of one minister and made no mention of the cabinet as a whole.

In a later instance the cabinet did act on its own and quickly experienced negative repercussion in party support. Before the 1964 election, in response to increasing pressure from Roman Catholics, the cabinet announced changes to be made in the system of grants to separate high schools. Except for the normal presence of members of the legislative advisory committee during caucus discussion, none of the customary consultation with the NDP council or other party organs had occurred on this matter before the public announcement. This was obviously a difficult situation for the cabinet, with pressure and publicity on the grants issue mounting and the matter itself too complicated to be quickly and simply explained to either party or public, especially since there were religious differences and the question of conscience among party members to complicate a decision. The cabinet presumably concluded that of the unpalatable alternatives open to it, lack of consultation was a lesser evil than possible rejection by the party of the proposed policy.

An election campaign was not the time for airing a party grievance, but the grievance over separate high school grants was considered a factor exerting at least a certain negative influence among party workers. Specifically, the personal defeat of the Minister of Education in his bid for re-election was interpreted within the party as rank-and-file response to cabinet failure to consult them.

The rarity of such instances of conflict underscores the remarkable degree of concurrence in the direction of party and of government. Throughout the twenty years of CCF rule, the cabinet carried out its executive and legislative duties with the leadership and decisiveness necessary in parliamentary government while paradoxically upholding consistently the principle of party supremacy. This reconciliation of executive decision and party control was accomplished through seemingly perpetual consultation between the two groups, including careful consideration by the cabinet of all CCF convention resolutions and equally careful explanation to the party for those it felt could not be implemented. The system was, in essence, a balance requiring adroit handling. Mr. Douglas, during seventeen years as premier, managed by consummate skill to avoid collision through keeping party and government running along parallel courses. The conclusions and compromises that were arrived at in party meetings at which government representatives were present, tended to coincide, after sufficient discussion at each, with the conclusions and compromises which were reached in government meetings at which party representatives were present.

The Liberals in opposition showed little inclination toward change in the traditional relations within the party. After their defeat in 1944 they were slow to reassess party structure and practices. Within the province, they were preoccupied for several years with frequent leadership changes. From outside, the yet strong hand of the Hon. James G. Gardiner continued to reach from Ottawa with his long-standing influence. Until Ross Thatcher became leader in 1959, the Liberal party remained basically unaltered. Even the fairly extensive changes which Mr. Thatcher initiated, described in earlier chapters, arose neither out of the party ranks nor became embedded in the party itself. Furthermore, although they were borrowed from the CCF, the practices of democratization were applied in the Liberal tradition, simply as a means to victory rather than as having importance in themselves.

While in opposition, Mr. Thatcher, showed a readiness to accord substantial priority to party direction. As leader he followed closely the guidance given in convention resolutions and executive meetings. He was interested in increasing the general activity of the party as well as in having a corps of effective party officers to provide strong leadership.

After the Liberals achieved power in 1964, the role of the party declined in two ways. As premier, Mr. Thatcher now was much less inclined to turn to the party for guidance. Second, the traditionally important function of the party as the vehicle carrying its leader to power had been reduced. The new premier gave substantial credit for his electoral success to the professional consulting firm which had conspicuously shared the 1964 campaign duties. This association did not stop with the election. Premier Thatcher retained as his executive assistant one of those who had helped to direct the election campaign, Jim Moore, in whom he placed a trust and confidence unusual for the premier to accord, and which he withheld from cabinet and party colleagues.

Both Liberal party tradition and Premier Thatcher's personal inclinations contrasted with the CCF philosophy of active participation of the party in the conduct of government business. In Mr. Thatcher's view, the government should operate within the general framework of Liberal policy, without specific reference back to the party organization.[9] Despite earlier party innovations which were continued, the spirit and the basic realities of party-government relations followed the traditional pattern. The main outlines of party policy were adopted at the annual convention. The government felt no necessity for direct accounting or explanation to the party for any deviation from particular aspects of convention resolutions. Meetings between the government and the party executive, held usually every few months, provided an opportunity for mutual exchange of information and opinions, but nothing more. There was no thought on either side that these meetings were decision-making or that the views of the executive were mandatory. There was furthermore no provision for regular party consultation beyond the executive. The real weakness in avenues of communication in the Liberal party lay in the resulting gap between the executive and the grass roots.

In administrative as well as in party relationships, Liberal and CCF governments exhibited sharp contrast. The narrower role of government during early Liberal tenures in office required relatively simple organization. The cabinet gave little thought to the establishment of central administrative or planning agencies. Its own overall direction of government activity provided whatever planning and co-ordination were seen to be necessary. Experts were limited to the technical and professional personnel within the various departments. The means for obtaining economic advice tended to be the ad hoc practice of calling in specialists on particular phases of economic problems as they arose in legislation.

The CCF not only gave high priority to central administrative agencies but also directed careful attention to government-administrative relationships, in accordance with their concern that proper methods be used to achieve proper results. Furthermore, administrative organization was an area more readily within government and party control than was the legislative fulfillment of ideological policies.

In the implementation of its legislative program, the CCF operated under a threefold limitation. It was a provincial government within a federal system; it was dependent upon outside capital for development; and its electorate consisted largely of a pragmatic and conservative farming population. Party realists were aware that it was pragmatic and not ideological considerations which would keep it in power or turn it out. With limited capital available within the province, any plans to develop and diversify the economy had to depend upon outside sources. Since it was these very financial sources which were most suspicious of socialist policies, government programs must attempt to ameliorate the distrust. As a provincial government, its area of jurisdiction was restricted accordingly. Thus in implementation of policy, the new government faced practical checks both from within and outside the province.

Like party organization, government administrative procedures were free of these practical restrictions. Whatever the extent to which this freedom was responsible for innovation, these innovations in party organization and in administration processes, and in the relations of each with the cabinet, were the most remarkable aspects of the CCF regime.

Whereas the basic principle in party-government relations was party democracy, in the administrative field the basic principle was the application of rationality. The development of the administrative structure, in the views of those involved, started with the CCF belief in the positive role of government. According to this view, the party philosophy attracted people who wanted to use rationality in forming public policy that would give practical expression to their ideological convictions. After such personnel had been obtained, the machinery was developed around them to facilitate this process of making policy by the use of rationality.[10]

There was a frank recognition that administrative officials play a positive role in decision-making. General acknowledgment of this role has only more recently been made elsewhere by public administrators, both theoretical and practical. In the mid 1940s the dictum that politicians make the policy and administrators carry it out continued, in general, to cloak the reality of the part played by administration. In contrast, CCF theory and planning in Saskatchewan were based on the premise that the administrative level had a part in the formulation as well as in the implementation of policy. The institutional structures and practices were developed therefore not solely in the light of the specific functions which each exercised. Their form was shaped also by the interrelationships of the respective agencies, political and administrative, as they were employed in the decision-making process.

A key institution in the CCF formulation of public policy was the annual cabinet conference on planning and budgeting. This conference was a formally constituted procedure for the political and administrative consideration of general policy. The conference brought members of the cabinet and representatives from the caucus into joint session with senior civil servants, including the deputy provincial treasurer, the secretary of the Economic Advisory and Planning Board, and the director of the Budget Bureau, with the premier serving as chairman.

The conference usually was held in November or December for a period of four or five days, with deputy ministers and accompanying senior personnel attending during discussion of their respective areas of jurisdiction. Before the conference the general outline of departmental programs was drawn up, and briefs and studies of particular areas of concern were prepared by the Planning Board, the Budget Bureau, and departments or other government agencies or committees. As a background to conference deliberations, the state of the provincial economy was reviewed, and departmental proposals and programs were examined in the light of economic planning.

The purpose of the conference was to examine the broad outlines of the program for the next session of the legislature, from the long-range point of view of the party's social goals. The conference was not a decision-making body, but the discussions and conclusions it arrived at provided a general framework for the guidance of the Treasury Board and the cabinet in their decisions on expenditures, programs, and legislation.

The spirit of administrative unity exemplified in the cabinet conference was evident also in the close relationship which existed among the personnel of the administrative agencies themselves. The provincial treasurer was chairman of the Treasury Board and was also a member of the Planning Board; the premier was chairman of the Planning Board and was a member of the Treasury Board. The deputy provincial treasurer was secretary of the Treasury Board and was a member of the Planning Board; the secretary of the Planning Board was a member of the Treasury Board. Both of these last were key public servants with membership in a variety of other agencies composed of both cabinet ministers and civil servants. The Budget Bureau served as staff for the Treasury Board, and the director of the Budget Bureau attended Treasury Board meetings. It was these close relationships and common purpose which involved all who participated in a feeling of collective responsibility.

Another device that provided liaison was the common background of training which many of the public service received in the Planning Board. The prestige of the Board and the challenge and opportunity which it offered readily attracted recruits. It became customary for personnel to move from Planning to other areas of the government, being by then already trained and having ready-made avenues of liaison.

Both similarity and contrast may be seen in the nature of the CCF party-government and of the government-administration relations. In each relationship there was the same close communion of personnel, but in the relations of government to party this closeness was achieved through reciprocal attendance at meetings, while in the relations of government to administration it was achieved through overlapping of positions.

The party's concern with maintaining its independence led it to avoid an overlapping of personnel between party and government. With only a few exceptions, such as the premier's position as party leader and the presence of two M.L.A. representatives on the CCF council, government (and legislative) members were, as noted earlier, barred from party office. The method of reciprocal attendance was used instead to provide close association, with one group (or its representatives) being present at the meetings of another body, and with the former group reciprocating hospitality during its own meetings. The clear identity of each as host or guest was always maintained.

Within the administrative area, the cabinet's dominant position over civil servants was undoubted. Here, in the absence of any necessity for maintaining a delicate balance as in party-government relations, government-administration liaison could be established by the overlapping of positions. Cabinet ministers and administrative officials could sit on the same committee, and the same person could serve on a large number of agencies, since it was clear that the cabinet had ultimate control of the appointments and of the resulting relationships and lines of authority.

Just as the Liberals resisted any basic change in traditional party-government relationships, they also tended to cling to their previous pattern of government-administration practices upon coming to power in 1964. A return to less structured administrative practice was accentuated by the personal inclinations of Premier Thatcher.

After twenty years in opposition, the victorious Liberals returned to a world of government vastly different from the one they had left. In the interval there had been extensive change and expansion in government everywhere. In Saskatchewan the general trend had been sharply accelerated through the CCF's conscious expansion of the role of government and through its emphasis on techniques of organization. It would be an understatement to say that the Thatcher government did not share the CCF interest in administrative method.

As premier, Mr. Thatcher's view of the role of the civil service was less that it should search into the rationality of proposed programs than that it should carry out decisions made at the political level.

The result of this Liberal outlook was not only the demise of the Economic Advisory and Planning Board and the restriction of the role of the Treasury Board, noted earlier, but also a shift in emphasis of the functions of the Budget Bureau. This body was now relied upon less to examine programs than to reduce estimates, and it served also as an extension of the cabinet secretariat. Premier Thatcher furthermore showed little concern even for widely accepted administrative procedures. In any matter claiming the premier's particular interest, the channel through his office superseded all others. In general there was a marked disinclination to share with the administrative service any substantial participation in policy formulation. No consistent pattern was applied, so that, depending on circumstances and personality, varying degrees of administrative participation might occur. The overall result, however, was that the political executive set policy to a greater extent than in most governments in Canada at that time.[11]

The NDP government under Premier Blakeney re-established the pattern set by the CCF both in party-government and in government-administration relationships. Differences under the NDP were limited mainly to changes in emphasis and detail that resulted from changing circumstances and different personalities.

In party-government relations, probably the greatest difference arose out of, or at least was intensified by the modern practice of probing and detailed questioning of political leaders. Bear-pit sessions, confrontations, and questioning on hot-line shows made it difficult to maintain the delicate balance of a theory of party supremacy against the realities of day-to-day government. In the 1940s, Premier Douglas's ringing statements to annual conventions proclaiming party supremacy over the government left room for individual interpretation. The idealists, including some within the cabinet, accepted the declaration literally. The realists, if the term may be used for contrast, assumed feasibility as a necessary qualification to the principle of party supremacy. Early in the 1970s, when he was confronted by student demonstrators who pointed to a recently passed NDP convention resolution to support their demands, Premier Blakeney publicly said that a convention resolution was not necessarily government policy.

That the premier's statement apparently elicited no reaction, or even notice, from the party faithful indicates less a change in party direction than a realistic acceptance of the need for government maneuverability. It is highly probable also that over the years the reality of a significant degree of party influence now allows a more mature approach than was possible in the party's more uncertain formative years.

This acceptance of a realistic approach to party supremacy by no means suggests the disappearance of a strongly ideological element within the party. The maintenance of at least a basic equilibrium between doctrinaire and moderate has been a consistent factor of CCF-NDP life, and of party-government balance. The major difference from the old CCF ideological group is that the later Wafflers, as the very fact of their having a name suggests, became a distinct group within the NDP party. They also were younger, more vocal, and had a radicalism combining, strangely, certain precepts from the American New Left with a fervent Canadian nationalism. The group shared with the former doctrinaire adherents of the CCF the narrower concept that equated socialism with government ownership. Wafflers also looked back with nostalgia to what they saw as the purity of the CCF. They regarded the early party as genuinely socialist and, like their older counterparts, they believed literally in CCF party control of the government. Wafflers were disillusioned that, as they saw it, the NDP neither upheld socialism nor exercised democratic direction over government policy.

The consistent CCF-NDP attitude has been an acceptance and tolerance of the radical element within its membership. Even those who do not agree with it point to its value as a conscience and as a reminder that the NDP has principles that set it apart from other parties. It is significant that the separation of the Waffle from the NDP in 1973 came from that group's own initiative, not the party's.

Government-administration relations in the NDP continued where those under the CCF had left off. Basically the aim and approach were the same, of facilitating participation of the public service in decision-making.[12] The annual cabinet conference which constituted a key link between government and administration was resumed by the NDP. The scope of the conference was moreover broadened to include direct representation from the party in the person of the party president. This introduction of the party closed, as it were, the third side of the triangle to create a government-administration-party relationship. The party view could scarcely be considered absent from the conference before, in a group which included cabinet, caucus representatives, and at least some staunchly partisan civil servants. The addition of the party president nevertheless gave the party representation in its own name. It also provided the only direct, formally constituted link between the party and the administration. Party influence otherwise was exerted through the cabinet, through informal association, or through ad hoc participation, as in party committees which were set up to enquire into such questions as surface rights or agricultural leases that were matters of particular government concern.

The NDP continued the relationships developed by the CCF in a framework of changed circumstances. There was not the excitement and flush of enthusiasm of a new party fresh in power. The searching for method and procedure which had characterized the early years of the CCF led gradually to a more structured administration in its latter years, which was built on by the NDP. To maintain, lubricate, and even extend existing machinery is a less dramatic task than to devise it.

The type of public servant has tended to change correspondingly. Furthermore, the NDP in the 1970s did not hold the unique position which the CCF had held. It had to compete for public service personnel not only with other NDP governments but also with greatly enhanced administrative structures in the federal and in other provincial governments.

The NDP also inherited unresolved problems from the CCF. A conflict with constitutional principles has always been inherent in the CCF-NDP concept of party-government relations. Party control of government unalterably contradicts the basic principle of responsible government.[13] A cabinet cannot be responsible at the same time to a party and to the legislature. A firm allegiance to the parliamentary principle, and the prior responsibility which CCF and NDP premiers accorded to the legislature, automatically diminished the practice if not the theory of party control.

Administratively and politically, the CCF established no method of assessing the merit of their programs as to aim, priority, and degree of success. Clear criteria were lacking as to whether particular ventures were primarily for economic benefit, social services, or for other purposes. There were also no criteria by which to judge priority, nor were there either interior or exterior criteria to judge the effectiveness of programs.[14]

The lack of these yardsticks to measure performance persisted even after the CCF's enthusiastic plunging into government-operated enterprises during its first years of office. In later years, in fact, there was less attention to goals, objectives, and the validity of programs than in the initial years in office. The results of early economic studies which were carried out were ignored. The early Economic Advisory Committee found that many of the enterprises which were under consideration by the government and were subsequently entered into, were not economically feasible.[15] At this initial stage, ideological exuberance and political necessity, not surprisingly, overrode all other considerations. Even after discontinuing some of the unsuccessful ventures and after more time for reflection, purposeful and precise guidelines as to aim and priority were lacking.

Neither were there clear-cut limits on how far investigation and planning should be carried. Planners and researchers tend to be carried further into tantalizing areas of exploration instead of imposing restrictions upon themselves. Increasingly detailed planning at the public service level may also be used as an outlet for frustration over delay in implementation at the political level. At either level, planning may be a means of avoiding a decision. A question of planning unsolved by the CCF and passed on into the lap of the NDP thus became the rationalization of planning itself: by whom and by what standards should the boundaries of planning be set?

The NDP government, then, continued from its CCF predecessor its general lines of party organization, its administrative approach, and the relationships between these two elements and the cabinet. NDP policy also followed the CCF pattern. Social services, agricultural requirements, and the development of resources continued to be emphasized, with the last requiring particular attention, as noted in the following pages. Similarly, the NDP faced the same limitations on the implementation of policy as had its CCF predecessor. The constraints inherent in a federal system remained, as discussed in the following chapter. Premier Blakeney, in appealing during the 1974 federal campaign for more substantial influence outside the province, made specific reference to the restrictions under which a provincial NDP government must operate. Economically, he said, even the most favorable conditions in agriculture and natural resource revenues can scarcely hope to render the province self-sufficient in development capital. The same limitation would apply whether activity was carried out by private enterprise or through the crown corporations that were established for oil, gas, and mineral development.

12

Saskatchewan, Ottawa, and the 1970s

The Saskatchewan elections of the 1970s reflected two outstanding political characteristics of the decade. One was the external relationship of the province and its long-standing and continuing differences with Ottawa. The other characteristic was internal, consisting in a new complexity that was developing for political parties in the province. This new complexity went beyond the normal shifts in party fortunes and the emergence of the Progressive Conservatives, to the more diversified concerns of the modern Saskatchewan electorate with which parties must keep pace.

The direct effect which federal government policy has always had on the welfare of individual westerners increased as a result of enlarged government activity over the years. The marketing of grain which in early years had been through the privately controlled Winnipeg Grain Exchange was taken over by the Canadian Wheat Board. The extent of government control over railway and freight rate policy increased. In financing of individual farm operations, private financial institutions were supplemented by federal as well as by provincial farm credit schemes. Later there were crop insurance and farm-stabilization programs. As these changes occurred, voter reaction became concentrated more closely on government actions and policy, shifting from earlier challenge and protest to individual corporations. General approval greeted some actions such as the establishment of the Wheat Board, but discontent continued over the long-term grievances of freight rates and the movement of grain, and later over policies of rail line abandonment and agricultural stabilization.

New areas of contention aside from agriculture arose with the development of mineral resources in the province. In this area it was the provincial government which came into conflict both with the corporations that were developing the resources and with the federal government over taxation policies, individual residents of the province to a considerable extent being left as interested bystanders.

The result of the overall greater extension of government activity was that the antagonism of earlier settlers, mentioned in chapter 1 as directed against both Ottawa and the private financial empires centered in Toronto and Montreal, showed itself by the 1970s to be concentrated to a greater degree against Ottawa. An electorate which for individual reasons had become incensed over Ottawa's policies was all the more ready to side with its provincial government in a government-to-government confrontation. For these reasons, issues which concerned the federal government spilled over to a greater or less degree into all three of the provincial elections of the decade.

In the 1971 election it was the general agricultural outlook which was foremost among provincial grievances against Ottawa. Although this was a contest in which the provincial Liberals largely defeated themselves, as noted in chapter 4, a significant advantage on the other side was the NDP championing of the family farm. Allan Blakeney and his party were articulate in denouncing recent federal farm stabilization proposals which pointed to a consolidation of smaller farms into larger units and to the consequent demise of a considerable number of existing farms. Although the NDP defense of the family farm attempted no definition of the precise size that was intended, the term upheld the concept sacred since homestead days of an individually controlled farm unit.

In 1975 Blakeney added energy to agriculture as an area in which he needed a mandate to resist federal policies. This new concern arose as a result of the disputes and court cases over the marketing of oil which had gone on for two years before the election. This time the call had impact only in certain areas. The constitutional implications of federal-provincial disagreements met with the normal indifference given to theoretical questions. Practical manifestations of the energy question were restricted mainly to the oil areas of the province. In the agricultural sector the impact of federal policies was less than in 1971. The proposed farm stabilization program had been withdrawn and reworked. Even if it was still not enthusiastically received by farmers, it did not now attract the downright antagonism which had been directed towards the earlier proposals.

The Crows Nest freight rate controversy which developed in the course of the 1975 election did however illustrate the readiness of the farming electorate to become aroused over a matter affecting it so directly. These long-standing statutory rates set at a low level for the shipping out of grain hold a special place in the economic affections of the Saskatchewan farmer. They are seen not as a special privilege to be tampered with unilaterally, but as one side of a firm bargain originally entered into with the CPR, for which the railway had received full benefit. A suggestion by Otto Lang, then the federal minister in charge of the Wheat Board, that consideration be given to altering the Crows Nest rates brought angry reaction from producers. Provincial Liberals were chagrined that the federal minister could not have kept the suggestion to himself for a few more months. The NDP took full advantage of the assistance thus handed to them by identifying federal and provincial Liberals in an accusation that "the Liberals plan to do away with the Crow Rates."

In announcing the October 18, 1978 election, Premier Blakeney declared the basic issue to be who would in fact have control over the natural resources which belonged to the province. His issue might have been lost in a host of other election issues had it not been unexpectedly highlighted by two Supreme Court decisions which came down during the campaign, striking down Saskatchewan legislation on the taxing of resources. One of the decisions of October 3 referred to potash, ruling illegal the prorationing legislation that originally had been brought in by Ross Thatcher's Liberal administration and included some later changes by the NDP. The other Supreme Court decision was on oil taxation. The previous November the court had ruled the province's tax structure on oil invalid. The decision now handed down was that Saskatchewan must pay interest on the revenue which it had collected from the company contesting the tax, Canadian Industrial Gas and Oil Limited.

Initially it seemed that these decisions might provide greater ammunition for the opposition in showing the shortcomings of provincial legislation. Instead, aided by a climate of sharp dissatisfaction with Ottawa, the NDP quickly turned them to reinforce its issue that the federal government was usurping control of natural resources. The public was not particularly concerned, or even aware, that the only way in which the federal government could legitimately be blamed for a court decision was because it had supported the company side of the action. Premier Blakeney suggested, however, that there was eastern orientation of the Supreme Court in such matters.

With the campaign question, "Who do you trust to best manage our resources?" the NDP now were able to turn voter attention more firmly to the issue of leadership and ability, not only in provincial administration but also in resisting Ottawa. The issue strengthened existing hestitancy about the Conservative leader, Dick Collver, and sharpened the voters' perception of Premier Blakeney as one who had already proven himself in the federal-provincial arena.

Throughout the 1970s personality had played an increasingly stronger role in the federal-provincial scene as it related to Saskatchewan. The two principals remained the same through most of the decade, with Mr. Trudeau still in his first term as Prime Minister when Mr. Blakeney became premier in 1971, and with Blakeney firmly re-installed in his third term when Trudeau was defeated in 1979. Western Canada preceded other sections of the country in antagonism toward Trudeau and his policies. Prairie residents early resented both the Prime Minister's evident failure to understand or appreciate western problems and what they came to see as an excess of attention to Quebec in contrast to continued ignoring of long-standing western grievances. Premier Blakeney emerged a competent champion of the western cause not only in election campaigns but also in federal-provincial conferences and in public statements.

Although Saskatchewan trailed far behind Alberta in economic power, it was Blakeney's personal qualities in discussion, maneuver, and counter-argument which gave him prominence as a western spokesman at these conferences. Eastern writers, not widely known even for cognizance of the west, much less for praise, pointed to Blakeney as the one premier who could stand toe to toe with Trudeau. Especially after receiving a strong mandate in the 1978 provincial election, the premier showed particular zest and confidence in the 1979 conference. Although no specific gains were made, in the way of federal-provincial meetings, Saskatchewan's views were firmly stated, and its ground was held in preparation for succeeding discussions.

A behind-the-scenes factor in strengthening Saskatchewan's position was the rebuilding of public service administrative staff to do the groundwork. This area of administration had suffered after 1964 from Premier Thatcher's general disregard for the public service and from his blindness to the need for adequate preparation and research in order to bolster the province's position in federal relations. Knowledgeable response to Ottawa and presentation of alternatives in conferences during the 1970s, however ably presented by the premier, also owed much to a rebuilt administrative staff in the area of federal-provincial relations. The office carrying on this work was elevated to become a full-fledged Department of Federal-Provincial Relations on July 1, 1979, parallelling similar departments in some of the other provinces.

The shifting of economic power to the west was the outstanding feature of inter-provincial and federal-provincial relations in the 1970s. Tangible evidence for this shift was the movement of head offices from Montreal and Toronto, particularly to Calgary, new business magazines about the western economy, and generally greater attention to the west in a variety of ways. In the economic shift Saskatchewan trailed in the glow of oil-rich Alberta, but it still found itself regarded as part of the "new rich" and given such newspaper captions as that in the *Financial Post* on September 1, 1979, "Saskatchewan blooms with rich resources."

Two sobering facts temper unbridled enthusiasm. The first is that the new riches are non-renewable. The second is that they are primary resources so that, as with agriculture, Saskatchewan's economic role continues to be as a primary producer, subject to the sharper downturns to which resource areas are subject compared to those areas that enjoy secondary industry. Even the safety of a greater variety—oil, potash, and uranium, instead of the single resource of agriculture as formerly—does not ensure stability. The reality exists that all resources are susceptible to a downswing, just as all have been buoyant at the same time.

Industrial development has been stressed successively by CCF and NDP governments from a socialist viewpoint and by Ross Thatcher's Liberal government from a private enterprise outlook. Encouragement and aid have been added by federal regional development programs. Despite the successes claimed by succeeding governments and certain increases in this area, the value of manufacturing in the gross domestic product of the province was less than sixteen per cent in 1978.

The second sobering fact is that an economic shift westward does not necessarily mean a similar political shift. As mentioned in chapter 1, from the earliest days resentment has existed over the west's exclusion from political as well as economic power. The sparse population of western Canada has not altered the slight voting power which it can wield in party caucus or in the House of Commons. The attention given to the shift in economic power has created an idea that political power has followed, but the truth of that idea remains to be seen. A sense of newly gained political power was enhanced by the substantial support that the west gave the winning Progressive Conservative party in the 1979 election. But the plain statistics are that the fourteen seats which the entire province has are less than one-sixth of Ontario's ninety-five seats, and that the ten members which Saskatchewan sent to the Conservative caucus were barely more than one-sixth of the fifty-eight Progressive Conservatives which Ontario sent to the same caucus. The city of Toronto alone has more than half as many members again as the province of Saskatchewan. Even the western provinces together fall far behind the weight of interests to be looked to in the central provinces.

More significantly in the post-election political scene in 1979, no change was evident in the real center of power, the cabinet. Even with no scarcity of Conservative members to choose from, western strength was not increased, the traditional heavy reliance on Ontario contin-ued, and in Quebec where voters denied the government material for cabinet choices, alternatives were explored to continue the province's customary role.

In the 1970s Saskatchewan felt defensive towards Quebec. Long regarding "the east" with its economic and political control as the common enemy to their interests, westerners viewed with astonish-ment the eastern interpretation arising out of the "Quebec fact" of the 1960s and 1970s. In the newly defined alignment of the country, the west now found itself grouped with Ontario as "English Canada", presumably with a special antagonism towards "French Canada". It is debatable whether frustration ran deeper at being regarded as a satellite of Ontario or at being unfairly castigated, as the west felt, for hostility towards Quebec. Saskatchewan residents may previously have been only vaguely aware of the nature of Quebec's distinctive culture, but they had no doubts of a prairie personality and culture different from Ontario's.

The newly alerted attitude of Saskatchewan residents to Quebec and to the French-speaking population in the 1960s and 1970s varied widely and it also changed over the years. Without attempting anything but the most superficial comment here, the attitude extended all the way from that of the "rednecks" with their outspoken opposition to what they saw as any concessions to Quebec as a province or to the French as a people, to those who were sympathetic to French Canada's complaints.

Ottawa, not Quebec, was the source of bilingual measures which created probably the greatest irritation in the province. Bilingual labelling as the most obvious of these measures is met every day, and it conflicts with two interrelated outlooks which still survive from pioneer days: the practical and the economic. To search through two languages for content or information seems less than practical in a section of the country where French-speaking residents form an extremely small part of the population—less than three per cent in Saskatchewan. Economically there is also the knowledge that either the bilingual labelling raises the price of items coming from outside the country which have to be re-labelled, or that alternatively consumers are denied the product.

In federal-provincial matters Saskatchewan is not at all hesitant to take any advantage offered in constitutional re-alignment that may arise out of Quebec militancy. In the late 1970s there was a greater willingness on Ottawa's part, at least verbally, to look at changes in federal and provincial powers, so Saskatchewan pressed forward its claims. These included clarification of control over natural resources and the right of the provinces to levy indirect taxes.

Premier Blakeney has repeated in public addresses the tenor of the views he expressed in federal-provincial conferences. In Montreal in June of 1979, addressing a meeting of the Council for Canadian Unity in which he dealt with the broader theme of the needs for Canada's future, he spoke of the economic relation between east and west. In this speech Premier Blakeney rejected the Quebec government's proposal of sovereignty association as a violation of one side of the economic bargain of Confederation while holding onto the other side. He pointed out that by western understanding, the economic basis of Confederation meant that the west accepted tariff protection for industry in Ontario and Quebec, and in return those provinces supported a strong central government which helped sell western products, provide a transportation network, and give some degree of economic security.

As a parallel to Quebec's legitimate complaints, the premier referred to the historic sense of injustice felt by the prairie provinces, and he noted that the sense of grievance has increased as the provinces have gained in prosperity and self-confidence. Westerners are strongly committed to the idea of a united Canada, but some of the alienation in the west, as in Quebec, comes from a sense of having been taken for granted and regarded as laborers by what the premier referred to as the rich landlords of Ontario and Quebec.[1] In addressing the convention of the federated Women's Institutes in Saskatoon in July of 1979, Premier Blakeney spoke of the prairie's viewpoint on Canada's racial foundations. He said the eastern Canadian idea of two founding races, built on two cultures, does not convince prairie people, because the French fact in Saskatchewan is largely confined to bilingual labels, radio, and television, and to small communities of French Canadians. He continued that "Saskatchewan is the only Canadian province in which people of British and French descent added together do not form a majority. We belong to neither of the two nations referred to in the current debate." Referring to the variety of provincial origins, the premier spoke of the need for a Confederation which takes into account the needs of all regions and the true multi-cultural basis of the country.[2]

Internally in Saskatchewan in the 1970s changing economic and social circumstances showed the beginnings of a more complex political situation. Agricultural concerns which have traditionally dominated the political scene were nudged by non-agricultural problems which increasingly competed for attention from political parties and government. Even while agriculture still held its prior position in the economy and there seemed little likelihood of its being replaced, the population had become more and more urban. Not only were a smaller number required on modern farms, but those in cities became more urban minded as direct connection with agriculture decreased. The second generation which came from farm families but took on urban occupations still had a feeling for or at least an understanding of rural concerns. An urban born third generation does not have this link.

In the 1970s the Saskatchewan government was substantially preoccupied with oil and gas, potash and uranium. This preoccupation included the disputes with potash firms over taxation which resulted in the eventual establishment of the Saskatchewan Potash Corporation and the nationalizing of a sufficient area of the industry to secure government control of potash development. In the latter half of the decade there was attention to uranium development and to the accompanying questioning and protests from those concerned with the safety of such development.

In addition to development policies, the government was concerned with strategy on two other fronts. In the short term it had to devise new legislation to circumvent, retroactively, the effect of Supreme Court rulings which would otherwise have deprived the province of a large amount of revenue from resource development. On the broader scene there were efforts towards the overall division and definition of taxation and resource revenue between the provincial and the federal authorities, referred to above.

Northern Saskatchewan and the native population of the province were other non-agricultural areas that increasingly competed for attention. To the extent that Indians and Metis moved into cities, the question of adjustment overlapped with other urban concerns. Creation of a Department of Indian and Metis Affairs by the Liberals, which the NDP replaced with the Department of Northern Development, reflected official recognition of special needs in these areas. On the eve of election day in 1978, the Association of Metis and non-status Indians of Saskatchewan complained that all three parties had ignored their concerns.

Another group, cutting across all sections of the province, was formed of senior citizens, whose proportion of the population is increasing and who are becoming more vocal. In the 1978 election they were wooed by all three parties. The Conservatives promised to adjust senior citizen pensions to the minimum wage, the Liberals proposed to freeze pensioners' utility costs at the level they paid at the age of sixty-five, and the NDP promised to remove school taxation on property owned by senior citizens.

Political parties cannot lose sight of the agrarian base of the province, but they must now effect a balance between agricultural and non-agricultural interests in order to attract the support of each without alienating one or the other. This double need is well illustrated in the varying approach of the NDP in the 1970s. In the 1971 election the preservation of the family farm was emphasized, as already noted. After the 1975 election, the rise of the Progressive Conservatives persuaded the NDP that they must give more attention to urban problems in another election. The NDP were not afraid of the Conservatives taking city seats, since Conservative strength was in rural areas, but they did fear that the Conservatives might split voting sufficiently in urban areas for the Liberals to win. In the 1978 election, without specific agricultural issues to demand particular attention, the NDP like the other parties spread their attention more widely among other issues. The result was that complaints were made that agriculture tended to be neglected by all three parties.

The 1978 election post-mortem quickly turned NDP attention again to rural areas. They had made an almost clean sweep of city seats, but their support in rural areas had dropped. A cabinet shift placed a tried and strong minister, Gordon MacMurchy, in the agriculture portfolio, in frank recognition of the need for a higher profile and rebuilding in that area.

In July of 1979 the new Minister of Agriculture laid down what was essentially a long term agricultural platform for the next election. He acknowledged that since 1971 the NDP had concentrated on its resource policies, and farmers had justifiably begun to feel they were being ignored. During the next four years, Mr. MacMurchy said, the government wanted agriculture restored to its place as the key to the Saskatchewan economy. The chief areas which he specified for attention were grain handling and transportation. His concern covered the province's support for implementation of the federal Hall royal commission report on grain handling and transportation which recommended, as part of its wide-reaching proposals on the railways, the retention of the country elevator system. The government's concern for grain handling and transportation also included strong defense of the Crows Nest freight rate on grain. Saskatchewan had already taken a stand on this question as the only province to favor retention of the Crow rate at a meeting of western transport ministers.

Other areas which Mr. MacMurchy singled out for future attention included further diversification of the farm economy into livestock and specialty crops. Although this diversification had been encouraged by government in the past they had, the minister said in good agricultural terms, "just scratched the surface." Drainage and flood control, which had become an increasing problem in recent years, was marked for immediate attention. He spoke also of land use and, in an issue harking back to the "family farm" ideal, of the difficult problem of limiting farm size.[3]

To compete successfully in the changed and changing Saskatchewan scene, all parties will have to attempt a balance between agricultural and non-agricultural concerns. Although the scope of the political game has thus become more complex, there is no indication that the basic rules have changed. Just as the dominant agricultural electorate of the past judged on practical grounds, the less homogeneous present generation continues in the main to demand that political parties meet them on pragmatic terms.

Appendix A
Supplement to Chapter 3
(The Separate Schools Controversy, 1905)

The 1905 separate school dispute was double-headed. In addition to the basic question of direction over separate schools, the second issue concerned financing, and it had far-reaching implications. It was in fact the financial aspect which reportedly was the subject of hottest debate in official confrontation, even though the spotlight of public attention was on various aspects of separate schools as such.

All that the North-West Territories Act of 1875 had to say about the financing of schools was in the single paragraph which guaranteed the existence of separate schools and which stated that in the establishment of school districts

... the minority of the rate-payers therein, whether Protestant or Roman Catholic, may establish separate schools therein, and that, in such latter case, the rate-payers establishing such Protestant or Roman Catholic separate schools shall be liable only to assessment of such rates as they may impose upon themselves ....

In practice, the Territories also paid school grants equally to public and to separate schools. Each type of school in the Territories thus operated on the same financial basis of taxes from its own ratepayers plus annual grants from the Territorial government.

The school land fund was a potential third source of revenue, but one for the future rather than for immediate availability. Revenue from the sale of school lands (the two sections in each township), was to form a trust fund which was entirely separate from the annual legislative grant that the government paid to public and separate schools. Also, the Dominion Lands Act specified that this trust fund was for public schools.

The original 1905 clause which Laurier included in the autonomy bills followed very closely the broad wording of the old North-West Territories Act, but with two additions. One was reference to Section 93 of the B.N.A. Act which protects those separate schools which are in existence when a province enters Confederation. The second was a spelling out of the new provinces' financial obligations to separate schools. Payment of legislative grants without discrimination to public and separate schools was spelled out, thus giving constitutional sanction to what had been legislative practice. A provision that future proceeds from the school lands trust fund were to be similarly distributed to both separate and public schools broke new ground.

The newly introduced clause 16 read in its entirety:

1. The provisions of Section 93 of the British North America Act, 1867 shall apply to the said Province as if, at the date upon which this Act comes into force, the Territory comprised therein were already a Province, the expression "the Union" in the said section being taken to mean the said date.

2. Subject to the provisions of the said Section 93, and in continuance of the principles heretofor sanctioned under the North-West Territories Act, it is enacted that the Legislature of the said Province shall pass all necessary laws in respect of education and that it shall therein always be provided.

(a) that a majority of the ratepayers of any district or portion of the said Province or of any less portion of the said Province or of any less portion of subdivision thereof by whatever name it is known, may establish such schools therein as they think fit, and make the necessary assessment and collection of rates therefor and

(b) that the minority of the ratepayers therein, whether Protestant or Roman Catholic may establish separate schools therein, and make the necessary assessment and collection of rates therefor, and

(c) that in such case the ratepayers establishing such Protestant or Roman Catholic separate schools shall be liable only to assessment of such rates as they impose upon themselves with respect thereto.

3. In the appropriation of public moneys by the Legislature in aid of education, and in the distribution of any moneys paid to the Government of the said Province arising from the school fund established by the Dominion Lands Act, there shall be no discrimination between the public schools and the separate schools and such moneys shall be applied to the support of public and separate schools in equitable shares or proportion.

Territorial members of Parliament completely overlooked the ambiguity in the legislation's references to the separate school system as such. The unexpected reference to the school lands fund puzzled them, however, and made them uneasy. Walter Scott wrote to a Regina friend the day after the bills were introduced:

Our expectation was that section 14 of the N.W.T. Act [relating to schools] would simply be embodied in the new measure and re-enacted but they have gone further and inserted additional language proposing to grant to minority schools their share of public grants ... [from] school land revenues. It is understood that they contend that the additional language does not alter the system that has existed at all, and if this is the case it probably means no difference. On the other hand there is a fear that the language must have some meaning and may mean some change and that otherwise it would not have been inserted. If it does mean any change it certainly also means trouble. Those of us from the North-West were united in intention to support the proposal to re-enact section 14, but I do not think we can stand for anything additional.[1]

The members' initial unease concerning the school lands fund was sharpened by Clifford Sifton's quick return to Ottawa, and their concern was broadened to include the nature of the schools themselves. In later correspondence Walter Scott explained that the Northwest members had relied upon the assurance that the existing system of separate schools would continue, and he admitted that when the bills were introduced, "Laurier's speech indicated nothing further to me, and I followed him closely . . . but Sifton's analyzing acumen quickly picked out the meaning of the clause, which, without question, would remove the separate schools from public regulation."[2] Having been thus startled into a reappraisal of the clause, western members held to their determination that separate school privileges should not extend beyond those actually in operation, and they backed Sifton's opposition to Clause 16.

Sifton himself expressed initial uncertainty as to the precise meaning of the separate school provision, even with his "experience in construing and arguing clauses of this kind." A long-standing feud with Fitzpatrick also sharpened Sifton's suspicions, as he admitted to his close personal and political friend, J. W. Dafoe: ". . . the fact that it was drawn by Fitzpatrick does not add anything to my confidence that the draftsman had in mind the same intention that we had. I do not accuse him of intentionally deceiving anyone, but he makes no secret of the fact that he is desirous of meeting the views of the Church."[3] Sifton came to a firm conclusion as to what the bill did not do, however. In a letter to Laurier the following day he referred to its ambiguity, and he told the Prime Minister "that he was quite satisfied that it does not safeguard the right of the legislature to fully regulate and control all the schools."[4]

From the beginning Sifton was single-minded in his opposition to the new provision on school lands. He regarded its inclusion in the financial provisions as indefensible, and he wrote indignantly to Dafoe:

This question was never discussed before, it has never been discussed at all between myself and any other Member of the Government, and the contents of the clause as it stands now in the Bill are altogether new to me.[5]

Two days later he again unburdened himself respecting the impropriety of the proposal:

. . . it constitutes a division of the proceeds of the enormous land subsidy for school purposes in the North West. The Dominion Lands Act reserves these lands for public schools. Laurier proposes to divert a portion of the amount, which in the whole will probably amount to from twenty to forty million dollars, to endow the separate schools of the Roman Catholic church. I am unalterably opposed to such a proposition. I cannot conceive of any serious minded man in the present stage of the history of Canada contemplating the possibility of such a measure.[6]

Sir William Mulock, the only Protestant representative on the federal negotiating committee, found himself at even greater loss than the western members to recognize the significance of the school clause. Unlike them he did not have Sifton's close advice and his enlightenment came eventually from a newspaper correspondent who wrote from Ottawa to his editor in Toronto:

Mulock wavered over the school clause. As far as I could gather from him, he trusted Laurier—was staggered at the scope of the clause when it was brought to his attention by the press—sought an explanation—received an unequivocal assurance that L. had no intention of going beyond the leg. of 1875—apparently got another assurance that the clause would be amended to make this plain—is disposed to think it all right to guarantee the continuance of the present excellent system. I put to him the difference between the present system and the sort of system that would be guaranteed by the leg. of 1875. He seemed struck by it, and made me repeat it.[7]

By contrast, Mulock's Catholic colleagues on the negotiating committee, Charles Fitzpatrick and Senator Scott, had clearly been kept informed by Roman Catholic officials of the changes made in the Territorial school system over the years. A nine-page typed memorandum prepared after the 1892 legislation, which traced changes in separate school provisions, had engaged Senator Scott's attention sufficiently for him to make marginal notes and at the end his angry, handwritten judgement:

The skeleton permitted to the minority by the men who framed this Draconian code—The minority have no control over their children—the books may misrepresent their faith.[8]

Senator Scott also received a copy of a letter of October 4, 1903, from the Bishop of St. Albert, Northwest Territories, to Archbishop Sbaretti, Apostolic Delegate in Canada, giving a historical summary and bringing changes in Territorial law up to date, as far as the establishment of the Department of Education in 1901. The letter included the Bishop's careful enumeration of the privileges lost by separate schools in the "radical modification" of the school law in 1892, the advantages still existing, and the further provisions "the Catholics have then the right to exact."[9]

Letters in March of 1904 to Justice Minister Fitzpatrick from Archbishop Sbaretti and from Henri Bourassa discussed a "document relative to the guaranteeing of Catholic Separate Schools in the Territories when they are erected into provinces," which Fitzpatrick was to draw up and which was to be signed by him and by Bourassa, and submitted to Prime Minister Laurier for his signature.[10]

A firm sense of their own right held by each side hardened positions in the ensuing struggle over the school clause. Sifton and the other western members felt betrayed at what they saw as a devious attempt to violate the earlier agreement. Fitzpatrick and Senator Scott felt deeply that Roman Catholic rights had been unjustly eroded over the years by restrictive Territorial legislation. They looked for a return to the earlier denominational separate school system, not as gaining any special privilege but as a simple restoration of right. Prime Minister Laurier, in addition to his own similar convictions, felt bound also by the earlier assurances he had given Roman Catholic officials which were in terms of the broadly worded 1875 North-West Territories Act. In the midst of the crisis which developed he wrote to a friend that although there might be some modifications to make in the bill they should be in form rather than in substance, and he indicated as his foremost aim the preservation of the rights of the minority.[11]

The real nature of the issues was obscured both by the complications involved, and by Laurier's early insistence that his clause did in fact represent what had been agreed to. The initial superficial view that a mere clearing up of a misunderstanding was all that was required was evident in correspondence which the Governor General had with both Laurier and Sifton. A general lack of awareness of the crucial points was represented in the Governor General's expressed optimism for a speedy resolution since, he noted, each wished only a clause "which will confirm the minority in the rights they at present enjoy."[12]

Basic policy decisions were in fact involved. The question of supervision of the schools required a choice to be made between two previously existing systems: government supervision, or a possible return to ecclesiastical direction of the separate schools. The other issue, that of distribution of funds from the school lands trust, required decision on an entirely new matter not previously considered in connection with establishment of the provinces. This proved the more difficult point, as Sifton reported in the course of discussions:

I have had to make a very determined fight about the School Lands Fund. This is in reality where the conflict was hottest. They did not expect to get much more in the way of separate schools than they have now, but they expected to get a declaration in the Constitution which could not be repealed, and which would give them a vested interest in the proceeds of the School Lands which would be an inducement to the Catholic people to organize as many schools as possible.[13]

A further financial point which Sifton also raised concerned the level of separate schools which should get government support. The existing practice within the Territories to pay legislative grants equally to separate and public schools was restricted to elementary schools, since the Schools Ordinance of 1892 required secondary education to be non-sectarian. This limitation was not included in Clause 16. Its wording referred in broad terms to "public moneys ... in aid of education" and "support of public and separate schools", potentially leaving it without limitation. Later, in House of Commons debate, Sifton explained that he had feared in the original clause a compulsion of division of moneys between Protestant and Roman Catholic institutions even up to and including university grants.

Slow and painful resolution of the issues extended from an initial meeting between Sifton and Laurier on February 24 to the introduc-

tion of an amended school clause into the House on March 22. Prime
Minister Laurier was reported to show a marked reluctance to discuss
the various points, and his renowned "sunny ways" were not evident
within the conference walls.

The February 24 meeting was reported by Sifton to be a one-sided
presentation of views:

> I have not discussed the matter with Sir Wilfrid at all further than that he
> called me into his room yesterday and spoke at some length of the difficulties
> which he had had. He did not ask me my opinion or what my views were. Sir
> Wilfrid's procedure in matters of this kind is always to assume that everyone
> agrees with him until they insist upon quarrelling. He finds this much the
> easiest way of getting on. He will not seek for an opportunity of allowing me
> to raise a dispute about it, but I shall of course be compelled to bring the
> subject up very soon.[14]

Sifton's letter to Laurier on February 26 in which he expressed his
dissatisfaction with the clause was followed by a visit to Laurier the
same day. Laurier refused to consider modifying the clause and
intimated that he would resign if Sifton did, although Sifton privately
expressed doubt that Laurier would do so. Sifton himself resigned
from the cabinet on February 27.

In announcing the resignation in the House on March 1, Laurier
stated that the disagreement between himself and his colleague was
confined to the education clause. Sifton followed immediately with a
brief explanation, saying that in the Prime Minister's address in
introducing the bills there were principles enunciated with which he
could not agree, nor could he endorse or support the principle of the
education clauses. In contrast to the restraint of the speeches in the
House, rumors ran riot of further resignations, and even that Sifton
would lead a party split against the Prime Minister.

The western members drew up a substitute clause, but subsequent
meetings and caucuses failed to secure any agreement with the Prime
Minister and his colleagues. A cabinet committee finally was
appointed on March 8 to try to break the deadlock.

Those engaged in the discussions reported privately on the extreme
difficulty of reaching agreement. Clifford Sifton wrote that it was
impossible for anyone not in touch with the "inner movement of
affairs" to realize the difficulties, and Walter Scott echoed this
viewpoint when he wrote on March 9:

> The position here during the past week has been very precarious, possibly
> more so in fact than anybody outside would think from the reports going out.
> Even yet it cannot be said that the solution has been reached, but I think the
> atmosphere is clearing and am hopeful that before long an unmistakable
> understanding will be arrived at, furnishing common ground on which all the
> elements of the party may safely stand.[15]

Senator Scott said later that "the Prime Minister was face to face with
the question whether he should accept the substituted clause or he and
his colleagues should resign".[16] By March 11 Sifton reported to Dafoe

that they had "practically agreed" upon a settlement. Following the Prime Minister's intimation on March 15 that a change was contemplated, he announced to the House on March 20 that he would introduce an amendment to clause 16.

The result was an amendment on March 22 which met the demands of Sifton and the other western members on both points of contention. The amended clause removed ambiguity as to the nature of the system by including specific reference to relevant Territorial legislation which would keep both public and separate schools under direct government administration. Financial provisions also were specifically restricted to prior Territorial practice. Reference to the school lands fund was deleted, and legislative grants were applied only to the level of schools provided for in existing legislation, which was the elementary level. The exclusion of separate high schools from government grants which was effected by the amended clause remained until 1964. Financial provisions in 1905 thus were specifically restricted to current Territorial practice, although payment of legislative grants on an equal basis to elementary public and separate schools now had the constitutional sanction of the Saskatchewan Act.

The amendment was subsequently adopted as clause 17 of the Act which read:

Section 93 of the British North America Act, 1867, shall apply to the said province, with the substitution for paragraph 1 of the said Section 93, of the following paragraph.

1. Nothing in any such law shall prejudicially affect any right or privilege with respect to separate schools which any class of persons have at the date of the passing of this Act, under the terms of Chapters 29 and 30 of the Ordinances of the North-West Territories, passed in the year 1901, or with respect to religious instruction in any public or separate schools as provided for in the said Ordinances.

2. In the appropriation by the Legislature or distribution by the Government of the Province of any moneys for the support of schools organized and carried on in accordance with the said Chapter 29, or any Act passed in amendment thereof, or in substitution therefor, there shall be no discrimination against schools of any class described in the said Chapter 29.

3. Where the expression "by law" is employed in paragraph 3 of the said Section 93 it shall be held to mean the law as set out in the said Chapters 29 and 30; and where the expression "at the Union" is employed in the said paragraph 3, it shall be held to mean the date at which this act comes into force.

Although commonly termed the "compromise clause", the amended clause was in no sense a compromise so far as the western members were concerned. They secured exactly what they understood as the original agreement, a continuation of the school system as it was then operating in the Territories. Even if that agreement itself had been regarded as a necessary compromise by members who would have preferred no provision at all for separate schools, within that framework western members did not move from their position. Clifford Sifton nevertheless remained outside the cabinet, despite the final acceptance of his arguments.

Settlement within official circles was only part of the defusing of the crisis. The public controversy and the agitation and counter-agitation in Ontario and Quebec had raged within such a framework of confrontation, suspicion, and plain misunderstanding of complicated issues that it was not readily susceptible to rational explanation.

Even though Sifton had carried the day in official discussions, he was concerned that his efforts might be scuttled by blind religious animosity among those presumably supporting him. Just as assistance from the Roman Catholic clergy had been enlisted by Laurier to prevent discussion of the separate school issue before the 1904 election, so Sifton in turn now sought support from the Protestant clergy to ensure acceptance of the amended school clause in 1905. On March 11, when a settlement had been "practically agreed" upon at Ottawa but was not yet to be made public, Sifton wrote to Dafoe in Winnipeg:

It is of the utmost importance that the Methodist, Presbyterian and Baptist clergymen in Winnipeg should be got to see the desirability of supporting this Provision before it is announced, and I would therefore like that you should either yourself or through someone else have them interviewed confidentially and fully informed as to what is under consideration. On the merits there is no objection to this proposal at all as you know. The only difficulty that we shall be in will be that some people will not be able to get themselves away from the blind adherence to catch words such as "provincial rights" and "separate schools", that is to say they will not take the trouble to analyze the proposition but will oppose it on theory. If, however, the clergy of Winnipeg support it I am not afraid of anything else.[17]

The legal arguments which each side had advanced in the dispute had in fact little substance, however impressive they may have sounded for political purposes. The Conservative opposition argued that inclusion of any school clause at all invaded provincial rights. Whatever moral substance the argument had, it had no constitutional basis, since Parliament had full legal power to determine the terms of entry of a new province. This power had been explicitly confirmed in the amendment to the B.N.A. Act in 1871, after doubts had arisen about Parliament's powers in creating the province of Manitoba.

Those favoring separate schools appealed to Section 93 of the B.N.A. Act which protected denominational schools that were in existence when a province entered Confederation. They disregarded the distinction between an existing province coming in, where the clause automatically applied, and a former Territory being created into a province, where the clause did not apply, unless specifically included in the legislation creating a new province, as was done in 1905.

Legally, therefore, no constitutional provisions applied which required any form of separate schools whatever to be included in the constitutions of the new provinces. Equally, there were no legal restrictions barring any kind of system which might be established. Whatever terms for separate schools were to be included in the constitutions of the new provinces rested entirely upon a combination of common justice and political expediency, to be worked out through negotiation. This was the way in which the question had started early in 1904 in agreement on the deceptive "existing system" and the way in which it concluded with the tense negotiations of March, 1905.

The question remains whether Prime Minister Laurier was part of a conscious effort to expand separate school rights in 1905 as Sifton believed, or whether the Prime Minister was unaware of the double interpretation afforded by the term "existing system" and genuinely thought it was represented by the 1875 legislation.

The conscious intent of Fitzpatrick and Senator Scott at least can scarcely be doubted. Walter Scott expressed a contemporary view when, while exonerating Laurier and all other cabinet ministers in his own mind, he specifically named Senator Scott and Fitzpatrick as those who did know the real purport of Section 16. A private letter of Senator Scott's two years later documented his clear intent in 1905 to broaden the latitude of separate schools. Writing to Archbishop Sbaretti on December 30, 1907 to resist some new action which the Archbishop was pressing upon him, the Senator referred to the 1905 situation and to the "honest effort to secure for the minority the unconditional school privileges to which I think we were entitled." Senator Scott spoke nostalgically of the 1875 legislation and reminded the Archbishop, "You cannot have forgotten the ministerial crisis that resulted in our attempt to re-enact the legislation of the former period," although as he noted, through pressures in the House of Commons it had been necessary to "practically adopt the law as it then stood in the Territories."[18]

That the Prime Minister was among those included in the reference to "our attempt" is also substantially documented, if not so conclusively as in Scott's admission. Laurier's position in the drawing up of the school clause was not detached or remote. On the contrary, he participated actively with Fitzpatrick and Archbishop Sbaretti in private and painstaking preparation of the clause in January and February of 1905. At the same time, official negotiations with Territorial representatives were under way on other aspects of the autonomy bills, and also at the same time, on January 26, Laurier turned aside Sifton's query about the school clause.

The clause was drafted by Fitzpatrick in consultation with Laurier and Sbaretti, and it was submitted to Sbaretti on January 10.[19] After suggestions from other Catholic officials and further representations from Sbaretti, Laurier met with Sbaretti on February 1. On February 7 Sbaretti wrote Laurier, pressing for a change in a revised clause just submitted to him by Fitzpatrick, and on February 10 Laurier gave Sbaretti another revised clause. After further communication between the two during the next few days, Laurier wrote to Sbaretti on February 16 rejecting a proposed addition on the ground that it contained new words which "opened the way for 'a somewhat dangerous attack.'" The main difficulties, he explained, had been with the wording of the financial provisions which broke new legislative ground, but Laurier now said that he saw his "way perfectly" before him.

The anticipated fulfilment of the Church's hopes by the original school clause is evident in Sbaretti's letter to Archbishop Langevin of St. Boniface on February 20, the day before Laurier introduced the bills into the House. He wrote, "If Parliament passes the clause as it stands, we shall have more in the Constitutional Acts of these Provinces than in any of the Constitutional Acts of the other provinces of the Dominion."[20]

That Laurier was a knowledgeable partner in these aspirations rather than a dupe is suggested also in two subsequent comments of Archbishop Langevin. During the first Saskatchewan election campaign in December 1905, Langevin privately described Walter Scott, now premier, as "a strange person who had practically cut Laurier's throat by objecting to his giving the minority confessional schools."[21] The second comment was a marginal note which the Archbishop added in 1907 to a letter of appreciation to Laurier written (but never mailed) on February 23, 1905, two days after the school clause had been made public and before there was any clear intimation of the fate which was to befall it. The 1907 addendum noted that fortunately the letter had not been sent "car Sir Wilfrid a, ensuite, capitulé."[22]

Appendix B

Supplement to Chapter 8
The Lieutenant Governor:
1905 and 1916

In 1905, Liberals concerned with western affairs clearly assumed that the choice of a new premier for Saskatchewan would be made in fact by Prime Minister Laurier and only formally by Lieutenant Governor Forget. During the tense weeks of maneuvering which preceded the formation of Alberta and Saskatchewan, Liberal leaders regarded the choice of premiers in both of the new provinces as a matter of political strategy. Correspondence shows that Haultain's chances for appointment in Saskatchewan had vanished by early July, and that the decision to by-pass him for either province was made in Ottawa later that month.

Opposition to Haultain's appointment in Saskatchewan was strong both at Ottawa and at Regina. As early as May of 1905, the choice was becoming a matter of some interest, though without any definite understanding as to what would be done. Haultain's active participation in two Ontario by-elections in June, in which he attacked the autonomy terms, did much to crystallize Liberal opposition against his selection. From Ottawa Walter Scott wrote to Bulyea in Regina:

His statement at Woodstock on election night containing the direct threat that, if put in power in one of the new provinces, he would go to any length to perpetuate trouble over the school question is about all the reason that is needed to excuse passing over him. . . . The fact of the matter is that his whole course since the issue of his letter of protestation has been of a sort to make it more and more difficult to our party to assent to his being called in either province. Between ourselves, Laurier would be strongly inclined to have Haultain called if there were a ghost of a chance that such action would be followed by Haultain's dropping the school question fight—at least so he has expressed himself to me. I had to tell him plainly that I would only consent to his being called upon the view that we could more certainly beat him in the election as head of a government than as leader of an opposition.[1]

In Regina G. W. Brown, a member of the Territorial assembly and later a lieutenant governor of Saskatchewan, similarly was convinced that the course which Haultain had pursued had "made it impossible for the Government to justify itself in calling him to form a Government in either of the Provinces. . . ."[2]

It is evident in correspondence that the choice for Saskatchewan had been made by early July and that it was to be Walter Scott, but Scott reported from Ottawa:

Laurier still seems to be imbued with the idea that Haultain ought to be called in Alberta. I think this is largely for the reason that we appear to lack any legitimate man in our party in Alberta to call. . . . With everybody here excepting only Laurier himself, Haultain's Woodstock threat has served to put him entirely out of the running so far as concerns his being called in either Province and in face of this unanimous feeling it is pretty certain that Laurier will not continue to stand out.[3]

The Prime Minister continued to "stand out" for a time, but by July 25 Scott reported that Haultain would not be called in either province, although Laurier very much regretted "the impossibility of doing what, under ordinary circumstances, would have been the obvious thing."

Prime Minister Laurier explained his sentiments on the same day in a letter to Regina, writing to Bulyea, the senior Liberal member of the Territorial cabinet:

The time is fast approaching, when the organization of the two new provinces must be seriously considered, and as the time is thus coming nearer and nearer to unavoidable action, I every day feel more keenly the difficulties of the task.

At the outset, I had indulged the hope of an easy solution, a solution which then seemed so natural as not even to suggest the possibility of another and different one.

When you and Haultain came to Ottawa, in the early part of January last, I thought, and indeed every one thought, that as soon as the two provinces came into existence, the then existing Government of the Territories would naturally become the government of Saskatchewan.

The attitude of Haultain has made this, in my judgment, an impossibility . . . especially when he announced his intention of carrying on the provincial elections on the avowed policy of destroying the school system of which some weeks before, he had said, that if he were a dictator, he would not change . . . he left us no alternative, but to accept the declaration of war.[4]

Lieutenant Governor Forget's sentiments echoed Laurier's. To whatever extent the lieutenant governor's assessment of the situation was his own or was influenced from outside, it is evident that Prime Minister Laurier had directed the lieutenant governor's attention to Scott as the new premier for Saskatchewan. In a letter accepting Laurier's offer of the position of lieutenant governor, Forget added:

The situation which we will have to deal with the first of next September is as you say not without difficulties.

It is infinitely regrettable, in particular, that Haultain, by his extreme hostility, has made himself impossible as Prime Minister of one of the new provinces.

The change from the old to the new regime would then have been made smoothly and general satisfaction would have reigned everywhere. Unfortunately this is no longer possible and with a few exceptions, the general desire is that the new governments be constituted on the basis of federal party divisions.

The Lieutenant-Governors then have, in my opinion, no other alternative, than to choose their prime minister from that of the two political parties which, for the moment, seems to have the majority.

In both provinces, they fortunately have to guide them the very recent results of the last federal elections, which leave no doubt. In spite of that it will still be necessary that those who are chosen as members of the executive in both provinces inspire sufficient confidence, especially the prime minister. If as you allow me to hope Mr. W. Scott will consent to take upon himself the administration for the province of Saskatchewan, what appeared to be the gravest difficulty will be happily resolved; for he is, in spite of his youth, the most influential politician in the province.

The Liberals of Saskatchewan are to have a convention . . . in a few days and there is every reason to believe that they will choose Mr. Scott as leader . . . it would not be possible for . . . [Haultain] to form a government like the one of which he is at present the head, for I do not believe that any Liberal, at least any influential Liberal, would agree to become a part of it. To invite him in these circumstances would serve no useful purpose unless to demonstrate the fact that no combination between the two parties is possible. Unless then you have a different opinion, my intention is to call immediately as first minister the leader whom the Liberals of Saskatchewan choose at their next convention.[5]

Friendly newspapers in the province naturally defended the choice of Scott over Haultain. One local editor openly swept aside constitutional propriety in defending political reality:

It is a well known fact that the selection of a Premier by the Lieutenant-Governor for any province in Canada is made on the recommendation of the party in power at Ottawa, and by the appointment of Walter Scott, Lieutenant-Governor Forget was simply following out established precedents.[6]

In Regina the *Leader* cautiously restricted its study of precedents to the federal Conservative administration in 1867. It wrote editorially:

Nobody can for a moment doubt that all the first Premiers were selected by the advisers of the Crown at Ottawa whose will the respective representatives of the Crown in the Province carried into effect.[7]

Prime Minister Laurier denied that he had interfered. In reply to a charge in the House of Commons from Mr. Borden, the national Conservative leader, the Prime Minister stated that Mr. Forget was not the kind of person who would accept such improper direction, and he referred to Haultain as not "being in sympathy with the constitution . . . [and] openly avowing his intention of putting a ruthless hand upon it." The lieutenant-governor, he stated, "could not do otherwise than to call to his counsels a man who would advise him to work the constitution harmoniously for the benefit of all." In the following session when the charge was repeated Laurier stated flatly, "I never had a word of communication with the Lieutenant-Governor of Saskatchewan as to the party whom he should call to his council.[8]

Aside from who decided, the question remains whether the choice itself was constitutionally correct. The established principle that the leader with a majority in the house should be chosen premier provided little guidance here. No local elections had been held since 1902, significant changes had since occurred in the political situation, the legislature had not met for more than a year, and at that time the two parties were evenly represented in a theoretically non-partisan house. In any event the Territorial assembly would automatically disappear on September 1, and the new government would be an interim one until elections were held.

As indicated in his letter, Forget looked instead for guidance to "the very recent results of the last federal elections," in which the Territories had elected seven out of ten Liberal members of Parliament. Furthermore, as Forget pointed out at the earliest possible opportunity, the choice was justified by subsequent events. At the swearing-in ceremony of Forget's successor five years later, the retiring lieutenant governor referred to his own assumption of office and his

difficult and most delicate duty ... connected with the formation of his Cabinet. It was his first act and the only one ... which had met with severe criticism on the part of the opponents of the present Provincial Government. Despite all that had been said in condemnation of this one act, he felt sure, in his conscience, that he had done his duty and that even those who found him most at fault, had they been in his position, with the circumstances as then existing, they would have acted as he did, he felt certain. But whether he made a mistake or not in the selection of his Ministers, his mistake if it was a mistake, was then and has since been approved by a great majority of the Province.[9]

This was the ground on which Laurier had justified the choice at the time. In the House of Commons he stated that the lieutenant governor "is not limited in any way in his choice. There is only one limit upon his choice, he can choose whom he pleases provided his choice is endorsed by the people of the province." He pointed out also that Borden's criticism of the lieutenant governor's choice was only on grounds of fairness and generosity—not of constitutionality.

It cannot be denied that subsequent approval of a lieutenant governor's choice provides the final test. The implication inherent in the defense of Forget's action, that any other choice would not have been similarly approved, is less valid. The evidence indicates that Haultain might well have emerged victorious had he enjoyed the advantages of office prior to the election. It was because Liberals at both Ottawa and Regina were acutely conscious of this probability that they were anxious to avoid its being put to the test.

Liberal correspondence during the anxious summer of 1905 was concerned not with any action which Haultain might take as premier in the interim period before the first election, but with subsequent developments. In Regina J. A. Calder, prominent in the Liberal organization and later the first Minister of Education in Saskatchewan, speculated on the unhappy possibilities:

If his [Haultain's] recent public utterances mean anything they mean that if he is given an opportunity he will at the convenient moment pass a Public School Act. I need not tell you what would follow—a suit in Court to test its constitutionality—an application for disallowance— and possibly an application for Remedial Legislation. If he should be returned to power in either of the provinces these matters would reach a head in about three years time—possibly four.[10]

The good showing of the Liberals in the 1904 federal election gave the lieutenant governor a convenient peg on which to hang his choice. Its reliability as an indicator of provincial Liberal strength was even less than usual in judging possible provincial support by federal voting results. Territorial elections had consistently been non-partisan, and Haultain had the local support of a substantial number of federal Liberals. The independent attitude which Territorial voters showed toward party labels in federal politics gave scant assurance that partisan considerations would shake their support of Haultain in a provincial election. It was Haultain's stand on autonomy which had turned Liberal leaders against him, and this stand was not likely to have a great impact on the electorate. Prairie indifference to constitutional issues had already been demonstrated, with the autonomy question appearing to have little influence in the federal election of 1904.

Haultain's electoral strength haunted the Liberals until the voting results were in on December 13. Even with the Liberal advantages of being the existing government, with control of patronage, control of election machinery, the choice of date theirs, and a friendly federal government, Liberal expressions of confidence were mixed with apprehension. Two days after the first Saskatchewan cabinet was sworn in, the newly appointed attorney general asked Laurier to hold a judicial appointment for him in case the Liberals were defeated in the forthcoming election. A month later he privately acknowledged a much harder fight than he had anticipated and admitted that "if the elections were on today ... we would be beaten" [11]

Provincial Liberal concern was evident also in the pressure put on the federal Liberal government for help. W. F. A. Turgeon, who later joined Scott's cabinet, appealed through his father, a Liberal M.P., for every possible help from Ottawa. It was, he urged, "their battle that we are fighting. If we are beaten here, the school question will cause the Liberal party in Ottawa to fall."[12] Premier Scott anxiously waited for announcements from Ottawa on railway construction before setting the election date. He berated Prime Minister Laurier for "an abundance of assurance that the importance of the contest is recognized" but found "no assurance . . . forthcoming" that the things required for success would be accomplished, and he finally threatened to resign as premier and go back to newspaper work.[13]

The final result of sixteen Liberal seats to nine Conservatives amply justified the choice that was made. From the other side of the election curtain, however, such a result was by no means a foregone conclusion, even with the advantage of office, and it would have been highly speculative without that advantage.

In 1916 when scandal threatened the government, the public proceedings were paralleled by a series of private meetings between the premier and the lieutenant governor.

Before specific charges were made in the legislature on February 21, as described in chapter 8, Premier Scott had gone to Lieutenant Governor Lake to inform him of "a most grave set of circumstances threatening scandal to the public life of the Province." The premier reported the current rumors to the effect that the lieutenant governor had accepted appointment on the understanding that occasion should be sought for the lieutenant governor to intervene as in Manitoba, and for Scott to be dismissed from office unless he agreed to the royal commission demanded by the Conservatives. The lieutenant governor denied that there was any truth to the rumors concerning himself, and he expressed approval of the government's conduct.[14]

On the evening of February 21 the leader of the opposition, Mr. Willoughby, privately presented a petition to the lieutenant governor requesting the appointment of a royal commission to investigate the specific charges made in the legislature earlier that day against government members.

The petition to the lieutenant governor led to contention between the premier and the lieutenant governor on two points: first, the necessity for the lieutenant governor to act in accordance with the premier's wishes, and secondly, the lieutenant governor's right to seek outside advice.

Scott initially wished to make Mr. Willoughby's petition public. The lieutenant governor did not agree. Two days later Scott told the lieutenant governor that he had now decided against publication, but the premier clearly enunciated his view that the decision as to the disposition of the petition lay with him, and not with the lieutenant governor.[15] In the meantime the lieutenant governor had told Mr. Willoughby that he could not grant the opposition request for a royal commission. (Those subsequently appointed were through the normal channels of a government request, not by a request from the opposition.)

The question of whether the lieutenant governor might properly seek advice outside his ministers arose out of the disagreement over publication of the petition. The lieutenant governor wanted to consult the chief justice of the province on that point. Scott reminded him that his counterpart in Manitoba had been criticized for similar action the year before, and that Governor Cameron's only justification for consulting the chief justice in Manitoba was that he had lost confidence in his attorney general. Lieutenant Governor Lake nevertheless remained unconvinced of any restrictions on his right to seek advice, and Scott reported that in subsequent discussion:

His Honor quoted Todd to effect that it was the right of the Governor to seek advice apart from the Attorney-General in the event of the Governor being of opinion that the views of the Attorney-General were unduly affected by such and such considerations.

Scott's response was that the "Attorney-General in such a case must be under the necessity of ceasing to hold office and in such a case it followed that the chief adviser should cease to hold office." The premier emphasized the point by noting that the personal responsibility of the crown began only "when the Crown's confidence in his chief adviser became disturbed."[16]

Failure of the lieutenant governor and the premier to reconcile their differing viewpoints led to no practical difficulties. The lieutenant governor did not intervene, and knowledge of the meetings with the premier was confined to a small circle. Oblique references in the legislature went unnoticed. Scott had intimated his intention of going to the lieutenant governor when he declared in assembly debate, "I want each of the estates of the realm to know exactly what the conduct of the members of the opposition is." The premier later challenged Mr. Willoughby to explain his absence from the assembly on the evening of February 21 (when Willoughby had gone to the lieutenant governor) but the opposition leader evaded the question. The assembly in general and the public were unaware of the opposition petition or of the discussions. The lieutenant governor's differences with the premier remained an academic rather than a practical matter.

A notable feature throughout the discussions was the uncertainty of both the premier and the lieutenant governor as to their respective positions and authority. "Because after more than ten years in public office he had never before been under a similar duty," the premier explained upon his first visit, he "craved indulgence in the matter of form or technique with which he might be unfamiliar."[17] This confession proved to be unnecessary, as it became evident that the lieutenant governor was in equally unfamiliar territory and doubtless would not recognize any oversights which might occur. He in turn admitted frankly that "he was entirely unfamiliar with the practices and usages of his official position" and "observed that it was exceedingly embarrassing at such a time to be unfamiliar with constitutional law and practice . . . ." The frequent grasping at Manitoba precedents emphasized the uncertainty which each felt respecting the rights, powers, and limitations of the lieutenant governor's position.

Within this framework of mutual uncertainty the premier, aided by his attorney general, showed the sounder grasp of constitutional principles in both points at issue. Scott's insistence that, as premier, it was his advice which the lieutenant governor must follow in the disposal of the Conservative petition was in line with established practice:

We have now a well-established tradition ... that, in the last resort, the occupant of the Throne accepts and acts on the advice of his ministers. ... He is entitled and bound to give his ministers all relevant information which comes to him; to point out objections which seem to him valid against the course which they advise; to suggest (if he thinks fit) an alternative policy. ... But, in the end the Sovereign always acts upon the advice which ministers after (if need be) reconsideration, feel it their duty to offer.[18]

To the extent that the lieutenant governor's remonstrances about the petition were advanced as advice and counsel, the lieutenant governor was not overstepping proper bounds; so far as his intention was to reject the premier's advice, the lieutenant governor was incorrect. Although not acted on, it seemed that the overriding of the premier's view was the intention which, with some uncertainty, the lieutenant governor held to, and which was opposed by Scott and Attorney General Turgeon.

The lieutenant governor seemed similarly mistaken in his belief that, under existing circumstances, he might properly seek advice from the chief justice of the province. Both he and Scott used Todd to support opposing views. In his *Parliamentary Government in the British Colonies,* Todd stated that if the governor has reason to believe that the legal judgment of his cabinet ministers

has been unconsciously biassed by political considerations, so that he cannot accept their interpretation of the law ... a governor is not bound by opinions given under such circumstances, but is free to ask further assistance from elsewhere to aid him in his judgment.[19]

Lake could certainly see that as supporting his view. But that is without taking into account the restriction in a footnote that the "indisputable right to the use of all instruments" is

subject always, and subject only, to the one vital condition that they do not disturb the relation, on which the whole machinery of the Constitution hinges, between those ministers and the Queen.[20]

The apparent suitability of the lieutenant governor's turning to the chief justice of the province for advice has to be weighed against the background of that incumbent. The chief justice was F. W. G. Haultain. Therefore the lieutenant governor was proposing to turn for advice to the man who had been leader of the opposition until his retirement from politics four years earlier, and who had opposed Premier Scott in bitter election campaigns as well as in the earlier autonomy controversy, in which Haultain each time had come out the loser. Within the existing climate of disquietude and rumor, the lieutenant governor's proposal to go beyond his constitutional advisers to their former political enemy could scarcely be reassuring to the premier. Although he "did not formally object," Scott's reluctance was evident, and it is difficult to see how such action could have avoided disturbing even further the "harmonious relations which should always subsist between the Crown and its constitutional advisers."

Even the suggestion of such consultation was among factors which altered Scott's original belief in the lieutenant governor's impartiality, which Scott had expressed in their original meetings. Within a few days the premier related to the lieutenant governor a "set of isolated, but possibly related, incidents" which had instilled doubt in his earlier "complete confidence in His Honor's perfect straightforwardness." Among the incidents enumerated were those connected with the presentation of the Conservative petition, and "His Honor's decision to consult Chief Justice Haultain who not very long ago was the Conservative party leader in Saskatchewan."[21] Despite the serious implications of these suspicions, the matter was not mentioned again, and there was no evidence that the lieutenant governor was in fact a party to any political plotting.

Notes

Chapter 1

1. James M. Minifie, *Homesteader* (Macmillan, 1972), p. 39.

Chapter 2

1. Lewis H. Thomas, *The Struggle for Responsible Government in the North-West Territories, 1870–97* (Toronto, 1956), p. 180.
2. Laurier papers, Prime Minister Laurier to G. H. V. Bulyea, July 24, 1899, p. 35561. Public Archives of Canada.
3. The *Leader* (Regina), Apr. 30, 1903.
4. Scott papers, Brown to Scott, May 5, 1903, pp. 1359-62. Archives of Saskatchewan.
5. *Ibid.,* Scott to Bulyea, Apr. 3, 1903, p. 1428.
6. *Ibid.,* Haultain to Scott, Apr. 25, 1901, pp. 530-32.
7. *Ibid.,* Scott to Bulyea, Apr. 6, 1903, pp. 1430-32; Scott to Brown, May 1, 1903, pp. 1356-58.
8. *Ibid.,* Scott to Bryce, Nov. 26, 1904, p. 3209.
9. *Ibid.,* Scott to Clifford Sifton, Nov. 23, 1903, pp. 2692-94.
10. *Ibid.,* Scott to Davis, Dec. 23, 1904, p. 3448.
11. Willison papers, Hamilton (Ottawa correspondent for the Toronto *News*) to Willison, Jan. 19, 1905. Public Archives of Canada.
12. C. C. Lingard, *Territorial Government in Canada* (Toronto, 1946), p. 132.
13. The *Leader*, Dec. 28, 1904.
14. *Journals of the Legislative Assembly for the North-West Territories* 1903, Appendix, Sifton to Haultain, Mar. 21, 1901, pp. 6-7.
15. *Ibid.* 1904, Appendix, Haultain to Laurier, June 1, 1904, p. 13.

Chapter 3

1. Laurier papers, Sifton to Laurier, Jan. 22, 1905, pp. 93969-73.
2. *Ibid.,* Sifton to Laurier, Feb. 1, 1905, p. 94354-57.

3. *Ibid.,* Sifton to Laurier, Jan. 22, 1905, pp. 93969-73.
4. Sifton papers, Sifton to Dafoe, Feb. 25, 1905, Vol. 263, p. 210. Public Archives of Canada.
5. Laurier papers, Sifton to Laurier, Jan. 22, 1905, pp. 93969-73; Laurier to Sifton, Jan. 26, 1905, pp. 93974-76.
6. Scott papers, Scott to Laurier, July 17, 1905, pp. 6064-65.
7. *Ibid.,* Scott to Laurier, May 26, 1905, p. 6051.
8. Laurier papers, [Fitzpatrick] to Laurier, Mar. 28, 1905, p. 96104.
9. *Journals of the Legislative Assembly of the Province of Saskatchewan,* 1906, p. 86.
10. Willison papers, Haultain to Willison, Aug. 5, 1906.
11. *Statutes of Canada,* 1930, c. 41, "The Saskatchewan Natural Resources Act".

Chapter 4

1. The *Leader,* Aug. 30, 1905, reprinted from the Toronto *Star.*
2. Laurier papers, De Veber to Laurier, May 2, 1903, p. 208708.
3. Scott papers, Scott to Sifton, Dec. 18, 1903, p. 2709.
4. Sifton papers, Scott to Sifton, Jan. 15, 1904, Vol. 171, p. 138909.
5. Scott papers, Sifton to Scott, Oct. 25, 1905, p. 37864.
6. *Ibid.,* Laurier to Scott, Aug. 20, 1910, p. 50496.
7. *Ibid.,* Scott to Shea, July 24, 1908, p. 38226.
8. The *Morning Leader,* Dec. 6, 1919.
9. F. W. Anderson, "Farmers in Politics, 1915-35," unpublished Master of Arts thesis, University of Saskatchewan, 1949, pp. 56-60.
10. Martin papers, Martin to Langley, Dec. 31, 1920, pp. 33330-33. Archives of Saskatchewan.
11. Scott papers, Turgeon to Scott, Oct. 3, 1919, pp. 78179-85.
12. *Canadian Annual Review,* 1921, p. 781.
13. David E. Smith, *Prairie Liberalism: The Liberal Party in Saskatchewan 1905-71,* (Toronto, 1975), pp. 109-114.
14. See Patrick Kyba, "Ballots and Burning Crosses," Ward and Spafford (eds.), *Politics in Saskatchewan* (Don Mills, 1968), for an account of the 1929 election campaign.
15. See Peter R. Sinclair, "The Saskatchewan C.C.F. and the Communist Party in the 1930s," *Saskatchewan History,* Vol. XXVI, No. 1, Winter, 1973.
16. S. M. Lipset, *Agrarian Socialism, the Co-operative Commonwealth Federation in Saskatchewan* (New York, 1968), p. 187.
17. Edwin A. Tollefson, "The Medicare Dispute," Ward and Spafford (eds.), *Politics in Saskatchewan,* p. 267.

Chapter 5

1. Scott papers, Scott to McColl, Jan. 24, 1906, p. 38105.
2. Escott M. Reid, "The Saskatchewan Liberal Machine before 1929," Ward and Spafford (eds.), *Politics in Saskatchewan.*
3. Turgeon papers, Hill to Turgeon, May 27, 1913, Personal. Archives of Saskatchewan.
4. Scott papers, Scott to Robertson, Aug. 26, 1907, p. 31141.

5. W. L. Morton, *The Progressive Party in Canada,* (Toronto, 1967), p. 118.
6. The *Leader-Post,* Nov. 6, 1953.
7. Reid, *op. cit.,* p. 96.

Chapter 6

1. The *Moose-Jaw News,* May 22, 1908.
2. Scott papers, Scott to Callender, Sept. 3, 1908, pp. 8017-18.
3. *Ibid.,* Scott to Alex Ross, Nov. 27, 1905, p. 37952.
4. The *Morning Leader,* Nov. 20, 1912.
5. Scott papers, Scott to Bryce, Dec. 5, 1912, pp. 11273-4.
6. Lewis H. Thomas, *The Struggle for Responsible Government in the North-West Territories 1870-97,* p. 243.
7. Scott papers, Scott to MacNutt, Nov. 15, 1905, pp. 37921-22.
8. Norman Ward, "Gardiner and Estevan, 1929-34," *Saskatchewan History,* Vol. XXVII, No. 2 (Spring, 1974).

Chapter 7

1. David E. Smith, "The Membership of the Saskatchewan Legislative Assembly: 1905-1966," *Politics in Saskatchewan,* Ward and Spafford (eds.), p. 204.
2. Scott papers, Scott to MacNeill, Dec. 10, 1910, pp. 46134-35.
3. *Ibid.,* Scott to Stevenson, Dec. 20, 1910, pp. 46136-37.
4. *Journals of the Legislative Assembly of the Province of Saskatchewan,* 1953, p. 131.
5. "Questions and Returns," prepared by Gordon Barnhart, Clerk of the Legislative Assembly, Oct., 1973.
6. Scott papers, Scott to Pearce, Feb. 17, 1911, p. 10966.
7. The *Leader-Post,* Mar. 29, 1941, reporting Mr. Speaker Agar.
8. *Rules, Orders and Forms of Proceeding of the Legislative Assembly of Saskatchewan,* 1906, s. 99.

Chapter 8

1. Scott papers, Ross to Scott, Aug. 24, 1910, p. 10071.
2. *Ibid.,* Rutan to Scott, Oct. 24, 1910, p. 25677.
3. *Ibid.,* Scott to McGuire, June 2, 1910, p. 25634.
4. Laurier papers, Laurier to Davis, Aug. 27, 1910, pp. 174170-71.
5. John T. Saywell, *The Office of Lieutenant-Governor* (Toronto, 1957), p. 25.
6. The *Leader-Post,* Jan. 10, 1938.
7. Earl of Halsbury, *The Laws of England, being a Complete Statement of the Whole Law of England* (London, 1909), Vol. X, p. 527.

Chapter 9

1. Scott papers, Scott to Rimmer, June 27, 1907, p. 7747.
2. *Ibid.*, Lottie Craig to Scott, Apr. 29, 1920, p. 17133.
3. The *Morning Leader,* Dec. 13, 1921, quoting Maharg to Martin, Dec. 7, 1921.
4. Fines papers, "Cabinet-Planning Board Conference, Sept. 13-20, 1948," Archives of Saskatchewan.
5. Lloyd papers, "The Role of the Cabinet Secretariat," Lecture delivered to the 1956 Budget Bureau Public Administration Training Course [by a senior civil servant]. Archives of Saskatchewan.
6. Interview with Woodrow S. Lloyd, Leader of the Opposition, May 1, 1970.
7. Lloyd papers, Minutes of meeting of Cabinet Committee on Cabinet Procedures, Apr. 9, 1963, 1-11; Cabinet Minutes, No. 2301, May 3, 1963, 1-3-96.
8. Gordon Robertson, *The Changing Role of the Privy Council Office,* a paper presented to the 23rd. meeting of the Institute of Public Administration of Canada, Sept. 8, 1971, p. 20.
9. Scott papers, Scott to Calder, June 28, 1910, pp. 9581-82.
10. *Ibid.,* Scott to Langley, Jan. 12, 1916, p. 14084.
11. Lloyd papers, Lloyd to Kramer, Dec. 5, 1963, (11) Premier, 1-1 Misc.
12. Laurier papers, Motherwell to Laurier, Dec. 20, 1918, pp. 202198-200.
13. Scott papers, Scott to Laurier, Dec. 27, 1918.
14. The *Leader-Post,* May 4, 1962.

Chapter 10

1. Scott papers, "Public Health Work in Saskatchewan," report enclosed with letter, Seymour to Scott, Mar. 14, 1914.
2. Thomas H. M. McLeod, "Public Enterprise in Saskatchewan: The Development of Public Policy and Administrative Controls," Ph.D. thesis, Harvard University, 1958, p. 198.
3. *Ibid.,* p. 193.
4. Douglas papers, Minutes of 6th. meeting of Committee Studying Methods of Organizing Government Operated Enterprises, Feb. 28, 1946. Archives of Saskatchewan
5. McLeod, *op. cit.,* p. 205.
6. *Ibid.,* p. 208.
7. Douglas papers, Cadbury to Douglas, August 9, 1948. E.A.P.B., 152, Crown Corps.
8. Lloyd papers, Work Program for Fiscal Year 1963-64. (11), 2, Ex. Council.
9. Albert W. Johnson, "Biography of a Government: Policy Formulation in Saskatchewan 1944–1961," Ph.D. thesis, Harvard University, 1963. ch. 7.
10. Douglas papers, Douglas to prospective staff member, Nov. 6, 1948. E.A.P.B. , 138.
11. Lloyd papers, Minutes of Cabinet Conference on Planning and Budgeting, Nov. 20, 21, Dec. 14, 15/61, Minutes of Conference, Reference Number 58, L-1-Sec., 13-2, Cab. Planning Brd. Conf. Nov. 1961.

12. Scott papers, Scott to Ashe, Oct. 26, 1909, p. 31796.
13. Martin papers, Martin to Bishop, Dec. 11, 1917, p. 288.
14. The *Morning Leader,* Jan. 27, 1926.
15. The *Leader-Post,* Aug. 7, 1944.
16. The *West* (Regina), May 17, 1906.
17. Scott papers, Secretary-Treasurer, Regina Liberal Club to Regina Liberal Association, Nov. 23, 1911, p. 47487; Scott to Secretary-Treasurer, Regina Liberal Club, Nov. 24, 1911, p. 47490.
18. The *Leader-Post,* Aug. 19, 1935.
19. R. Brown papers, "Outline of Present Checking Procedure," Nov. 27, 1962, V18-19-1, Checking Procedures, p. 4.
20. The *Commonwealth,* Aug. 29, 1962.
21. Martin papers, Memorandum to the President of the Council [from the Civil Service Commissioner], Aug. 10, 1917, p. 14297.

Chapter 11

1. See Evelyn Eager, "The Paradox of Power in the Saskatchewan CCF, 1944–61," *The Political Process in Canada,* ed. J. H. Aitchison (Toronto, 1963), pp. 118-35.
2. Papers of the United Farmers of Canada (Sask. Section), Farmer-Labour Group Convention Minutes, July 27, 1934. Archives of Saskatchewan.
3. Albert W. Johnson, "Biography of a Government: Policy Formulation in Saskatchewan 1944–1961," Ph.D. thesis, Harvard University, 1963, pp. 125-71, relating to the CCF drawing up of the program.
4. CCF papers, Council Minutes, July 27, 1946. Archives of Saskatchewan.
5. Interview with Woodrow S. Lloyd, Leader of the Opposition, May 1, 1970.
6. CCF Convention Minutes, 1946.
7. Lloyd papers, Cabinet Minutes 1371, Feb. 19, 1962, 1-Sec., 1-3-96.
8. CCF Convention Minutes, 1952.
9. Interview with Premier W. R. Thatcher, Dec. 10, 1964.
10. Interview with Paul Leger, Budget Bureau, June, 1964.
11. Interview with the Hon. D. G. Steuart, Deputy Premier and Provincial Treasurer, Apr. 22, 1970.
12. Interview with Premier A. E. Blakeney, Feb. 21, 1973.
13. Eager, *op. cit.*
14. Interviews with Paul Leger, June 1964; Dr. T. H. McLeod (formerly secretary of the Economic Advisory and Planning Board, Director of the Budget Bureau, Deputy Provincial Treasurer), July 15, 1965; Opposition Leader Lloyd, May 1, 1970.
15. Interview with Dr. G. E. Britnell, Saskatoon (member of the Economic Advisory Committee, 1944–45), Nov. 1956.

Chapter 12

1. The *Western Producer,* July 5, 1979, p. 7.
2. *Ibid.,* July 19, 1979, p. 18.
3. The *Leader-Post,* July 14, 1979.

Appendix A
Supplement to Chapter 3

1. Scott papers, Scott to Kerr, Feb. 22, 1905.
2. Scott to J. K. McInnes, Mar. 14, 1905, published in the *Leader*, Dec. 11, 1905.
3. Sifton papers, Sifton to Dafoe, Feb. 25, 1905, p. 211.
4. *Ibid.*, Sifton to Laurier, Vol. 263, Feb. 26, 1905, p. 214.
5. *Ibid.*, Sifton to Dafoe, Feb. 25, 1905, p. 211.
6. *Ibid.*, Feb. 27, 1905, p. 229.
7. Willison papers, Hamilton to Willison, Mar. 3, 1905.
8. R. W. Scott papers, "Memo. Separate Schools, North West Territories," n.d. but apparently prepared between 1892 and 1901, Vol. 1.
9. *Ibid.*, Bishop of St. Albert to Sbarretti, Oct. 4, 1903 (copy) Vol. 21, pp. 685-91.
10. Fitzpatrick papers, Sbarretti to Fitzpatrick, Mar. 5, 1904; Bourassa to Fitzpatrick, Mar. 2, 1904.
11. Laurier papers, Laurier to O. Turgeon, Mar. 7, 1905, p. 208971.
12. *Ibid.*, Lord Grey to Laurier, Mar. 2, 1905, pp. 202922-29.
13. Sifton papers, Sifton to Dafoe, Mar. 11, 1905, p. 428.
14. *Ibid.*, Feb. 25, 1905, p. 212.
15. Scott papers, Scott to Burton, Mar. 9, 1905, pp. 5354-56.
16. R. W. Scott papers, R. W. Scott to Cardinal Merry Del Val, Apr. 15, 1905, p. 723.
17. Sifton papers, Sifton to Dafoe, Mar. 11, 1905, pp. 429-30.
18. R. W. Scott papers, R. W. Scott to Sbaretti, Dec. 30, 1907. I am indebted to Professor Mary Hallett, University of Saskatchewan, for bringing this letter to my attention.
19. The sequence of events in this paragraph is from Manoly R. Lupul, *The Roman Catholic Church and the North-West School question: A Study in Church-State Relations in Western Canada 1875-1905* (Toronto, 1974), pp. 172-74. Our conclusions differ, however.
20. *Ibid.*, p. 175.
21. *Ibid.*, p. 210, quoting Langevin à M. Taillon, Dec. 5, 1905.
22. *Ibid.*, p. 183, Feb. 23, 1905.

Appendix B
Supplement to Chapter 8

1. Scott papers, Scott to Bulyea, June 17, 1905, pp. 5312-13.
2. *Ibid.*, Brown to Scott, June 28, 1905, pp. 5312-13.
3. *Ibid.*, Scott to Dafoe, July 3, 1905, pp. 5519-21.
4. Laurier papers, Laurier to Bulyea, July 25, 1905, pp. 100389-91.
5. *Ibid.*, Forget to Laurier, July 10, 1905, pp. 99633-35. Translated from French.
6. The *Melfort Moon*, Oct. 4, 1905.
7. The *Leader*, Oct. 4, 1905.
8. *Canadian House of Commons Debates*, Nov. 23, 1906, p. 40.
9. The *Morning Leader*, Oct. 15, 1910.
10. Scott papers, Calder to Scott, June 20, 1905, p. 5383.
11. Laurier papers, Lamont to Fitzpatrick Oct. 17, 1905, pp. 102236-38.
12. *Ibid.*, W. F. A. Turgeon to O. Turgeon, Sept. 26 [or 20], 1905, p. 101779. Translated from French.

13. *Ibid.,* Scott to Laurier, Oct. 28, 1905, pp. 102537-39.
14. Scott papers, "Memorandum of Conference with His Honor the Lieutenant Governor, "Feb. 19-Feb. 25, 1916 (a record of the discussions, made by Scott and approved by Lieutenant Governor Lake), pp. 48078-48108. Cited as "Memorandum" in following references.
15. *Ibid.,* Feb. 24, 1916, pp. 48102-06.
16. *Ibid.*
17. *Ibid.,* Feb. 19, 1916, p. 48078.
18. Sir Ivor Jennings, *Cabinet Government* (Cambridge, 1969), pp. 336-7, quoting from *Life of Lord Oxford and Asquith,* 11, pp. 29-31.
19. Alpheus Todd, *Parliamentary Government in the British Colonies,* (London, 1894), pp. 58-59.
20. Ibid., p. 9.
21. Memorandum, Feb. 23, 1916, pp. 48098-99.

Bibliographical Outline

This bibliographical outline is intended to suggest only the main areas and balance of source material and is not exhaustive. In a work that has extended over as long a period as this one has, with re-working, changing of shape and updating, any attempt to include all the sources used at any time would be not only impossible but misleading.

ARCHIVAL MATERIAL

Archival material provided the core of information for the book, the Saskatchewan Archives being a rich source for the province's political development, which was supplemented from the Public Archives of Canada.

Correspondence and papers, to a varying extent, of all the provincial premiers from 1905 to 1964 were available, except those of Premier Anderson (1929–1934). Papers of many cabinet ministers were used as well.

In particular, circumstances and personality combined to make the papers of the first premier, Walter Scott, singularly valuable. His incumbency, from 1905–1916, was preceded by membership in the House of Commons from the time that provincial status was first seriously discussed, and it continued through autonomy talks. His correspondence as M.P. and then as premier falls into the fortunate period after use of the typewriter and of carbon copies had become common, but before extensive use of the telephone partially overtook the written medium. Furthermore, since the provincial and federal governments were of the same political color until 1911, correspondence between officials of the two Liberal governments was frank and sympathetic in those first years of provincial establishment.

Scott himself must be regarded as a natural letter-writer, judging from the full and far-reaching accounts and comments that are characteristic of his correspondence. He was also less politically cautious then some of his colleagues. Messages on currently sensitive topics from his cabinet colleague and chief party man, J. A. Calder, for example, still remain in the archives, complete with Calder's injunction to destroy the item immediately. A fortunate circumstance for researchers, if a less happy one for Scott, was the premier's less than robust health, particularly the respiratory problems which frequently sent him south in winter weather, with resulting correspondence between Scott and his colleagues on matters which would normally have been dealt with verbally.

The exceptionally rich source of the Scott papers in themselves is supplemented by holdings of the Public Archives of Canada, including Prime Minister Laurier's papers and (in the events leading to autonomy) the papers of Clifford Sifton and J. W. Dafoe, Fitzpatrick and Senator Scott, Governor General Grey, and newspaperman Willison.

Within the provincial archival holdings, the papers of Scott's cabinet colleagues, Calder and W. F. A. Turgeon in the early years, expand the already extensive view made possible through the premier's papers. Further development of the political scene is continued in the papers of Scott's successors in office, W. M. Martin and then C. A. Dunning, whose papers were divided between Saskatchewan and Queen's University.

The unhappy loss of both premier's and ministerial papers of the 1929-1934 Anderson administration, presumably in the bonfires behind the legislative building that were reported by spectators after the 1934 election, leaves the most serious gap in provincial documentation. And only a limited number of papers were available of the premier who both immediately preceded and succeeded Anderson, J. G. Gardiner, because the main body of his papers were not open for general use at the time of research for this study. The papers of W. J. Patterson, a minister in the Gardiner cabinet and his successor as premier, are thin, and they are only partly supplemented by papers of other ministers in his cabinet.

Like the first years of the province, the CCF era beginning in 1944 is again richly documented through the papers of Premier T. C. Douglas, those of Premier W. S. Lloyd, and those of other cabinet ministers and M.L.A.'s, as well as through the papers of the Saskatchewan CCF party.

PERSONAL INTERVIEWS

Interviews were extremely valuable for the years through the CCF, Thatcher, and the present NDP administrations. They served to fill in and round out the already abundant written record of the CCF period and to give a fuller understanding of the philosophical approach and administrative practices which were introduced at that time and continued afterwards by the NDP.

Those interviewed included Premiers T. C. Douglas, W. S. Lloyd, and later Premier Blakeney, and a number of cabinet ministers of the respective administrations, as well as assembly members and a wide range of public service administrative personnel.

Similarly during the Thatcher Liberal administration from 1964 to 1971, when current records of course were not available but when rumor and report abounded of unconventional practices in the government arena, interviews and cross-checking of interviews were indispensable. These included the same range of personnel as previously (and sometimes the same persons) among public servants and former public servants, as well as M.L.A.'s, cabinet ministers, and Premier Thatcher.

For activities and practices in all political parties, interviews filled many gaps. Party leaders, presidents, and other party officials of the Liberal, CCF, NDP, Conservative, and Social Credit parties were generous with their time in explaining details and changes in party organization and election practices. In addition to those within the upper echelons of the party, interviews with party workers whose interests were concentrated on details of electoral persuasion within a particular constituency or even poll were equally rewarding in the insights they provided at the grass-roots level of the individual worker.

There were other interviews with those who had recollections of earlier periods, such as former premiers W. M. Martin and W. J. Patterson, and with a few long-time public servants who had served over a long period of the province's history, such as Tom Lax. Others were interviewed who were in particular positions or areas of activity, as lieutenant governors, the speaker of the assembly, successive clerks of the assembly, or one who was serving as a member of the electoral boundaries commission.

Throughout, the helpfulness of those interviewed, their sometimes surprising openness and frankness, the perspectives given, and the generosity in allowing time made the interviews a rewarding and stimulating avenue of information.

BOOKS, THESES, AND SIMILAR WORKS

Books used naturally cover a wide range, from those that provide general background information to those that relate to narrowly specialized areas of study, and from those that cover the early periods of provincial development to those that deal with the most recent times. Specific mention of titles here is not therefore in any sense exhaustive, but is intended to give an indication of the types of sources drawn from.

Of those dealing with a significant area of relevant subject matter, the one heavily relied on for the earliest period was *The Struggle for*

Responsible Government in the North-West Territories 1870–97 (Toronto, 1956), by Lewis H. Thomas, whose thorough study provided the substance for my chapter on Territorial government. On the political scene were S. M. Lipset's *Agrarian Socialism: The Co-operative Commonwealth Federation in Saskatchewan,* and W. L. Morton's *The Progressive Party in Canada,* both first published in 1950, and more recently David E. Smith's *Prairie Liberalism: The Liberal Party in Saskatchewan* (Toronto, 1975).

Early studies dealing with a single issue include *The Natural Resources Question* (Winnipeg, 1920), by Chester Martin, and George Weir's *Evolution of the Separate School Law in the Prairie Provinces* (Saskatoon, 1917). A much later and broader study, which also included the separate school issue, was *The Roman Catholic Church and the North-West School Question: A Study in Church-State Relations in Western Canada 1874–1905* (Toronto, 1974), by Manoly R. Lupul.

Books that provided a new slant or insight into situations which are generally well known were James H. Gray's excellent *Men Against the Desert* (Saskatoon, 1967), detailing both the man-made share of responsibility for conditions in the 1930s and the recognition of it, and James M. Minifie's *Homesteader* (Toronto, 1972), which recounts his father's experiences in early problems of grain marketing.

Politics in Saskatchewan (Don Mills, 1968), edited by Norman Ward and Duff Spafford, was drawn upon for a wide variety of areas dealt with by the various contributors to the volume, the "Left Wing" in the 1920s, the Liberal party machine before 1929, the Ku Klux Klan and the 1929 election, the medicare dispute, an overview of the 1960s contemporary political scene, and legislative assembly membership. This volume also contains my own article on the conservatism of the Saskatchewan electorate, which is an earlier publication of my thesis of the pragmatic and conservative nature of the general population of Saskatchewan, the same thesis that is the basis of this present book.

Other volumes that are composed of contributions from various writers include *Canadian Political Parties* (Scarsborough, 1972), edited by Martin Robin, which contains "Saskatchewan Parties in a Politically Competitive Province," by John C. Courtney and David E. Smith. *One Prairie Province? Conference Proceedings and Selected Papers* (Lethbridge, 1970), edited by David K. Elton, includes a variety of perspectives and background studies presented in the conference held at the University of Lethbridge in 1970 to study the feasibility of there being one prairie province. The publication of papers presented at the annual Western Canadian Studies Conference at the University of Calgary provided similarly useful material.

Books which did not necessarily deal specifically with Saskatchewan were valuable for comparative purposes or for providing a model for a particular area of political study. One such was F. F. Schindeler's *Responsible Government in Ontario* (Toronto, 1969), an excellent exploration into executive-legislative relations. Applicable to all provinces is John T. Saywell's *The Office of Lieutenant-Governor* (Toronto, 1957). *Collective Bargaining in the Public Service* (Toronto, 1973), published by The Institute of Public Administration of Canada, contains Saskatchewan material as well as that on other provinces. Two studies which give insight into political activities in neighboring provinces are *The Liberal Party in Alberta* (Toronto, 1959), by Lewis G. Thomas, and *The Government of Manitoba* (Toronto, 1963), by M. S. Donnelly.

University theses provided specifically researched areas. Thomas H. McLeod's "Public Enterprise in Saskatchewan: The Development of Public Policy and Administrative Controls" (1958), and Albert W. Johnson's "Biography of a Government: Policy Formulation in Saskatchewan 1944–1961" (1963), both Ph.D. theses for Harvard University, provided inside pictures of administrative innovations in which the authors had themselves participated in senior government positions. Also valuable for an earlier period was F. W. Anderson's Master of Arts thesis for the University of Saskatchewan, "Farmers in Politics, 1915–35" (1949).

The *Canadian Annual Review* must be included here. Starting as an annual publication in 1901 and continuing for years under the capable hand of J. Castell Hopkins, it included an authoritative annual summary of political and governmental events in the province as a part of its general overview of each part of the country. Its title varied in the earliest years, and the last two volumes of the original series each spanned two years, 1935 and 1936, and 1937 and 1938. It was revived as a new series in 1960 with John T. Saywell as editor.

NEWSPAPERS AND PERIODICALS

The Regina daily paper, from its origin as the *Leader* in its first edition in 1883 to the *Leader-Post* of the present time was examined on microfilm, in old bound volumes or current form in circulation. Its coverage of legislative debates was particularly full in earlier years when there was no official record of legislative debate, and throughout publication, its reporting on political events, even if it did not supply all the information necessary, pointed to areas which might be further explored in more official sources. Its reports of legislative debates, clipped and joined with similar reports from rival Regina papers, from Saskatoon, and from newspapers published in other centers, formed the so-called "Scrapbook Debates" in the legislative library which served as an unofficial Hansard until debates were first officially recorded in 1947.

Other newspapers and periodicals were examined substantially, if not as consistently as the Regina paper. Aside from daily papers these included such publications as the *Grain Growers Guide*, the *Commonwealth*, and *The Western Producer*.

Useful articles were used from both popular and academic journals. Those from such publications as *Maclean's, Saturday Night* and the

Canadian Forum tended to be general. Some of the articles in academic journals on specific topics include J. R. Mallory, "The Lieutenant-Governor's Discretionary Powers: The Reservation of Bill 56," in *The Canadian Journal of Economics and Political Science,* XXVII, No. 4 (Nov. 1961), and Peter R. Sinclair, "The Saskatchewan CCF: Ascent to Power and the Decline of Socialism," in the *Canadian Historical Review,* LIV, No. 4 (Dec. 1973). The Spring 1972 (vol. 5, no. 1) issue of the *Lakehead University Review* included among the articles featuring Saskatchewan's 1971 election, "The Changing of Spots in Saskatchewan," by Norman Ward, which deals with the Liberal leadership convention not long after the election, and "Saskatchewan Returns to Agrarian Socialism," by Harold E. Bronson.

Particular mention should be made of *Saskatchewan History,* which published many articles relevant to this study. Among these were "The Provincial Capital Controversy in Saskatchewan," by Jean E. Murray, in vol. V, No. 3 (Autumn, 1952); "The Saskatchewan CCF and the Communist Party in the 1930s," by Peter R. Sinclair, in vol. XXVI, No. 1 (Winter, 1973); "Gardiner and Estevan, 1929–34," by Norman Ward, in vol. XXVII, No. 2 (Spring, 1974); and "Colonization Work in Last Mountain Valley," by William Pearson, in vol. XXXI, No. 3 (Autumn, 1978).

OFFICIAL PUBLICATIONS AND REFERENCE SOURCES

Statutes, journals, sessional papers, and (after 1947) official recording of assembly proceedings were the framework of reference for official legislative happenings. For procedure in the House, the publication *Rules, Orders and Forms of Proceeding of the Legislative Assembly of Saskatchewan* was supplemented by special studies as "Questions and Returns" prepared by the clerk of the legislative assembly. The Chief Electoral Office in 1979 combined material from earlier reports of individual elections into an all-inclusive compilation of election statistics, *Provincial Elections in Saskatchewan, 1905–1979.*

In the administrative and executive areas were the annual reports of government departments and individual agencies, and publications that give an overview of conditions such as the Department of Finance's annual publication, *Saskatchewan's Financial and Economic Position.* Among the many royal comission investigations on a variety of subjects is the report of the *Royal Commission on Government Administration (1965).* Various published presentations of the Saskatchewan government to federal-provincial conferences periodically stated the government's position in this field.

Just as the clerk of the assembly has upon occasion pulled together procedural practices in the assembly and put them in orderly written form for the information of those concerned, so officials in the executive area have prepared what are, in effect, working manuals as a guide to procedures that are to be followed. An example of this type of manual is the "Procedures for Recommendations for Orders in Council," prepared by the clerk of the executive council in 1974.

Publications of the Saskatchewan Archives Board: the *Saskatchewan Executive and Legislative Directory 1905-1970,* and the *Supplement 1964-1977,* as well as the *Directory of Members of Parliament and Federal Elections for the North-West Territories and Saskatchewan 1887-1953,* were indispensable handbooks for reference and for checking of elected personnel in legislative and executive positions.

Index